LOVE IS POWER

AND A WARM SMORGASBORD FOR GLOBAL VILLAGERS

WARREN
DOUGLAS
PHEGAN

iUniverse, Inc.
Bloomington

Love Is Power
And a Warm Smorgasbord for Global Villagers

iUniverse books may be ordered through booksellers or by contacting:

iUniverse
1663 Liberty Drive
Bloomington, IN 47403
www.iuniverse.com
1-800-Authors (1-800-288-4677)

ISBN: 978-0-5954-6633-7 (sc)
ISBN: 978-0-5959-0928-5 (ebk)

Printed in the United States of America

iUniverse rev. date: 03/19/2012

DISCLAIMER:

The views expressed in this work are solely those of the author and do not necessarily reflect the views of the publisher, and the publisher hereby disclaims any responsibility from them. The contents of this book are not advice. They are options to be considered by the reader in making choices in his or her life. How it feels to you is often your best guide. Add to that, watchful thinking as you go. How-it-feels and watchful thinking are the tools you ordinarily use in thinking. *Love Is Power* is a way to expand your style of living. Consume it with glee.

Scripture quotations marked NIV are taken from the Holy Bible, New International Version. NIV. Copyright © 1973, 1978, 1984 by International Bible Society. Used by permission. All rights reserved worldwide.

Scripture taken from "The Message," a modern English version of the Bible by Eugene H. Peterson. NavPress Publishing Group, 1993, 1994, 1995, 1996, 2000, 2001. Used by permission.

Some quotations from Buddhism are from *The Teaching of Buddha*, provided by the courtesy of Bukkyō Dendō Kyōkai, Tokyo.

Scarboro Missions of Toronto collected thirteen different versions of "the Golden Rule" on a poster. These versions are reprinted here with permission.

Three quotations from C. S. Lewis are presented with permission, © C. S. Lewis Pte. Ltd.

To Susan, whose support made this book possible.
It is also dedicated to the largely untapped potential within you, the reader. No matter what you have yet done or haven't done, there is far more inside of you waiting to be tapped.

Contents

ACKNOWLEDGMENTS

My first inkling of nurturing one's own self came from my father. He used to quote a phrase: "Every day in every way, I'm getting better and better."

In the early 1970s, a self-nurturing poster appeared, created by Virginia Satir, a pioneering family therapist. This, she turned into a book (Satir 1975). The beginning material for the present pages was given to me by transactional analyst colleague H. Capers, at a retreat in 1976. Subsequently, material from Mel Boyce, also a transactional analyst, was added to that (Boyce 1978). Material in sections here titled "Strong," "Perfect," "Pleasers," "Rushing," and "Trying" grew out of an article on "Mini Script Drivers" by T. Kahler with H. Capers in 1974 (Kahler 1974).

For many of the quotations from the world's religions, I am indebted to Juliet Mabey, who had compiled them in a tiny book called *God's BIG Instruction Book: Timeless Wisdom on How to Follow the Spiritual Path* (Mabley 1996).

Scripture quotations marked NIV are taken from the *Holy Bible, New International Version, NIV.* Copyright © 1973, 1978, 1984 by International Bible Society. Used by permission. All rights reserved worldwide.

One quotation, following "Leaders and Followers," comes from an interesting version of the bible written in modern language, by Eugene H. Peterson: Scripture taken from *The Message.* Copyright © 1993, 1994, 1995, 1996, 2000, 2001. Used by permission of NavPress Publishing Group.

Some quotations from Buddhism (labeled "The Teaching of Buddha") are from *The Teaching of Buddha,* a book provided by the courtesy of Bukkyō Dendō Kyōkai, Tokyo.

Scarboro Missions of Toronto collected thirteen different versions of The Golden Rule on a poster (McKenna). These versions are reprinted here with permission.

Three quotations from C. S. Lewis are presented with permission: extracts by C. S. Lewis © C. S. Lewis, Pte. Ltd.

For the concept, mentioned in the Introduction, that alcoholism is a "disease" of not knowing how to live (for which alcohol is the attempted "cure"), I am indebted to Dr. Graeme Cunningham, director Addiction Division, Homewood Health Centre and past president of the College of Physicians and Surgeons of Ontario.

I am indebted to Don Hunkin for some of the elements found in "The Now Exercise."

But by far the greatest contribution has been discussions with people coming to a psychiatrist for help to put their lives together. The wisdom in this book derives from that. I learned something from every one of you. I remain forever in your debt.

I am indebted to Paul Cameron, when he was professor of psychiatry at the University of Ottawa, for feedback about an earlier version of the present book.

I am grateful to my secretaries, Lesley Pergau and Kathy Bowering, for their ongoing support and organizing skills, and to Kimberly Williston and students Patrick Casey, Anna Yueh-Chun Chen, Ahsan Khan, and Iris Cao for their typing.

ABOUT THIS BOOK

The deepest, most profound nutrition we require is not physical at all. It is the nourishment available from genuine, warm contact between people. We can feel starved of that. It is easy to confuse that feeling of starvation with the far more trivial, yet visible, problem of food nutrition. See the section "Physical Nutrition Mistaken for Love" for more about that.

Love Is Power is multifaceted. It arises from and grounds itself in centuries' old traditions, which I have made evident by including many quotations from the world's religions. It offers experiences of healing with creative text, poetry, and images. These are designed to transform previous negative experiences in our lives and upgrade our consciousness. Allow that. If problems like pollution that are plaguing our planet are to be solved, we must begin to employ the power within us and the deliberate use of goodwill and emotional warmth toward others. People so upgraded are capable of much more. People are doing the polluting. People need to be maximally empowered to solve it. Helped by the Internet, contact between people of the "global village" has multiplied to unprecedented levels. We are effectively global villagers rubbing shoulders across the planet. We cannot afford to mimic the computers and stay at the level of cold facts, ignoring the versatility of warm emotions. A computer, fast at transferring facts, never understands what it is doing. It is a good servant, an incompetent master. Understanding, which makes our actions relevant, comes through the sharing of emotional warmth. The segment "Understanding Must Be Earned" explores these ideas. *Love Is Power* offers a smorgasbord for global villagers to feast upon.

UNIQUE CONSTRUCTION AND CONTROLS

Unique to this book is that several topics are presented with a two-page spread. The material presented on these pages makes a point, one angle on the chosen topic. As you read on, you will find material on the same topic, but from a different angle. This is user-friendly. It is easy to swallow, simple to digest. There is a logic to the sequencing that I have chosen for the topics. However, this may prove to be heavy going. Many topics yield a more complete understanding at a second reading. If this becomes tiresome, you can bookmark the page and return later after you have let it sink in. Or you can open the book to a completely different page, for a breather.

Love Is Power is the most complete book written on the human condition. There is hardly a topic to do with the self and relating to others that is not at least mentioned in these pages. The best way to read it is to follow cross-references of interest. That keeps you, the reader, true to your own best interests.

WHY POETRY?

Poetry can fly like a bird, embody life-energy, freed in part from the grammatical cage, while still standing on a word-base. Poetry brings back life to text made dead by conformity. Positive imagery seems to fly. Rhythm, rhyme, and alliteration evoke play. Play has a natural way of disrupting structure ("Let's try it this way"), that again has a freeing effect. The text-article "Excitement" and the accompanying poem "Weak Excitement, *Powerful* Love" shows how the same information can be presented in the two forms. The same occurs in "Growth Jitters" and "I Want to Change." Rhythm varies. One poem, "In the Flow of Life," has three different rhythms. In some poems, the rhythm is replaced by the intensity of the topic, for example, "I Am a Refinery." Numerous double limericks, a couple of triple limericks, and one four-limerick poem, "Teenagering," can be found. Free verse in various rhyming and metric patterns, e.g., ABCB, AABB, AAAAAAAA, and rhymes mixed with rhythms are all present. The poem "Laughter, Laughter" has seventeen lines that rhyme. There are many constructions. Always, I let the subject and the way the words tend to flow around it dictate the final form. Each time, with a little help, the poem appeared to write itself.

MUSIC

As a composer, I am free to turn poetry into lyrics and create piano/guitar music. I have done this with "You Can't Set Alight to a Satellite" and with the poem "My Fear." Music has two properties that overlap with living feelings. It is both invisible and unbounded. As you listen to it, music borrows the power of emotions.

WHY HUMOR?

Humor, (the belly-laugh better than the snicker) tends to relax that part of structure represented in the body as armoring (Schreibman): a set of tense muscles. A belly-laugh gives you a free massage, from the inside.

Those readers not yet ready to do the releasing that might disrupt their *safety zone* can choose to by-pass humor and poetry. There is much information elsewhere in *Love Is Power* that will be of value.

IMAGERY

Love Is Power is full of imagery. I have arranged always for the imagery to favor the positive, the creative, the healing. Imagery, the picture worth a thousand words, is powerful. You cannot afford to retain negative pictures. Too powerful. They blight your life unnecessarily.

CARTOONS

It is always great to lighten things up with humor. The thousand-word picture, as a cartoon, does that admirably. A few cartoons add that levity to *Love Is Power*.

MEDITATION

Meditations are usually based on imagery. There are three meditations in this book: "The Cleansing Meditation," "The Now Exercise," and "The Rejuvenating Fear Exercise." For those of you who like to meditate and those others willing to try it, you may be pleasantly surprised.

SOURCES

I have dedicated my life to collecting the facts and describing the experiences we all need to get our acts together. As it is wisdom collected over thirty years of my professional life as a family psychiatrist, it offers psychotherapists of all disciplines optional ways of approaching many problems. That annoying problem counter-transference—negative feelings psychotherapists can have about their patients—can be alleviated and upgraded by practicing the principles laid out in this book. *Love Is Power*, from cover to cover, is about manifesting life force. Your ability as a psychotherapist to keep your finger on that pulse helps you to stay relevant to what is happening. This does not make you identical to every other psychotherapist. You have your own unique sensitivity and interests that flavor what you do and how you do it. You are your own instrument of help.

The psychotherapist who has become familiar with the contents of this book will have material to support most therapy situations. This does not remove the need for the therapist to stay in the moment, respectful, sensitive to the ever-changing needs of the patient, supporting an upward spiral of developing mutuality that will sooner or later meet the needs of both. The healing-involved therapist does not stay untouched by the therapeutic process. Readers can become their own psychotherapists as they gather understanding of the process, picking and choosing what is useful from things read and overheard.

Some of the information in this book derives from a healing technique called Emotion Exchange that I developed. Particularly, this applies to the qualities and power within friendly, warm emotions and the relationship between the thinking process and warm emotions, as you would find in unconditional love. It is not my intention to present the healing method here; that is for a subsequent book. Sneak previews of the method can be found, however, in "Changing an Old Habit Using Healing Emotions," "I Am a Refinery," "Richness for Connecting," "Dryness of Details," and "Be a Friend." I invite you to explore your experiences for evidence of available healing power—much is self-evident if you will allow it to be that way. Unless you prioritize it, healing can be moved to a back burner or replaced by the urge to maintain the status quo. And that is as much as I will say about the method.

Another important source has been Transactional Analysis (Kahler 1974) and its concept of the *mini script*. These have been expanded as "Strong"; "Perfect"; "Trying"; "Pleasing;" and "Rushing." Also relevant are the articles "Intensifying," "De-intensifying." Also from Transactional Analysis is Stephen Karpman's Drama Triangle (Karpman). The TA term *rescuer* is also used a lot in this book.

SECTIONS

The sections group articles that overlap on various topics. Articles may overlap into other sections, but they had to be put somewhere. Introductions to each section bridge the articles in the section. In the case of "Recaps" and "Expansions," they bridge back to the previous parallel section and recall it. The introduction is often used to supply information not detailed in the articles of the section.

SCIENCE

Science is examined in this book from new points of view. One is the habit science has of graphing time (see "Measuring Time"). Another is laid out in the article "Scientific Inexactness."

You have here an encyclopedia on living for people who want to live life to the fullest. It covers a variety of topics from across the spectrum of human experience. The topics are serious. But the way of approaching them is fun: opening and closing the book at random. As the cultural philosopher Marshall McLuhan said, "The medium is the message." Make this a fun learning experience. Deliberately invest your joy.

SELF-READER

WHO SHOULD READ THIS BOOK?

If you are a bartender, a hair stylist, or an accountant who wishes you'd had in your training how to help people alongside all those figures, or a neighbor who wants to know how most to be helpful over the back fence, then a thorough grounding in the contents of *Love Is Power* is your way forward. Anyone who wants to can benefit.

CHILDREN SHOULD BENEFIT.

Ideally, every child should be given a grounding in the principles of *Love Is Power*. There is a deep reality and power that global villagers need to understand and use. That will come best from the bottom up, starting with childhood training.

There are several difficulties blocking and slowing that down. The first is that it is not information. You can't teach the Puppy Principle to kindergarteners and leave Spiral Mountain for a higher grade. The whole enriched book aims at a far higher level than dry information. *Love Is Power* is above all, an experience. Information derives from experience, not the other way around.

The second is that children are immature and not independent. They make choices through the filter of those on whom they depend. A school teacher, sensitive to the nature of the class and the needs of the pupils, can offer a healing experience. But inside every pupil's head is the firm understanding of the parental person or persons on whom he or she is relying. For survival reasons, nothing must interfere with that bond. The more tenuous that bond is, the more crucial it is in the child's mind not to act or even think in ways that could threaten survival. Better to worship pathological parents than to upset them. Better to accept a problem-filled role in a family than reject it and risk being rejected in turn and possibly dying.

Yet the child deeply needs emotional closeness and seeks that. This can leave a child disconnected, with would-be closeness energy left over and unused. It is common to turn that energy into a wall of anger. Held onto, that wall of energy becomes hatred in imitation of the parent who did a similar thing a generation before. The pattern of being unconnected and creating an anger wall is faithfully passed on from generation to generation unless someone puts an end to it.

Some children are born with a deep understanding of the power within love. These children can stay with this certainty, this understanding, while also experiencing the disconnection and the associated invitation to convert energy into anger. If the parent also understood love but was not allowed in the previous generation to process anger, that experience stays unlearned. Complex patterns. Choices.

It is hard, understanding all this, observing all this, for you and me not to feel compassion for all the participants. It is the natural response. That flow of compassion is the warm emotional reality that this book is all about.

For children, there are particular parts of *Love Is Power* that can be useful. For those in the lower grades of school, an interpretation in simplified terms may be necessary. "Child," "Puppy Principle," "Child Communication," "Giving Your Power Away," and "Healing Warmth from the Conductor to His Own Beleaguered Soul" may be useful. "Mouse to Cheese Mountain" has a freshness and vitality that will be inviting. The rhythm and sparkle of poetry can be attractive to a child. Try "Fear Harvested," "Policed to Meet You," "Gratitude" (the poem), "Mess Makers," "How Can I Say to You 'You Are Worthwhile'," "Sadness Sharing," "The Child Matures," and "Spring Thaw." When poetry combines with music, you get the sing-along, great fun for a child; see "Satellites Afire."

WHAT PERSONAL PROBLEMS CAN BE HELPED BY READING *LOVE IS POWER?*

Are you plagued by guilt? Can you see that as an internal pattern of self-punishment, beating on yourself? Putting that aside for a moment, in other situations are you truly convinced that punishment is the best solution to problems? Have you been selling yourself a useless bill of goods? Would you like to examine these questions more closely and open up the possibility of more options? All of this book can help. You may start with reading "Guilt, Blame, Shame and Punishment," and its poem "Policed to Meet You." Go on to "God's Task," and "Love and the Friendly Feelings." That is where the healing power is. You can practice that power by using your ability to feel gratitude; see "Gratitude" and the accompanying poems and then "Gratitude Re-Visited." "Healing the Self-Critic" is also relevant.

Do you ever think forgiveness has bypassed you forever? Is there something you have done that you believe to be unforgivable, leaving you with a lifetime of suffering? Does a part of you ever question whether you have been duped? You have. You can reclaim the lost power. You can develop a deeper understanding. Read "Drawing Out," then "Head Puppets," and then "Forgiveness."

Does your problem of mistrust ever expand to paranoia? Do you ever feel terrified behind a mantle of loneliness? Does all of this appear to have condemned you? Reach out. You can bridge the gap. Start by reading "Mistrusting." The power, the red carpet you can start walking upon, the river you can place under your canoe begins with evoking friendliness and emotional warmth. See "Love and the Friendly Feelings."

If you are into self-actualization, meditation, or in training to become the best you that you can possibly be, you will find a wealth of support in these pages. You might start with "The Now Exercise." "Cleansing Imagery" flushes you out. Practice gratitude as the back-bone of your efforts by spending time with "Gratitude" and "Gratitude Revisited." The poem "The Child Matures" covers a broad cross-section.

Do you ever feel useless? Or a failure? Are you afraid to believe in yourself? Would you be prepared to make a jump-shift in the way you have been looking at yourself? Read the poem "My Fear." Feel the sensitive compassion built into it. No machine, no robot or computer could express such compassion and understanding. You are alive. You are a living power awaiting your willingness to start using it. Feel for the compassion, the warmth in "My Fear." Use a little, even the tiniest little bit of that warmth, right now. Send it into your fear. It is designed to mop up and absorb fear's useless crud and lift you to a new level. See "I Am a Refinery."

Are you troubled by destructive fantasies? Do you fear you may act them out? See "Destructive Fantasies."

Does your push always to be perfect threaten to drive you insane? See the article "Perfect" and the accompanying dialogue "Not Perfect." Then read "Mouse to Cheese Mountain."

Does jealousy ever seem so extreme that you fear it might consume you? Don't fear. It is merely something you are doing, an error you are maintaining. You can correct the error; see "Jealousy."

Do you feel stuck in the past? Do memories of past events anchor you back there, stop you from living in the present? There is a wealth of present-living throughout this book. Turn to random pages and let yourself soak in the experiences. These are now. Try the meditation "The Now Exercise." That could do it. To understand what memory tries to do for you, what it can do for you, and what it can't, see "Memory," "The Past," and "Experience: The Trap."

Do you worry incessantly? Do you always have something to worry about? Do you sometimes believe that if you didn't have something to worry about, then you'd be really worried!? Are you trying to use worry to force yourself to be alive? No problem. You *are* alive. No force required. All of *Love Is Power* is dedicated to celebrating your life. You don't need the self-imposed task of thinking excessively to make this so; see "Worry," "Bobby McFerrin Revisited," and "Worry: Healing a Long-standing Bad Habit."

Are you usually tight and grumpy? Is that your way of living? If you have been doing it for a long time, you may have become smooth and efficient—very good at it. Good at being tight and grumpy! Are you happy to be that way? Would you like to try a different routine? It is okay not be ready; see "Prematurity." Anything you do will improve with practice. "Float Along Those Chores" may be helpful. "Experience: The Trap" may explain things. "Can I Help? Said the Body," and "Love: Water to the Dry Creek Bed" may also be useful.

People with marital problems may find help in "Marital Love Base," "Feed Your Primary Relationship," "Child," "The Child Matures," "Validating Anger," "Be Thankful to Your Enemies," "When Behavior Replaces Communication," and many others.

People who are ill can find help in "Love Your Body," "Can I Help? Said the Body," "Experiences: All Good," "The Illness Paradox," "The School of Hard Knocks," and "Love: Your Power Center." Many things can stress us to the point of physical illness. These can be external—"You make me sick!"—see "Drawing Out," or internal; see "Don't Unravel," "Worry," and "Humility." All the articles in *Love Is Power* are designed to point you toward ultimate health.

This book is about how to regain control of your life. If you have an addiction or any process that feels like it controls you (for example, street drugs, alcohol, nicotine, caffeine, sugar, salt [which raises high blood pressure], good-tasting fat [LDL cholesterol], food, sex, pleasure (Hatterer 1980), look-at-me [attention-getting], love of money, or any piece of behavior that runs your life out of control), you may find support in "Spiral Mountain," and the articles preceding it, "Love Your Body," "Can I Help?, Said the Body," and "Love: Your Power Center."

Alcoholics drink to cover the pain of not knowing how to live; see "The Alcoholic." The alcohol is the supposed cure for the problem. *Love Is Power* touches the spectrum, from A to Z, of the range of knowing how to live. Consume this book, not alcohol.

WHAT PROFESSIONALS COULD BE HELPED BY *LOVE IS POWER?*

Would-be creative writers, journalists, anyone with writer's block could be helped by "My Own Worst Enemy," "Lost Creativity;" "Creativity Lost and Creativity Regained," and "The Versatility of Warm Emotions."

For people doing research on human beings, it will be useful to understand the function and limitations of the thinking process; see "Mind," "You Can't Get There from Here," and "Comfort Zones/Safety Zones." Then, to add to that the expansion into feelings, see "Unconditional Love" and "The Versatility of Warm Emotions"; then for creativity, see "Lost Creativity." See also "A Perspective," appearing later in this introduction.

Because of the many quotations from scriptures, each identified by the spiritual tradition of the text to which they refer, religious leaders may find material here for teaching.

For physicians and other health-care workers, *Love Is Power* illustrates how to use the basic healing power you already possess. For their patients, *Love Is Power* is a representative sampling of healthy attitudes and information. Nurses and other allied professionals need a deep understanding of the extensive tool-kit presented here for their own good and the welfare of those they tend.

For business people and the shareholders who back them, I recommend reading this entire book. You will find many useful items here. There are two book references, both mentioned in "The Golden Rule in Business." One ("Developing Your Company Culture: The Joy of Leadership, a Handbook for Leaders and Managers," Phegan 1994) draws attention to the peculiar fact that management frequently behaves in ways that reduce efficiency and profits. The other ("Love Is *the* Killer App"), shows the advantages of being a *lovecat*.

Even the most hardened business person will gain from "God's Task," "Healing Speed," "Forty Percent," "Jealousy; Times and Choices," "Spiral Mountain," "Trying," "The Puppy Principle," "Conducting the Me-Orchestra" (which becomes "Getting Your Act Together"), "Understanding Must Be Earned," and "Animal Love" (for those who have a pet).

FEEDING

Love Is Power is the ideal interpersonal diet for everyone. Try your warmth. You may be surprised how it relaxes you. (You burn energy tightening muscles to stay tense and cold). You may be surprised how your genuine warmth, flowing from your heart, opens others' ears to hear you, eyes to see you, and arms to accept you, as well as giving your own powers of perception a good clean-out.

You cannot package courage, goodwill, or amazing grace. You cannot even see them. Yet we live in a Garden of Eden where these invisible, unbounded fruits can be picked freely from the trees and consumed at leisure (see "Courage: Unseen Yet Oh-So-Useful.") They are there. But you do have to identify them and deliberately use them. Otherwise you reduce the lot to theory and academic information, a tragic endeavor ("Love Argument.")

In such a land of plenty, there is no need to narrow your range or cramp your style with specific expectations. What you need will be there for you in timely fashion, particularly as you clear more and more of the inertia, the habitual debris of your daily style of living.

Fed and Clothed for Living

This book has the ingredients for a novel-in-waiting. You are the hero or heroine. The story is the story of your life. That life is worth understanding and enriching. Here you will find rainwear for wet days, warmth for cold days, fog-clearers when you can't see, stress-reducers for stressful days, and snacks to keep you nourished on your trip. This book catalogues your needs.

Please don't *eat* the whole book or force yourself to *buy* what you don't need. On the other hand, bring with you a readiness to expand, to look outside-the-box, as you tackle the complexities life brings. A well-lived life leaves you experienced and strengthened by working through it.

Alive Human Beings

Central is the power built into the warm emotions; ultimately it's love. See the articles "Love and the Friendly Feelings," and "The Versatility of Warm Emotions." In contrast to inanimate objects, we feel. Two computers connected by a line can transfer huge amounts of data. But they feel nothing about what they are doing.

Invisible human feelings make emotional contact, unlike the two computers; see "Feelings as Colors for Connecting." From there, they rapidly expand. When you share your warm emotions, they nourish the other person. The benefits of this extend into tense situations. They lubricate communication gone cold. Shared, they offer support to all concerned—that is, everyone open to it (See "Love: Water to the Dry Creek Bed.")

Much centers on the word *love*. As commonly thought of, love is a confusing mish-mash of soft and pappy, fantasies and sex. Saying "I love you" becomes something to avoid. *Love Is Power* throws that out. Love becomes the power to get things done—sustainably—to energize delivery, smooth passage, healing all involved as the doing happens. Excitement is commonly used as a substitute for love's power. But it doesn't have the sustainability and is often associated with a backlash or hangover, reversing the advantage.

A Feast

Love Is Power is like a tree covered with fruit and blossoms. You can take the non-living book and give it life. You provide the invisible sap, the investment of life energy into what otherwise would merely be something of the same shape: a dead tree. You give meaning to what you read, measure its relevance to your life. You water the dry words to stand up as living plants.

Experience Supreme—the Ultimate Nourishment of Life

Supreme for the human being is the experience. It has color, depth, movement, and evolution that are barely glimpsed by a photograph taken at the time. We function at our fullest when grappling with an experience. We tend naturally, barring inhibitions, to revert or expand to this level. Life lived to the fullest brings a series of overlapping experiences in a seamless continuum. Experiences are to be milked for the value in them, sometimes with a little help from our friends (see "Experiences: All Good").

We live our lives as experiences, not facts. The living experience is the rich source from which we draw dry information and facts, a point to remember while so easy to forget. The derivatives of information and facts—opinions, beliefs, attitudes that were designed originally to help—can interrupt the full awareness needed to cope effectively with complex situations. The thinking mind can faithfully chatter these derivatives out, until instructed to stop by someone who has developed enough understanding to desire a balance (see "Conducting the Me-Orchestra").

Experiences contain information in a way that builds toward understanding. Understanding leads directly to competence in many situations, where dry facts and information build merely to knowledge. The link from the dry data of the computer to understanding is provided by the living continuity of the human being. You can do it.

By participating in life, we proactively create our own experiences and present them as gifts to others. We do this through an invisible glow called *presence*. If someone always comes to a get-together and then one time doesn't show up, we miss them. We miss their presence, even if they usually say little. Sometimes we are sensitively aware of this presence: "I know he's here somewhere, but I haven't seen him yet."

SPEAKING

The musicality of our speech provides *Love Is Power* for all within listening distance. If you speak in a monotone, you prevent feeding others with your message, just as you give yourself a headache. You will not be appreciated for deliberately depleting a universal experience. It would be an interesting way to observe the process of stuffing feelings, called somatization, to do PET scans on subjects instructed to speak monotonously.

Your hidden potential is tapped as you participate fully in your experiences. The direction is a coming-out: the expressing of yourself into the world. This is exactly opposite to monotonously stuffing feelings into the body (often driven by the thinking mind, based on fear as the fuel).

If you think of yourself as a no-fun person, then read the poem "Bobby McFerrin Revisited." If you then say "But that's not me," read "Who You Think You Are—Role Confinement" and follow that with "True to Self: A Balancing Act, A Work in Progress." You may become able to open yourself up to a vast potential. (You can be just a little vast if you like).

ENERGY MISUSE

The body is a good and faithful servant (see "Can I Help? Said the Body"), quickly expressing in its unique language of tension and excitement, a monologue of what is going on. This the conductor/observer can analyze; see "Conducting the Me-Orchestra."

If events or people are presenting problems, this is commonly felt as an upset stomach. It is as if we are being asked to *swallow* something that is objectionable. We *feel upset* about it. If our word or label-of-choice is that we feel *hurt,* we may be taking it as a threat. This invites fear and anger responses (see the articles and poems on fear and anger). This moves us to the feelings and continuing-reality level, where the conductor is invited to upgrade the *oil* of fear or anger into the more-efficient water of warm emotions; see "I Am a Refinery."

Each entry is a garment. Try it on for size. If it does not fit you properly, pass it on to someone else. No need to trash it. It may fit someone else perfectly; see "Don't Unravel."

Find the articles that work for you. As you open the book to exactly the page you need to read, rejoice and be grateful for your increasing skill at doing that. Notice that you can't *make* that happen, ("Trying"), but if you simply allow it to happen, the frequency rises (Kahler 1974).

POWERFUL LOVE

Love Is Power. This power is frequently misunderstood; see "Love Argument." Spread throughout our lives are many opportunities to use this power, experience this power, and grow in strength, certainty, and permanent effectiveness. Spread throughout this book are many illustrations of the use of love: "Handing Out Healing Love to Your Body" and "Marital Love Base." Particular lists of love's unique qualities occur in "Love and the Friendly Feelings" and "The Versatility of Warm Emotions." The use of any skill improves with practice. Consume this book. Practice your loving to explore the marvels of this power.

You want only the best for your family. Love is the best. So you love your family. Love is the multi-functional Swiss army knife—always with one more tool to display. It is a supportive cushion. In an environment full of love, you feel free to relax and be yourself. Love nourishes, emotionally. Love has holding power for relationships that might otherwise drift apart; see "Feed Your Primary Relationship" and "Two People." It makes for the best contact between people; see "Love: Water to the Dry Creek Bed." It lubricates tight situations, allowing them to flow more smoothly; see "Validating Anger." It moves physical illness in a healing direction; see the poem "The Illness Paradox." All of these work if they are allowed to do so, but they can be blocked—see "Holding and Blocking Out" and "Love: Water to the Dry Creek Bed." This book repeatedly returns to emphasize the power built into love.

Life is seamless. We move smoothly from one event to another, coloring each with our emotional reactions like a rainbow. The seamlessness is natural and invisible. There are parts of each experience to be seen. But our total reaction, our feeling response, is larger than the visible and extends beyond it. Different people, with different natures and sensitivities, take in each situation in different ways ("God's Task"). What is vital to one (color it red) may matter little to someone else (color it drab), who may in turn react intensely to some other situation. The seamlessness of the rainbow reality affects all. All live in it, reacting to different parts of it.

Cutting across the seamless reality of life is the process of thinking. Preferring the visible, the thinking mind is neatly adapted to what can be seen; see "Courage: Unseen, Yet Oh-So-Useful." With the left side of the brain equipped with words, we can quickly describe, define, reduce, and desiccate the richness of being alive down to word-fragments: facts stuck in black-and-white characters on a page. Inside a book, the written sentence sits obscurely on a library shelf. When someone lifts the book down, the written sentence borrows aliveness from the reader to leap back to the vibrant level. We imbue it with meaning. That gives it relevance to our lives. How we feel, matters. Feelings are unseen. We cannot pick up a compassion or buy a length of gratitude. Because they are invisible, feelings present difficulties in processing for a thinking mind that wants to visualize. Seamless, as they blend one into another, feelings present further difficulties for a mind bent on applying boundaries, defining and explaining, all using word-fragments. The containment and control sought by the thinking process does not do justice to the larger-than-that seamlessness of being alive.

The mind, carving out territory for itself, tends to apply conditions; see "Unconditional Love." When the mind uses the cold emotion of fear, then relationships—the warm cross-connections between people—can be disrupted (see "Mistrusting"). Anger can be a magical attempt to strengthen the weakness of fear.

Living Life

You are entitled to observe all this and make your own choices about how you will use your aliveness, your mind, your feelings, and your body that reacts to it all (see "Conducting the Me-Orchestra"). As you observe, assess, and choose, you use language, the same language used by the thinking mind (see "Mind"). The same language is used to think about life (see "Thinking About Experience") and then to stock memory (see "Memory") with habits. Habits can be useful, saving energy, freeing you to attend to matters of importance. Habits of walking and talking carry on automatically. But when a habit has become a problem ("Hang-Ups), you have the option to observe, drop automatic behavior, and rethink the error ("Confronting a Bad Habit," "Holding and Blocking Out," and "Guilt, Blame, Shame, and Punishment.")

As observer, you take input from the mind, from sensing awareness of what is going on outside of you and from your own body reactions. Retaining mind as your servant, you can use the human healing built into the warm feelings to relax your body, allowing it to heal, and to relax tense situations; see "Love and the Friendly Feelings." There will be a timeliness to doing all this ("Times and Choices"). For each of us, some waiting is necessary, ("Prematurity"). Meanwhile, life continues ("School of Hard Knocks").

As you learn to cope with life, you can insert a balance into how you learn ("Balance"). You will learn best canoeing a river of warmth of your own making. Practicing gratitude is the simplest way to evoke this; see "Gratitude" and "Gratitude Revisited."

Getting It: Being Aware

Awareness, and all its valuable input, rises as you attend to each of these (see "Unawareness," "Awareness Retrieved," "The World Is My Rorschach Test," "Selective Awareness," and "Aspire to Sense.") In an aware life, fully lived, sensing and feeling blend into a total-awareness mechanism. This provides for us information before all the facts are in. Awareness of self expands hugely beyond narrow thinking (see "Who You Think You Are") to untold possibilities (see "The Tennis Game"). Narrowness of thinking can be extended to punishing, cramping levels by a memory that has become full of dysfunctional examples (see "Memory" and "Experience: The Trap").

Inner Child Re-Experiences

Cutting across our experiences is the child. Our entry to life is as a child, dependent and in need of care. Children are learning machines, eagerly soaking up everything that is happening so they can play their parts, belong, and get the care they cannot supply to themselves.

Adulthood leaps us out of that state. No longer children, we may resent being treated like one. Yet the urgency at that younger age to develop well-oiled patterns can hold over from childhood. We all know adults who do childish things. In small ways, we all can be that way (see "Child" and "True to Self: a Balancing Act, a Work in Progress").

The child inside of each of us, besides being the life-spark—source of our curiosity, creativity, and spontaneity—can also carry parts that were unrecognized or inhibited by the previous generation and in need of the nourishment of validation.

SELF-HEALING

You start by validating yourself. You bridge the gap left from childhood. You may repeat a piece of childhood learning. But the support you give to yourself now is the appropriate, updated, relevant-to-this-moment support you need. You then go on to validate others. You spend extra time with those others who also self-validate and so lose nothing by validating you.

Parents teach us what they know. After that, we're on our own. Some parents know more than others. So some of us, having learned less, have more to learn than others do. It is not our fault. It is merely our task. We, as fully matured adults, assemble slowly and carefully the best combination of skills and outlook to suit our purposes (see "God's Task").

The ultimate balance is achieved by responsibility, stepping up to the podium as the conductor, bringing together disparate parts of yourself into one beautiful symphony of your life (see "Conducting of the Me-Orchestra" and "Healing Warmth from the Conductor to His Own Beleaguered Soul").

WORKING THE FEELINGS

In *Love Is Power,* the word *feelings* is used interchangeably with the word *emotions.* In a later, more complete book on feelings and emotions, they will be defined separately. Fear and anger (problem feelings) and sadness (the way out from problems) are dealt with extensively here. Gratitude, love, and forgiveness are key emotions in healing. Much emphasis is given to them in *Love Is Power.* Worry, guilt, hatred, resentment, and mistrust have mental and physical body components that intrude. These need releasing and extracting if the healing power is to flow freely.

The partial list of feelings mentioned in this book can be summarized as follows, with articles to refer to in quotations:

Acceptance—the gift that is delicious to receive, empowering to give:
"Acceptance"

Anger—instant hardness, the artificial protector of fear, the too-quick solution that
  actually maintains the fear as a toughened scab maintains a boil
"Anger"
"Validating Anger"
"Prematurity"

Caring—the simple, turned-on state: the warm-water tap of human emotion in action.
  Bothering to care raises proceedings to the living, human level of life-experienced.
  Your functioning expands. You grow in effectiveness
"Caring"

Compassion—the natural healing response to fear

Confusion—the mind jumping back and forth between topics
"Confusion"

Courage—the balm, the overriding behavioral feeling that can be used to overcome fear's
  inaction and make things happen
"Courage: Unseen Yet-Oh-So-Useful"

Despair—the darkness of despair hides a rewarding lighter side if you will breathe slowly and deeply and allow yourself to go through it
"Despair"

Disappointment—the feeling associated with a failure to connect (emotionally or physically), or separation and the sadness, anger, or fear that may follow

Embarrassment—has a weak, passive idea behind it: the person who is red in the face and shrunken in posture. That person is certainly doing something that probably includes a self-suffocating restriction of breathing. To achieve an action from it, go back to the origins of the word. It is from the Portuguese *baraco,* meaning halter. Hence, it meant to hinder or impede. When you hinder yourself, that is active voice, an action, something you do. So the embarrassed person is hindering self. How do you do that? Do you fell tense? Is your mind provoking tension? You can take over to stop the nonsense.

Empathy—makes a genuine connection with another person
"Empathy"

Excitement—a commonly used substitute for love. But a mere vibration can never have the power, the range, the versatility of love
"Excitement"
"Weak Excitement, Powerful Love"

Fear—that weak, incompetent feeling, all too commonly used to stay in a bad place, frozen
"Fear"
"Terrified"

Forgiveness—the releaser, from our own personal prison
"Forgiveness"

Friendship—warmth, activated to the personal, living, useful level

Frustration—the sense of pushing hard against a wall of resistance and nothing happens; raw, cold, useless energy. It is the result of holding on to the original gift, the initial energy response to a person or event. There is a need for mature people to decide what can be done, to do that, and then to release the energy not needed. Trust that there will be more available when needed. When energy is held onto although nothing can be done, the energy itself becomes the problem.
"Frustration and Despair"

Gratitude—being grateful or thankful, is an easy and controllable way to practice opening yourself to the power within warm emotion. Gratitude elevates everything to the living level and validates it.
"Gratitude"
"Gratitude Revisited"
"Be Thankful to Your Enemies"

Guilt—the behavior of internal self-punishment disguised as a feeling (and who wouldn't feel bad after they have beaten themselves up?). *Blame* is looking outside at others, hoping for temporary relief from personal guilt. While doing nothing to change the attitude of self-beating, blaming someone invites someone else to join the party and so distract the self-punisher, momentarily, from what she is doing to herself
"Guilt, Blame, Shame, and Punishment"
"Policed to Meet You"

Hatred—the hoped-for solace that has all the comfort of hugging a rock
"Hatred Is the Holder"

Hurt—a beginning feeling, an early stage in the development of an energetic response to an event. As the event is likely interpersonal, the unstated response of "You hurt me!" is likely to take the form of an emotion like anger, fear, or sadness.

Love—the all-inclusive term for the power in all the warm, healing emotions
"Love: Water to the Dry Creek Bed"
"Love Argument"
"Experiences: All Good"
"Love Base"

Mistrust—normal trust into which rotting fear has been installed
"Mistrusting"

Resentment—the holding action that extends a momentary feeling (often anger) into a life-long pattern of internal tension that drains and weakens you. Let it go.
"Holding"
"Blocking-Out"
"Releasing Holding"
"Jealousy"

Sadness—the melting, dissolving, relaxing pathway to walk out of the states of fear and anger
"Ferreting Out the Sadness"

Stress—a combination of mind and body reactions that can seem devastating until the deliberate choice is made to bring in love
"It's All Your Fault"

Sympathy—has a meaning of two pendulums swinging harmoniously together. It comes in cold and warm forms. Cold sympathy is a product of the thinking mind and lacks true nutritional contact value. It feels more like meddling in the affairs of others and may generate an angry "I don't want your sympathy!" The warm form, genuine sympathy, comes from the heart and has the power to be sustaining and emotionally nutritious. Unfortunately, if it is met with the rejecting, self-protective response by someone who has been hurt before by coldness, its value can be lost.

Understanding—the powerful healer at multiple levels, the goal to be achieved "Understanding Must Be Earned"

Upset—a beginning feeling—an early stage in the development of an energetic response to an event. As we commonly refer to having a stomach-upset, the upset response, more than hurt, indicates a physical element. It may develop into anger, fear, or sadness; the more experienced person can shift hurt or upset into a more meaningful response (a warm emotion) that connects to the situation with awareness and relevance

Warmth—the common ingredient of all the healing emotions

Worry—the excessive, energy-consuming mind activity that masquerades as a feeling "Worry"

FEELINGS CAN MAKE THE CASTING VOTE

Feelings are frequently the basis on which decisions are made. Actions follow. Whether you feel like it or not can be the determining factor as to whether you finally do it or not. Yet feelings, themselves, can be confusing.

The power within the heartfelt, warm emotions is undeniable. Placing that flowing river under your canoe, allows it to support you. Many potentially effective actions become easier, smoother, and more successful. Compassion, if it is allowed to, can mop up fear, which is the frequent source of our ineffectiveness. Practicing gratitude can quick-start the flowing of the supportive river. With that experience, a deep understanding develops, growing the roots that hold the tree of life erect and strong. Many useless actions come from a lack of those roots of understanding. The "tree" of such a life tends to fall over.

The blanket term for all the heartfelt warm emotions is love. The voyage of discovery toward love's truth can become a thrilling experience.

MONSTERS

There are many hazards along the way: monsters on life's path.

Holding actions (see "Holding and Blocking-Out") can become the anchor that is never raised. This ship cannot sail.

Guilt can knock us repeatedly into the ditch and off life's pathway.

Experience can teach us. How many times do we have to be knocked by life before we freeze in a fix and say "Enough is enough!"? This becomes an anchor that slows us down forever— until we realize what we are doing and release the anchor. The anchor is carried faithfully by a belief system that is trying hard to do the best it can with the task it was given. The dead end of anger as a way of life (enforcing the anchor) can be a result.

EXTRACTS OF EXPERIENCES

Experience is to be distinguished clearly from facts. Facts are word-extracts taken from the flow of experience. Spoken or written, the fact stands or falls on the base of the experience that underpins it. You already understand that. You went to a fantastic place and you are trying to explain it to your friend. But your friend has had no such experience. No matter what way you describe or explain it, your friend looks at you in disbelief (Belief itself stands on a base of experience.)

Finally, you turn away, saying, "You'll have to go there yourself," realizing that your words cannot give to your friend, your experience. Their fragmentary nature cannot bridge the gap.

Facts, made up of words (such facts as we choose to call important), we string together in sequences called logic. From such logical string we can fashion rafts, to which we give the job of underpinning much of our lives. Yet the logical string can never quite contain the invisible, diffuse, fog-like nature of our feelings' experience of life. Words are too rigid.

The words are fixed, like a cage for a bird. The bird is the metaphor for the flow of life: living, moving, breathing. You let the bird out of the cage when you allow in for yourself a new experience. "Now I have so much more to talk about!" you say. You can be excited. You give yourself another experience, a way of functioning in the world that people all-too-commonly suppress: their aliveness.

The topics in *Love Is Power* are designed to cover sufficiently wide a territory, that selections of them can become bases on which the legs of subsequent books I will write, like little Eiffel Towers, can stand and expand into cities on this continent-book.

See "Love Argument," "Experiences: All Good," and "Love Base"

NETWORKS

As cell phones, e-mails, and chat lines for common-interest groups enable us to reach instantly across the world, as blogs are maintained by people with a passion for them, as cell phones with video capability enable us to know what is going on through vehicles like YouTube and Facebook, networks condense to become the fabric of the global village. This is as close an approximation as will be achieved in this lifetime to the deep, common reality from which we all arise: love and its extensions, goodwill, understanding, human warmth, etc. It is our willingness to draw instantly upon this energy that will carry us past forces that would fragment and tear the fabric. This amazing love is the whole focus of this book.

LAW OF ATTRACTION

The Law of Attraction (as described in the book and film *The Secret*) overlaps with principles laid out in this book, *Love Is Power*. We pick a life course. We might go through a period of sensing that our needs not being met. We don't have perfect childhoods. Childhood is a time of immaturity, where we attempt to substitute for the unmet needs by taking on holding patterns. The pus of fear, a natural childhood weakness, can stay unidentified. The boil expands slowly. The holding pattern, driven by fear, can gradually increase, represented metaphorically by an ever more armor-plated scab of anger. This scab attempts to contain the fear, but does nothing to heal it.

We enter a period of developing understanding. During this time, it is not against the rules to gather information. In parallel with that, we build for ourselves a feeling for what is going on. We resist well-meaning attempts by others to bounce us out of this period of hard-knock training that life can be for us. We are not yet ready to forego this learning experience.

Meanwhile, we have an effect on people, we draw them out. From our experiences with others we construct a unique puppet of each one, in our heads. Working at this highest, living level we draw to ourselves both confrontational and supportive people and things. The successful people mentioned in *The Secret*, were sufficiently developed on their life-paths to be able to create that success.

BY-PASSING NEGATIVITY

If the experience you are here to have is an intensely negative, perhaps potentially lethal one, you can avoid the physical consequences of it by using your imagination, creating movies in your mind. Your mind cannot tell the difference between what you imagine or picture in your mind and the real thing.

You allow yourself to gradually come to understand the details of the negative experience. Then you method-act them. You desensitize yourself to them by gently, progressively immersing yourself in them.

If ever this gets to be too upsetting, take a break with someone loving with whom you have a good relationship. I don't mean sex; it may even be your pet. Allow the break to be distracting enough to put you into this very positive frame. That will lubricate and nourish your path.

NATURAL HEALING

It should come as no surprise that physical healing is connected to our aliveness. If a chair, which is not alive, has a broken leg, it cannot fix it. If you have a broken leg, trillions of cells, chemicals for clotting and cell support move into the area. These are helped if a physician aligns the parts and holds them with a plaster cast. The best physician does not interfere (*primum non nocere*). He does what is needed, stands back, and watches with admiration what the body then does. In parallel, if you are suffering from malnutrition, you can "splint" that by attending to your dietary needs. The body contains the wisdom to apply it. Be that good physician for yourself. Eat what your body can actually use.

It may present a difficulty for some to make the jump from this level of understanding of aliveness to the quality of emotional warmth and love. Love is inconveniently not visible and not bounded. This can make it hard for words to encompass it, especially for the thinking mind, which loves to assemble those words, attempting to reach around, grasp, contain, and appear to control the process, and so miss the vital implications of the word *love*.

HELPFUL ARTICLES

"Spiral Mountain" presents a useful concept. It offers hope. "Healing Speed" can be practical. "Don't Unravel" can bring some to a bolt upright position, as this oh-so-common habit is confronted early in the book. "Conducting the Me-Orchestra" is worth the time and trouble to reach out and take charge of a life gone haywire. That will require patience, tolerance, and forgiveness to achieve. The greatness of your potential is described in "The Tennis Game." Don't overlook your untapped possibilities. Challenges? You can handle them! Many useful principles are presented in the section "Principles." These are echoed and expanded in "Recaps and Expansions," an entire section of the book that re-addresses what has been dealt with before.

A PERSPECTIVE

We live in a world marked by *thing-ness* and separation. Objects, as seen by the naked eye, appear bounded and separate from one another. The mind and its thinking process is a tool well adapted to dealing with the separation, particularly when it uses as its fuels either fleeing fear, which creates distance, or the separating walls of anger.

Yet we are not confined to this separated world. Just as the colors of the rainbow blend imperceptibly into one another, we can access a continuing, vital reality. Mopping and dusting are lifted to a new level when we plug in a vacuum cleaner. We can reach out to create effectiveness and sustainability in living human relationships (where the action is) by deliberately using the power of friendliness and goodwill. Love has enormous power.

The objectifying part of the thinking process becomes a way to refine the crude fuels of fear and anger to more effective grades. Once we understand this, we gain for ourselves purpose for a life that can seem at times pointless in its separation, its isolation. The article "You Can't Get There from Here" indicates the difference between the downgrading from experience to facts, and the skill to be able to upgrade, to infuse life when people and relationships are involved.

I have long observed that people who are troubled often lack certain information. There is something about life they don't know. If they found out and practiced what they learned, they could lift themselves out of the mire. This applies both to children too immature to see and adults repeating patterns taken on years ago when they were children. Children can benefit from guidance. Adults can be open to self-observation, then apply the same guidance to themselves.

This book does not try to prove any points. It invites you to rise to the living level where you have experiences. Then you can examine how you feel about it in a far more personal way. You make your own decisions. No one proves you wrong or right.

This book is a collection of short entries into the knowledge of how to *work* life. As you read this book and go about living, you can expect to knit the two more and more together.

The sections are broached in the first part of the book, then recapped and expanded in the second part. The sections are as follows:

Beginnings

No Lecturing

Love Is Power

Love Interrupted

Energy, E

Awareness: Essential

Now

Life as Experienced

Body: Breathing

Body: Heart

Body

Mind-Meanings

Mind and the Things It Deals with Well

INTRODUCTION

HOPE

This book is grounded in optimism. As any seedling will tell you, there is always room for hope (just add water). Optimism is based on an accurate assessment of the possibilities. It is the mischievous mind that can sow doubt and reap a harvest of weeds, useless dead ends.

Does your life ever feel like you are groping your way forwards in the darkness? Each two-page spread in *Love Is Power* can become a point of light, if you will let it. Allow your selection of these fireflies to light your way!

THE PATHWAY TO HEALING

You can re-enrich the word extracts of *Love Is Power* by infusing the dry words with your meanings, giving them relevance to your life, as you are currently living it. Life, the way we naturally live it, tends to create hard knocks. In the sense of what-goes-around-comes-around, you can generate correcting reactions (from others) to what you are putting out. This becomes for you the School of Hard Knocks, which initially creates despair.

Living through despair in order to utilize its function of loosening holding patterns, you can reach for the invisible tools of patience, tolerance, and humility. You say "Here goes nothing" as you take a deep breath and chew on a little humble pie; see poem HUMBLE PIE.

This generates awareness. With greater awareness you increase the relevance and accuracy of your responses to what is going on around you. You move yourself to operate from greater understanding.

From the position of awareness, you can see better how words can cheapen what you are doing. You are not doing it to reap gratitude. You are doing it because service to others benefits giver and receiver, and you have come to relish serving humanity.

ENTERING INTO THE SPIRIT OF *LOVE IS POWER*

Developing a routine of self-care gives you continuity. No one else can do it for you. You would resent it if they tried. A pattern of planned selfishness is needed. Some people would give you the shirt off their back. Such generosity is wonderful. But if they have no plans to put another shirt on their back, that is the end of their giving.

In the struggles of life, we frequently seem stuck in a blind alley, trying to find a way forward. Interestingly, the movement out of stagnation always involves practicing a way that is being nicer to ourselves. Indeed, there could be no other way. We are each a part of life, no matter how many ways we discount it. There is a place in the flow of things for each of us to fill.

Some people basically think well of themselves and don't need to improve that thinking. Other people, while they may be nice to others—loving and generous—can be the opposite to themselves. If you kick yourself and find that really helps, go right ahead. It would be a shame to stop a good thing. But if on careful examination, you find it doesn't help, you can decide to stop and look for alternatives.

Body's bleeding?
Mind is freezing?
Friendship's fallen
on hard times?
No sense wishin'
needs nutrition.
Being respectful
life sublimes.

It is okay to expand your generosity and to include yourself as a recipient of it. You are a magnificent automobile with an amazing array of knobs and dials on the instrument panel, begging to be understood. It is a shame you would simply put your foot up and down on the accelerator. Add richness to your life.

It is important to do that even when you don't feel like it, particularly when you don't feel like it. Comfort zones can be seductive. The problem is that the less full your tank is (the less emotional fuel you have in your tank), the less you feel like filling your tank. Sometimes you have to pull yourself up by your own bootstraps. You feel so good when you do!

Within this book lies a smorgasbord of goodies. Take from it each day the item that seems most nourishing for you. Take two! If you develop the attitude that within every difficulty lies an opportunity, life becomes a feast. This book is a feast.

If you are well-fed
you will do better
when you visit countries
where starvation is the norm.
If you are emotionally well-fed
you will do better
when you have to keep company
with people used to emotional starvation.

If you will constantly and consistently keep returning to nurture yourself through your trials and tribulations, through pain and suffering, as well as through the good times, you tell yourself deeply that you are worthwhile, that no mistake was made the day you were created. This can be a basis for a profound long-term healing and self-strengthening that will stand you in good stead for the rest of your life.

BEGINNINGS

INTRODUCTION

Beginnings. The focus of "Beginnings" is on you, the reader. It is important to like yourself and not to pull that apart with self-criticism. With these problems mastered, you can feel free to celebrate your uniqueness. With your own beauty in full view, it becomes possible to recognize the beauty in others. You can all be human.

But it is always possible to return to self-criticism and believe bad things about yourself. Let that go. You are evolving. You have choices to make.

It is okay to commit yourself to something and go at it whole-heartedly. But you don't need to drag along with painful ways of doing things. If you need permission to take a break, you have it. Take a break. The important thing is that you are on your own side. Look in the mirror and read the following pages to yourself. You need to know you feel this way about you:

LIKING

I like you. I am your new friend. Our friendship will grow. There is no hurry. Take it at your own speed. I am not going anywhere. I will always be here for you. I will not leave you.

WORTHWHILE.

You are worthwhile. You have your own unique value as a human being.

GOOD HEAD.

You have good head on your shoulders. You will get better with practice at using it. Use it. Be in charge of when and how.

DON'T UNRAVEL

If someone knits a sweater or woolen pullover and gives it to you as a present, you may see if you like the color and try it on for size. You don't begin unraveling it.

This is the fourth topic in this section. Are you restating the last three topics with negative statements such as: "I 'like' you? I don't like you. I hate you. Nobody could like you. You're impossible to like."

"Worthwhile? You aren't worthwhile. You are worthless. There is no less worthy person on the planet!"

"You have a lousy head. You're stupid!"

When you make such judgments, you effectively unravel the meaning and the healing potential of the originals.

Don't unravel. Know the power in your every thought. How many rocks do you want to add to your rock cake? Saying *I don't like you* (meaning "I hate myself") may be conformable in the sense that it is familiar; that is, you say that often. But the purpose of these pages is to remove the weeds from the garden.

Block each negative unraveling statement. "I was only pulling wool over my eyes, stopping myself from seeing the beauty in the construction that is me."

This time, relax the muscles that tighten up and drive the negatives home uselessly, mischievously, ridiculously. Breathe in the fresh air, the value in the statements that contain true oxygen.

The sections in this book are all gifts. If one does not fit, pass it on. Do not unravel it. It may fit someone else exactly.

If you find you *have* to unravel these gifts repeatedly, look at your life. Do you tend to unravel other good things? Could there be gifts of untold potential that you do not receive because of your unraveling habit? Your first step in conquering that habit may be to pass by it. This time, deliberately refuse to practice the habit. As you create more and more *this times,* somewhere down the line this new behavior will take hold inside. The penny will drop.

The message of this book is the power of love. Regard the Unraveler, the Insulter, the Over-Critical Critic within you as a small child who feels ignored and has adopted a boring plan to drain your energies in order to get attention. Tell the child he or she can have your attention, but not in that way. Tell the child he or she is good, worthy of receiving attention; he or she is deserving, but must cool the way he or she has been acting. Tell the child that you love him or her, that your love is always available, that he or she can expect good things from you and feel safe about that. But he or she can no longer give you a hard time.

Be like "Sir" in the movie *To Sir, With Love.* The new teacher wins over an unruly class with patience and warmth. Patiently befriend each element (the Unraveler, the Insulter) and allow them to begin trusting you. Keep clearly in mind the picture of the prodigal son who eventually returns and is welcomed back into the family. You are the one who welcomes you. With each stop along the way, draw even closer to that picture. Use your love, practice your patience, keep your insistence clear: a happy ending is in sight for all.

Then take the weeks and the months to reel in that big fish, without breaking the line. ("Oh! I broke the line!" No, you didn't. That is just the fish trying to get out of what you are doing, so it can continue its boring routine. The line was merely a metaphor. Stay the course.)

QUOTATION FROM SCRIPTURE

> *If I am not for myself, who will be for me?*
> *But if I am only for myself, what am I?*
> *If not now, when?*

JUDAISM: Hillel the Elder (*Ethics of the Fathers*, 1:14)

BE YOURSELF

It's essential to be yourself here, now, in the presence of others. You are who you are at *this* point, not yesterday, not tomorrow. You feel what you feel *right now*, not what you *should* feel or what you try hard to feel. Your expression of feelings is your way to reach someone and make emotional contact with her or him the way you are right now.

When you don't do that with someone, you both miss out. Your *self,* despite any discouragement you may have heard, is a source of vast treasures, most of which are not mined in a lifetime.

PRESENCE

You make a difference. Your specialness shows. Whether people seem to respond or not, you are noticed. You have presence. Know that. Be secure in that. Never discount it.

DIFFERENT

It's essential to be different— to be different from others and sometimes to differ with others. Your way of doing things is okay. You are not the same as anyone. Differences keep things interesting. *Vive la difference!*

BEAUTIFUL

You are beautiful. You have an inner beauty that transcends your outward appearance. It is okay to sense this inner beauty and to radiate more and more of it each day. It is your glow. Love evens out worry lines drawn by the habit of tensing muscles as if to achieve something. The ultimate glow is to become a hollow vessel through which love passes.

OTHERS' BEAUTY

It is okay to sense this beauty within others, even if they are not used to sensing it in themselves. When you use your beauty to sense theirs, you are benefiting both.

BE HUMAN

It's important to be human. Do not act like a robot. People sometimes do that, trying to avoid feelings. You are not a robot. You are far greater. Learn to deal with feelings. Join the human race.

SOMETHING BAD INSIDE

So you believe there is something bad deep inside you. You see the badness as unworthy, as weak, as useless. You are as horrible as a human being can be. You tell yourself that to investigate this would court disaster. You would be laughed at, rejected, criticized, punished, or killed. And you'd deserve it. You have developed so much fear about this that you have not even dared to look at it, to face the awful truth, lest your worst fears be realized.

Good news! You're wrong! You are from top to toe an incredible being, worthy of worship, not denigration. You were born unique, with your own personality, your own way of seeing things and approaching things. Top that off with all you have gone through, how you reacted to it, what you've learned by this point in your life, and the resulting strategies you now use. There has never been anyone like you. You are amazing.

We sometimes learn things that are wrong, from parent-people who should not have been teaching such lessons. We take on what we choose in order to cope, to adjust, to feel acceptable, and to survive until we are grown up. In this process, we can take on false beliefs.

Let it all go. Start by being you: your uniqueness, your special ability to be who you are, your capacity to contribute to the world in a way you may not yet have fully worked out. Let that flower. If someone else cannot cope with that, that is their problem.

Become who you are: an individual human being at this place in this moment of your evolution.

EVOLVING ME

I used to believe
that I was defective
wrong shape, wrong size,
bad parts, inferior construction
unworthy, rejectable
ugly, disgusting in all ways
guilty as charged
I suffered mental and emotional starvation
as if I ate rocks for breakfast
emotional nutrition
was what I was lacking
the giving, receiving of
nourishing lubricant.
I practiced my gratitude
emotional warmth
got my love flowing
canoed that river
with ever more skill
riding the wave
that I was creating.
I now believe
that I am just right
a unique person
with a special viewpoint
my own sensitivity
worthy and beautiful
in my own way
not in need of correction
having a purpose
that I keep uncovering
excited at becoming
ever more Me!

WHAT YOU WANT

You are okay when you choose what you want to do and take the responsibility for what you do as you do it.

You think it through. You consider the options. You make your plans. You carry them out. It is easier then to see the results of your actions. The learning sequence, wants > results > adapt for better-next-time, becomes the way to shape your life to a professional caliber.

LIVING DANGEROUSLY

A behavior common to teenagers, but also carried on by many grownups, is living dangerously. It is as if the intensity of rebellion, combined with my-way-at-any-cost, obscures an exact appreciation of what you are doing. The following anecdote clarifies the issue:

Let's say you are an excellent cyclist. You are so good that you could ride your bike close to the edge of a cliff a thousand times and not fall over. So off you go, a hundred, two hundred, three hundred times. No fall. Five hundred, eight hundred, a thousand times. You are doing fine.

Twelve hundred times, fifteen hundred times, still no problem. Twenty-two hundred, twenty-nine hundred times. You are pushing your luck!

Thirty-seven hundred times. And off you go. Dead!

If you knew you would end up that way, why would you do it even once? Are you a loser? Are you self-destructive? Look at the issues you are dealing with (or avoiding). Pick over your choices. Which ones yield the best results? Is there something in that for you?

CHANGE

It's okay to change. We are all changing constantly in tiny ways. It's possible to change yourself, your beliefs, if they don't fit. Change your behaviors, if you need to. Don't despair if results are not instantaneous. You can only improve with practice. No one ever got worse by doing it right again and again.

The model for change is the dancing of Fred Astaire and Ginger Rogers. They flow across the dance floor in a wonderful way, constantly changing direction, evolving their movements, as they respond in intimate ways to the tiniest push here, pull there, turn, or swing. But the thinking mind is unable to grasp that. So it flash-freezes heaven into a statue of the couple. The mind may require some coaxing, some understanding, to release its hold and allow life to flow back in.

Breaking New Ground

When you practice something new
aimed at healing and growing you
it will be different, that's for sure
you won't be used to what's in store
You'll feel like saying "This is strange
it isn't 'me,' I feel deranged
this isn't like the life I know
let's go back to the status quo."
Knowing that is how you'll see it
you're forewarned to let you be it
practice makes you more familiar
lets you shift. It didn't kill ya.

Committed

It is good to be committed to something you believe in. You have the capacity to be committed. Exercise that capacity. Don't let it go to rust. It's stimulating to experience the vitality that you generate within yourself by commitment, the focus that uplifts. It's useful to examine your commitments. You don't have to retain commitments that have become destructive and pointless. Let those ones go.

All events can be turned to good. Like the conductor of an orchestra, you can monitor constantly and direct the details, the effectiveness of your commitment to doing something worthwhile just as that conductor blends together a living, swelling performance of the music.

Time Out

It is valuable to take time out, quiet time, when you can be with yourself. Plan regular time to do this. In this way build calmness into your life.

Pain Habit

We all have habits learned in childhood, preferences established at that stage and brought into adulthood. Some of those habits can be painful, yet we continue them and cause our own pain. By focusing on these habits and distancing ourselves a little, we can examine what we are doing and turn it around.

People say "Grow Up!" But we don't grow up. We are not ready to grow up. There is more to be understood, more to be learned by waiting a little longer inside the childhood pattern and re-working it. "So take your well-meaning advice and give it to someone who wants it," we feel like saying. As we get it wrong once again, we begrudgingly admit that the pain we have piled upon ourselves must last a little longer. Then we try to loosen and free up stuff that we have been living under—beliefs and their bodily expressions that have protected us, even while restricting us.

NO LECTURING

Introduction
Understanding Must Be Earned
The Three-Way Healing of Understanding
Misunderstanding Explained

9

INTRODUCTION

No Lecturing. No Lecturing says this book. *Love Is Power* never tells you what to do. You are you, a unique individual with specific sensitivities, interests, and awareness, here on this planet to have the experiences most useful to you.

A lecturer can drive a point hard by repeating it, in a my-will-be-done type of way. At no point is it my intention to lecture you or tell you what to do. It would be highly inappropriate. A book cannot know what you are dealing with or what you are feeling. It cannot know your situation. The best a book can do is offer suggestions. Take them or leave them. You will know what to do.

Your task in life is to go through it, gleaning bits of information that will assist you in dealing with life from your point of view. No expert can ever tell you what your perspective, your angle on this, really is. You know that already. You can tell the expert. You are gaining understanding.

You have a brain. Use it. No amount of passing off responsibility like a child might can ever shift you away from the need to see what is going on, to reach an understanding about it all, to use your brain to decide what to do. Be free to say "In this situation, at this time, with me doing it, this particular suggestion (from anyone trying to be helpful) is exactly what I will not do."

There is a flip side to this. If you read something in this book and it feels to you that you are being lectured, look again. Have you placed a skew on the process? Do you take out a microscope and enlarge the intensity of the suggestion way beyond the original intent? Does that happen elsewhere in your life? Do you often feel lectured to? Where did your habit of being the lecturee arise? Do you want to continue it any longer? What would be a next step you could take toward the ultimate goal of growing yourself up?

The article "Understanding Must Be Earned" points out the key role that understanding plays in a life that is being allowed to evolve. See also the poem "The Three-Way Healing of Understanding." If you don't want to gain that understanding, if you choose to stay weak for the rest of your life, it's easy. Just refuse to open the book. Case closed. But please, oh please, before you make that terrible mistake, read the poem "Misunderstanding Explained." It might make all the difference.

UNDERSTANDING MUST BE EARNED

Understanding is a profound emotion because of the empathy bound up in it. We can look with awe at someone who, time and again, demonstrates the depth and breadth of his or her understanding.

We all seek understanding. We want its healing. We cry out when it is missing. "Is there no one who understands me?!"

What is on the outside—the people and things in life to which we give importance and meaning—we also react to on the inside. We feel and react inside to the whole world. We want understanding from others. We have a responsibility to expect and create understanding within ourselves.

Understanding has deep qualities of healing at three different levels. It works on the thinking mind, the emotional heart, and the physical body.

The best of understanding has a thinking component. There are words that can be put to it. Yet it is, above all, action-oriented. There are people who use no words. They move in, do the job expertly, and then move back with a smile on their face. We admire them. We go to them for help. But being able to talk about things is important, particularly when the understanding we want involves people and relationships. Not so much talk that it squeezes the rich life out of it all, turning a plum into a prune; not so little talk that appreciation is not shown. But a balance.

Understanding has a living, heartfelt component. It is healing for the emotional heart. Without that, it is hardly understanding. The person who talks your head off trying to enforce his or her point of view may come across dry and devoid of humanity. This is cookie-cutter understanding, aiming to carve out a piece of territory, to be proved right. This is unreal. True understanding has a flowing, enlivening richness whose quality is undeniable, way beyond the dryness of facts and information or the mind-derived agenda.

Deep within understanding is the physical component—the sense of *standing-under*; the solidly grounded physical base that supports the whole structure. This part lies within the physical body. This third component rounds out the balance of the three elements.

One problem with someone who professes understanding is the instant expert. This is the teenager who has discovered something fresh and new and wishes to convince everyone. He sees the world in a grain of sand. Perhaps the world does lie within a grain of sand. But you think, *Not yet. Wait a while. You have more to learn.* Your understanding is greater than his. Yet you honor his excitement of discovery.

Another problem person who believes she understands is the person who has actually had a lot of experience, but always from the same point of view. She began gathering the experience from a certain angle. This remains her slant on things. The narrowness of this excludes a full understanding. Aspects inconsistent with the point of view have been edited out. They simply didn't happen. This is denial, the thinking mind blocking full awareness.

Understanding must be earned. It is the living, vibrant, enriched extension of simple knowledge, raw information. Must you forever struggle in the *Land of Unawareness,* dominated by a fear-driven, agenda-pushing mind? Understanding can be created if you are willing to invest your life energy in it; i.e., make it an experience. Full openness is necessary. This can require humility. Humility pries open eyelids previously closed to seeing, changing a mind-set that would otherwise railroad true understanding out of town. To gain this in-depth grasp of what is really going on, requires consistent, focused effort extended over a period of time. Understanding steadily melts hard holding actions.

This effort at focusing involves relaxing habits and holding patterns. Such misused energy creates noise that interferes with awareness. Without awareness—remaining emotionally blind, deaf, or insensitive—true understanding becomes impossible.

There is not an endpoint called "full understanding" at which you can stop. Endpoints and stopping are evidence of the thinking mind claiming territory for its efforts, chopping off natural interconnectedness. Rather, understanding is a process, a pathway you can feel privileged to be on, where you gain more and more power, more and more grasp of the process of life, and more and more ability to bring words to describe what is going on.

Be open. Be patient. You are gleaning for yourself a power that will last a lifetime. If you want understanding, you don't have to chase it. Openness will do. It will come to you. With deepening understanding, you leave behind excessive concern about details. This understanding has a vibrant life of its own. You open progressively like a flower. It is from this wisdom that we observe, "To travel is better than to arrive." Every step of the journey *is the journey*.

THE THREE-WAY HEALING OF UNDERSTANDING

There's something for the mind in understanding,
the feeling heart's receiving something real
till and when you're grounded,
feeling standing–under your body's in there,
taking what is true.

MISUNDERSTANDING EXPLAINED

I said to this person
who lacked understanding
" 'been watching your statements
I think that they show
there's something you're missing
so here's what you're needing
there is something more
that I want you to know."
I'd seen he was able
to take information
so shameful to keep him
so blind, not abreast.
Some folks are distracted
yet open to reason
you give them a clue
and they'll fill in the rest.
I told him, I filled him
with missed information
I saw him relax
hearing what I could say
his face bore a grin
I'd been gentle and kindly
he knew I was with him
there's no other way.

LOVE IS POWER

Introduction
Compassion
Compassion Is in Fashion
Quotations from Scriptures

13

INTRODUCTION

Love Is Power. The power built into love is what this book is about. Love is invisible. Yet that doesn't stop you from deliberately choosing to tap it and use it for the power it has to heal people and situations. It is equivalent to fuel. Fuel supplies power to get things done.

Fuel is a product of crude oil, the black gold that can be refined to higher, usable grades. Other upgraded products include perfumes, lubricants, and plastics.

Crude-oil feelings can be upgraded too. Fuel, in this case, is the invisible, unbounded feelings that extend far beyond the range of the physical. The mind understands and uses the crudest of the living feelings—fear and anger—to drive its simple yet far-ranging actions. Between the actions of fear and of anger, we can feel hog-tied to incompetence, hopelessness, and a belief in our own ineffectiveness. Underneath that load lies a potential fuel that is unique to each of us, but which goes untapped until we take deliberate action. That potential lies with love.

Through easing crude feelings—relaxing and upgrading them—love goes on to sort out and prioritize what you do, while at the same time, making it pleasurable. Love helps you filter people and situations to best advantage for all.

COMPASSION

Compassion is your beautiful gift. It can be received. It can be given. When someone shows us compassion, we can relax, breathe easier, and say, "At last, someone understands." We feel the healing as we openly receive compassion. When you let your compassion flow out from you, you raise your power to a healing level. You open yourself to be *relevant to the needs of another.*

Compassion is the sponge for fear. Fear, the crippler, experiences its enlightening rejuvenation when compassion enters. Transformed, it can throw away the crutches.

COMPASSION IS IN FASHION

Compassion is in fashion
and there will be no more bashin'
or people looking ashen
for the passion that's so smashin'
it's so nice that it's in style.

QUOTATIONS FROM SCRIPTURE

To act like the beasts of the field is unworthy of man. Those virtues that befit his dignity are forbearance, mercy, compassion, and loving-kindness toward all the peoples and kindreds of the earth.

BAHA'I FAITH: *Gleanings* 109

Who is incapable of hatred toward any being, who is kind and compassionate, free from selfishness … such a devotee of Mine is My beloved.

HINDUISM: Bhagavad-Gita 12:13–14

Finally, all of you, live in harmony with one another; be sympathetic, love as brothers, be compassionate and humble. Do not repay evil with evil, or insult for insult; but with blessing, because to this you were called so that you may inherit a blessing.

CHRISTIANITY: 1 Peter 3:8–9 NIV

LOVE INTERRUPTED

INTRODUCTION

Love Interrupted. There are many ways in which energy, which would normally be freely available for us to use as the power in love, can be diverted, stored, used-up, or turned into a noisy distraction. It can also be intensified beyond usability with too much energy. Many of these are holdovers from childhood that need upgrading and updating; see "In a Hole." Trying hard can be a problem; see "Trying." Being strong can achieve a parallel result, see "Strong," and its "Quotations from Scripture." The power in love is much superior to the phoniness of trying or being strong.

The following articles illustrate the points made above. Follow the cross-references to other articles. They in turn will have cross-references. Follow the chain of cross-references that interest you.

INTENSIFYING, DE-INTENSIFYING.

Children can have problems. Sometimes the problems come from the parents. These problems are hand-me-downs from a previous generation. Sometimes the child has a problem that has no obvious connection to the parents. The child brought it with her into this life. It is part of her skill set: who she is, what she is sensitive to, and how she likes to react.

Children try to solve problems. Children use childlike ways to do so. Using a flood of energy is one such way. Every child can intensify emotions and reactions. They're not just wounded, they're mortally wounded. They're not just wrong, they're permanently, unforgivably, dejectedly wrong. Disaster! Disaster! "Try! Try harder!" binds it all up. The intensification becomes a holding, a squeezing, and then a stranglehold on some issue. The body can be a place where the intensity takes hold. Muscles tighten. They may even tremble. Airways, arteries, bowels can spasm—all in the service of solving some problem. Grownups, years later, can be still doing the same thing.

It is all right. You can de-intensify. More intensity never was going to solve anything. Take some breaths. Breathe slowly. Breathe deeply. Gently ease into the pressure, the intensity. Imagine each breath you let out carrying a little more, and a little more, and then a little more of the intensity you have been holding. Take your time. There's no rush. Add a new meaning. From now on, every breath out takes with it a little of the unnecessary intensifying, holding, or trying you are still doing.

IN A HOLE

Patient:	Doctor! Doctor! You have to help me.
Doctor:	I'll do my best.
Patient:	You know me well. I'm trying so hard. Nothing's working.
Doctor:	You are standing in a hole. The way you are going about it is denying you success.
Patient:	Can't you see how hard I'm trying?
Doctor:	But you're standing in a hole.
Patient:	Nobody can accuse me of not trying. No one could put in more effort that I do.
Doctor:	*But you are standing in a hole!*
Patient(frustrated):	You're not listening to me!

Who is not listening to whom is in question here. Sometimes, with eyes fixed on unreachable clouds, we may need to turn our vision 180° to the hole, in order to begin a genuine healing. A simple step out of the hole, removes any further need for supreme effort. The main distracter to doing that can be all the wasted effort: the habit. Its noise is deafening.

Switch to validating the aliveness, the feeling itself. As the doctor, you may say, "I can see how frustrated you feel." You validate the aliveness, the person who is feeling, you. That may be all the response needed to loosen the holding-on.

Standing in a hole is self-degrading. If you stand in a hole three-feet deep, someone five-feet tall looks eight-feet tall to you.

Breathe quietly. Relax. It is all right. There is life. There is hope. Let things settle. Too much hard work is strangling things. Let it go. The gardener wrenching at the plant to make it grow does nothing for a process that has its own beautiful, relaxed agenda.

TRYING

I try and I try and I try ... and I try
I can't get no ... satisfaction ...[1]

—Mick Jagger, Keith Richards
of the Rolling Stones

First Term Report: Trying.
Second Term Report: Still trying.
Third Term Report: Still very trying.

We are all familiar with the idea of trying. We can say to a friend "You didn't even try!", sometimes with obvious justification. Your friend put out no effort.

> The word *trying* is a hazardous word to use. It implies strain, such as muscles that might move. So nothing happens, despite the effort. One foot on the brake and one foot on the accelerator.

We understand this so clearly that we do not tolerate the word "try" under many circumstances. How would you feel if the doctor said, "I'll try to take out your gall bladder"? Would you let him have a shot? Suppose he said later, "I'm sorry. I tried." Could you console him? No! You wanted the gall bladder out. "There'll be no 'trying' on me," you say.

There are many situations where the task is near to impossible. You might say, "I'll try to scale the east face of Mt. Everest without oxygen." The strain is built into the task.

There are many situations where the task is readily achievable with appropriate effort. If someone says "I'll try," you then question their motivation. "Do you really want to do it?" you might ask. Perhaps some further discussion will clarify their mixed feelings about the job. After that, the person may be able to say, "I'll do it," or perhaps, "I don't want to do it; so I won't." Both of these are clearer. You know where you stand. No one is "trying."

---

1   The raw-sounding musical accompaniment to the Rolling Stone's song lyric, with the rising and collapsing root note and the accompanying fifth above or fourth below, adds to the feeling of hopelessness. The emotional third in between is avoided. The message is that failing to deal with emotions while adding lots of try energy gets you nowhere.

Try is often used by people wanting to make an impression without committing to doing the job. "I only said I'd try," is their out. They never said they *would* do it, just that they would *try* to. Try energy shreds genuine talk down to a mulch of phoniness.

The mind has the agenda of trying. That agenda forces the pace. The body double-teams with the mind to create muscle tension. The noise sent back to the brain by muscles screaming, "I'm tight, I'm tight!" can be deafening and distracting.

Pull the energy. Invest less. Breathe slowly and deeply. Relax. Take it easy. If you find you simply have to attack someone verbally because you feel incapable of doing otherwise, turn sideways and do it from that angle; literally talking over your shoulder reduces the impact.

The word *try* is full of problems. Learn to avoid using the word yourself. If someone else uses it, be prepared for some discussion to help clear murky waters. If they feel your genuine interest, they may feel free to talk about their mixed feelings, clear their ambivalence, and go ahead to do an effective job.

The energy within trying can be built into holding actions in the body. Often, the thinking mind is behind this, prompting the body and attempting to exert control over it.

Ten finalists have been selected in a competition to sing the role of Maria in *The Sound of Music*. The two who gained the least points must sing to decide who is to be eliminated. One has lots of animation and facial expression. The other gives a wooden performance. The wooden one is eliminated. She must now sing "Farewell."

She is unrecognizable! She sings her heart out. The mask is off. The woodenness is gone. She *is* Maria.

Previously she had been *trying hard to be* Maria. The program from the thinking mind dictated intense holding. This was represented faithfully by the body as tense, expressionless facial muscles and rigidity in the diaphragm. The diaphragm sucks life-giving oxygen into the lungs. From there, the blood delivers the oxygen to all parts. An unmoving diaphragm stole the life from the contestant's voice.

Behind the mind's programming, she had long studied the role. She deeply understood Maria. After losing the part, she now switched to method acting, well able to express and be the Maria her aliveness knew so well, the aliveness no thinking process could ever simulate. She became her true self, the one she knew so well.

An example of trying in classical music is Tchaikovsky's *Sixth Symphony*. Tchaikovsky tries hard to look on the bright side. Yet repeatedly, the death music comes back and back. The composer died just over a year after writing it.

STRONG

A highly prized quality in our society is the ability to be strong. This quality will hopefully override difficulties and help us survive through threatening situations. Relaxed and tense ways to do this quickly separate us into two camps with very different outcomes.

When you are strong the tense way, you burn life energy 'round the clock to maintain total body muscle tension—as if to mimic the armor of knights of old. Movements, talk, even thinking become limited. It is as if you are at the starter's block; the starter raises his pistol and says, "Get ready! Get set!" … you wait … you wait … but the gun never goes off! People can spend a lifetime at the ready, tense all over, for no obvious gain. The brain is bombarded with I-am-tense messages from a billion muscle fibers, pouring their hearts out along the afferent feedback nerves. No wonder thinking becomes awkward. The whole person is agitated.

Relax. Breathe easily. Let out the tension a little more, a little more, with each exhaled breath. Limber up. Work out. Build muscle strength. Chronically tense muscles are fragile, not able to guard joints the way they deserve and need to be guarded. Save your energy for more useful messages than I-must-be-ready-danger-might-be-anywhere. Jumping at your own shadow invites attack, when you are already exhausted. Supple, relaxed responses bring much better results than cramped muscles can manage. Your strength is your ability to be agile, not your ability to imitate a rhinoceros.

> *Come to me, all you who are weary and burdened, and I will give you rest. Take my yoke upon you and learn from me, for I am gentle and humble at heart, and you will find rest for your souls. For my yoke is easy and my burden is light.*
>
> CHRISTIANITY: Matthew 11:28–30 NIV

ENERGY, E

INTRODUCTION

Energy, E refers to energy in its crudest form. This section looks at how we upgrade it to suit our needs. Energy is used for all movement, be it the erupting of a volcano or the energy you use to walk down the street or ponder some problem. Important, is to distinguish the quality of living, vibrant energy from the lesser, non-alive forms. Energy tends to be destructive unless and until it is deliberately transformed into love or supported in a profusion of love.

The equation $E = mc^2$ illustrates the relationship between a small number, matter (m) and a very large number, the speed of light multiplied by itself (c^2), demonstrating that Energy (E) is a huge amount. This was the principle behind the atomic bomb, which wreaked a great deal of destruction on Hiroshima and Nagasaki at the end of World War II.

Interestingly, there is a parallel within the human being where a lot of basically destructive energy can be released without the protection and support of vital healing love. It takes a lot of energy to have a mental health problem, a lot of energy to always be angry and scared.

Raw energy takes many forms. Tension and agitation serve no purpose for human beings. Sex and excitement can be mistaken for love. They are best when grounded in love.

In the first *Star Wars* movie, Obi-Won Kenobi says to Luke Skywalker, "May the force be with you." What he did not mention was that that force is love. Perhaps it would have been inappropriate in such a movie, a movie about war, conflict. Nonetheless, moviegoers were able to identify with Luke Skywalker and project their tension on to him.

A good skill to develop is the ability to recognize the moment when further effort begins to reverse the results so far achieved. Making too much or too little energy can be your body's attempt to solve the problem of depression. But neither works. Instead, they merely increase the depression. Sex involves lots of energy. Unfortunately, it can be misused. Excitement is raw energy, capable of being leavened with love. Until that happens, much mischief can be done. Another important skill is recognizing at what point speed becomes an issue. The speed of healing is slower than the speed of rushing. Exhaustion can be the payoff if the lesson is not learned.

TOO MUCH EFFORT

We live in an age that worships too much effort. So often the excess effort we put in defeats the purpose we intended. If your key won't turn in the lock, you can try forcing it. If the key breaks in the lock, then you really have a problem. If you are watering plants, the process is gentle and the plants do well. It is difficult to imagine what could force it or make this process hard (ice cubes? stomping on the plants?).

Worry wastes energy over time. Holding, being strong, and body armoring (Lowen 1958), which is muscle tension kept going over long periods, also add up to using too much effort. The habit of "catastrophizing," as described in Judith Beck's *Cognitive Behavior Therapy,* is another way to needlessly dissipate energy: It isn't difficult, it's impossible; it isn't awkward, it's life-threatening (Beck 1995).

Too much energy is often inconsiderate. It becomes a rough brutalizing of a situation, when a more measured touch would be much gentler . It can also be a deeply secret fanning of the flames of a fear driving the whole road show. Are you actually afraid of a bad result when you deliberately drown a situation with excess energy? Is your undisciplined excessiveness edging you away from the loving state that you fear might be too much? Is it love that you fear? Are you choosing the crudity of excess over the quality product? Could you instead, at this very moment, simply *choose* to be loving, and direct that love wherever you want to send it?

The nicest things in life—picking a flower, petting a puppy, giving and receiving a kiss—do not require smash-up energy. At such an intense level, all enjoyment is turned off. Survival responses, such as fear and anger, replace enjoyment. It all cries out for restraint. So often the gentle touch, the minimal-but-appropriate effort is what works. Conserve your efforts. Focus. Carry it through.

Do not fuss. Fussing over something can be exactly the excess energy that becomes your undoing.

HEALING SPEED

We function at three speeds: mind-speed, which is rapid and more conducive to agitation than to healing; emotional-speed which is slower and healing; and body-speed, the slowest, where physically damaged tissue is gradually replaced. Emotions are often held, static, in the body. It can be helpful to resolve emotions and release them. Then the body can follow its natural tendency to heal. Warm emotions are a living base. They upgrade and release stagnated, stored emotions.

You can't force yourself to be happy. You might say, "I want to be happy. I should be happy. Why aren't I happy?" If you are genuinely into investigating, understanding, and regaining control, this book may help. But there is much difference between your inner conductor (the truth-seeker) and automatic, controlling mind-speed— the same rapid speed as worry, as flashing yourself with scary images, as forcing an issue. You cannot force happy. It will not happen at a rapid speed.

Monitoring your speed is crucial. Thoughts are fast. They flutter like the wings of a bird in empty air. You can have a thousand thoughts very quickly.

Excitement works at that speed. We say, "I feel excited," but there is no calmness to it. You cannot stay excited for very long. It is too draining. Mind-driven excitement can exhaust you, requiring you to rest to replenish your energies. A mature grown-up is more likely to blend in understanding, gratitude, and some form of emotional warmth to leaven excitement. An immature child may become hyperactive.

If your life has been a weed patch lately, look for flowers, any aspect of anything you can use as an excuse to begin building your gratitude. It often begins with "At least I can …" or "At least I am not …"

You cannot feel sad, happy, grateful, angry, compassionate, or fearful in a hurry. These are feelings. You can feel their realness moving in. They are your vitality. That is for real. You must take your time. Each feeling must be savored for the value in it. You can say, "I know I'm alive. No machine can do this. This feels solid. I'm for-real now."

Pause a moment before you do each thing. Allow your frazzled focus to return, to settle, to relax.

When your body moves in, when you can *feel it in your bones*, your ultimate solidity is there. In this existence, we don't get any more real than that. This is the slowest speed: the tortoise doing the slow-and-steady to win the race.

EXCITEMENT GONE CRAZY

The fear that drives my racing
needs more speed to swallow fear
lest the impetus I'm racing from
might make me disappear.
At speed I can't smell roses
when my nose is slashed by thorns
and the thrill that spills and trips me
must be mourned on many morns.
For excitement can go crazy
lacking substance that maintains
without warmth it has no value
only sexiness remains.
So warm up your excitement
fold it in with pure love
you'll find others can connect with
what it is you're thinking of.

USING HEALING SPEED

Coordinate the following healing actions with your breathing. Breathing is a natural rhythm that is slower than the multitasking many-thoughts-a-second thinking. The rat-a-tat-tat speed irritates; it doesn't heal. Healing is slower: one receiving inhale followed by one releasing exhale at a time.. Settle down to breathing.

Sit relaxed. Close your eyes. Breathe out tension with each exhalation. Breathe in oxygen to relax tight muscles. Feel yourself, more and more with each breath, sinking into a relaxed state.

You are going to work directly with healing. Working with a healing partner (imagined), you will demonstrate the power of healing by its effect on others. Then you can do it for yourself. Put your wrist in front of your mouth and blow warm air onto it. Feel that warmth. That is the physical representation of your healing, emotional warmth. You can give out warmth.

Prime yourself with gratitude. Giving and receiving of any warm emotion are the same—twice blessed, as the Bible goes—benefiting both the one who gives and the one who takes. We will see below how to do this, by turns. As you inhale, line up in your imagination all the things you are grateful for. Feel the power begin to move within you. Exhale your healing breath into each image or memory, in succession. Feel the power of your gratitude flow more easily and more strongly with each breath.

Gratitude is a slow healer. Two other advantages to gratitude as a healer are its warmth and its controllability. You simply identify gratitude, gratefulness, and thankfulness; you just recognize it and show it, turn it on. You deliberately feel grateful, open the floodgates, let your gratitude flow.

Move your gratitude. Find any excuse, anywhere, anytime to be grateful. As you let it flow, feel its tingling throughout your body, enlivening you as you reach out to enliven someone else.

Choose someone you are can feel compassion toward. Picture the person in your mind. Breathe compassion into that person. See him or her healing, relaxing, easing, strengthening, expanding. It is the picture of the person in your head that you are healing. This improved personal representation will give you an enlivened head start before you meet them next time.

Is there someone you are willing to forgive? Start small. Breathe out a little warm forgiveness to that person (or perhaps it is a family pet). You are getting yourself in practice.

If you are not ambivalent about love, you may be willing to send out love. For most people, it is not too hard to think of someone they love. Watch the warmth of your love, in your mind's eye, bring that person to a warm glow!

Now comes the self-healing. It is your turn. You breathed out warmth. Breathe in warmth. Let the oxygen you take in light your own fires. Feel all evidence of suffocation—under-breathing—light up. Carbon dioxide leaves your body. You become cleaned out of this unwanted substance.

DISSIPATING VALUABLE ENERGY

We practice many tricks that can use up our energy, leaving us weak and exhausted, wondering why life is so hard.

The mind can exhaust its supply of energy with fruitless overwork. "What-ifs" are one way we do this. We imagine one disaster after another, when it is unlikely any of them have ever or will ever happen (and if by chance one did, the situation would likely be so unique it would require practiced awareness to respond, not worry). We diddle ourselves out of an accurate response, then, by installing a habit of being preoccupied.

Another exhausting mind trick is the "should" game: "I should do this," "I should do that," creating lots of noise to unsettle us, stop us thinking things through. When we say "I should have ..." we look back on an event now passed and out of reach and waste loads of present energy raining punishment on ourselves.

The body can dutifully echo this diatribe with holding actions, as if there were a storm—which there is, a storm inside of you—and you are holding on to the mast of a boat. Long-standing tensions of this nature burn up available calories. When you are so dissipated, even doing ordinary things can be difficult. The body has a heaviness that gives you the sensation that life itself is a punishment, as proposed by your mind.

TWO ENERGY MISUSES IN DEPRESSION

Energy up, energy down
you are bashed all over town
take back power, remove the strife
you'll create a happier life.

Depression is made of a complex of thinking, feeling, and physical factors that are uniquely expressed in each individual. No two people are depressed in the same identical way. As the objective conductor, you have the right to separate out the parts as they apply to yourself.

Physical body factors involving sleep, appetite and weight changes can be especially troublesome. The mind often plays the role of chief mischief-maker through its habit of chattering.

Last night I saw upon a stair
a little man who wasn't there
he wasn't there again today
oh, how I wish he'd go away.
—Anon.

The "little man who wasn't there" is the mind, invisible yet interfering.

The mind that never stops can keep you awake. This can intensify to worry. Losing sleep can disrupt your entire life.

The two energy misuses go in opposite directions. The first is increased energy: an upper. The second, decreased energy, is a turn-off, a real downer.

The first energy misuse comes, not surprisingly, from the thinking mind. The thinking goes something like this:

"I've been trying to solve this problem for a long time. I must be able to solve this problem. If I couldn't solve it, I'd be terrified."

"I know! What it needs is more energy. I can manage that."

The mind, unwilling to admit that the problem, (perhaps a relationship problem being expressed physically in the body), is beyond its capabilities, pumps in more and more energy to the point of exhaustion.

With the mind as usual convincing you it is the whole of you, you choose to expend more energy as it suggests, becoming more and more exhausted.

This cannot continue indefinitely. With the thinking process still in charge, a point of despair is reached:

"This way didn't work. That way didn't work. Nothing I can think of works. I'm a failure. I lose. I have to turn off all effort. I'll do nothing."

Depression's doom and gloom then gather around. This is unreal. It is denial of the true self that lies behind all of the nonsense.

The depression taking over begins to affect the physical body. Tensions, pains, aches, headaches, breathing difficulties, appetite and bowel upsets, weight changes can all follow—each driven by the thinking mind. The mind reacts to all of these with *more* effort, compounding the vicious cycle.

The extreme upper (more energy) and the extreme downer (no energy) are a polarization. The power of the true self, the power of love, lies between them. Love is a connector, not a separator. Separation is evidence that the mind is at work. It creates the polarized opposites, the extremes that are under governance of the mind. The power lies in love.

There is a way out. Love can do it. This may take time and patience. But since excessive speed is one of the errors of the thinking mind, this leech may need to be patiently, insistently pried away from its holding action.

SEX

Overheard in the dark of night: "Sorry dear. I thought it was the bedpost."

Sex is commonly mistaken for love. The expression *making love* might contribute to that error. When there is flowing love in abundance, having sex can be a delightful cherry on the top. The cleansing feeling that comes from an orgasm felt from head to toe adds to the delight.

In a life where love has not been given priority, sex is no substitute. A head full of ideas and fantasies can be the way love is excluded. In times past, the attitude of *doing her marital duty* could fill a woman's mind and so exclude her from loving. A man filling his mind with macho ideas and images of conquest doubles the error. Prostitution within a loveless marriage—where there is no cooperation to introduce even a little of the healing power within love—is still a problem today. Building body tensions can lead to violence.

The thinking mind is capable of becoming the solution to the problem it created in fear of losing control. It is possible, through a process of self-healing and maturing, to clear the *crude* energy from your body. Then having an orgasm, which raises awareness of putrid energy problems, without healing the habit that put such tensions there, can have the effect of encouraging the body to perform its historic role and accept feeling energy into itself, shoved there by the mind. This can be done even after your conductor has gained the confidence and trust of the thinking mind and so weaned it from its habit of colluding and double-teaming with the body. The body merely resorts to its old habit.

The solution to this is to have your "conductor"—your higher mind, the one in charge—bring the body to trust you. Love will do it. But it will cost you to upgrade your orgasms. It is likely that the bliss of divine orgasm, when love is flowing freely, requires you to be totally open and totally trusting of another human being. Are you ready for that? Can you be open and trusting of yourself? You may have become so in love with love, so entranced with its potential that you are willing to make that sacrifice. The expression *falling in love* is not enough. There is much that is childlike, dependent, and immature about that. Being in love successfully requires a wise, mature, planned use of love. But if you can do it, in the plentiful generosity of a greater reality, you can have your cake and eat it too. Practicing patience, forgiveness, gratitude, compassion, and self-awareness lay the pathway to uncover this.

Sexual excitement is not love. The speeded up energy intrinsic to excitement can temporarily shake loose, cleanse, and release tensions you are holding in the muscles and organs of your body. This can have the value of showing you that relaxation is achievable. But with no plan to heal and remove attitudes creating these tensions, they can only return. Cleansing dirties up again.

The supportive river of love provides tools to address these problems. With a loving base securely in place, sex becomes a delight, not a disappointing and false substitute for love. The river flows on to support many other human activities. This can loosen and heal an obsession with sex that was ruining your—or your partner's—life. Telling your partner how much you love him or her can become the basis for a real turn-on for you both, if you will allow that.

The contract when having sex requires that both participants make sure that their partner is getting his or her needs met. It is parallel to the attitude of giving in forgiveness: you need have no concern that you will get yours. It is your partner's job to ensure that. Mutuality is maintained.

QUOTATION FROM SCRIPTURE

The entire book: Song of Solomon, from Judaism, speaks to the beauty of sex. This is not commonly preached from the pulpit. We remain stuck in the tradition of Sigmund Freud's era. The spirit of good sex, like the spirit of this entire book, is in keeping with fostering the ability in each reader to glean from each situation, including sex, the fullest enjoyment possible.

EXCITEMENT

Excitement is a commonly accepted substitute for the power in love. But excitement does not rejuvenate. It exhausts you. That cannot be maintained for long. Excitement lacks the revitalizing aspect of emotional warmth, of simply being friendly. Excitement, like other feelings, is invisible and unbounded. So it can blend in with love and other warm feelings. But it lacks fundamental sophistication. Excitement alone simply vibrates.

Michael Moore, in his movie *Capitalism: A Love Story*, contrasts capitalism with democracy in an either/or, black-and-white way. I would expand that to a continuum: adding love. The banks in his examples were not being loving. They were not showing consideration for human beings. Add love, the more the better. The excitement the bankers felt at their financial success needed the upgrading of humanity added to their actions.

Small children are at risk. Without appropriate support they can learn the wrong lessons, blighting themselves for life. Immature and inexperienced, they can feel never so alive as when they are excited. They cling with glee to it. Good parents guide their children to associate excitement with success. All can experience joy in the successful accomplishment of initially small tasks, then larger and larger tasks. A momentum from "I can tackle this" can be trained into the growing, maturing person. The parent stays interested in what the current capability of the little one is and invites the child to discover that her own efforts can be successful.

Also invisible and capable of blending in is fear. Fear is hurtful. Children, unguided, can readily learn to invite the energy of bullying. Or they can learn to picture disasters for the "high" they begin to confuse with excitement. They can learn to be self-destructive. Excitement, blended with fear, becomes a snake that bites them.

As such a confused person matures to the age of sexual excitement, sadistic and masochistic elements blend in. Hurt becomes highly likely. The person who is sadistic in sex will get theirs, sooner or later. What goes around comes around. The sadistic person is unaware of the crime of confusion that he is perpetrating on his own self.

Excitement can heighten awareness. Dead to the world, the depressed person, for example, can be awakened by the adding in of excitement, if he or she will allow it. The dominating mind–body combination may be overcome, bounced out of its imprisoned life. The turn-off of imagining a magical drain of energy as a solution to the problem can require prolonged coaxing to realize holding on is a false prize.

WEAK EXCITEMENT, *POWERFUL* LOVE

We often use excitement as a substitute for love
but it can't achieve that power, so what were you thinking of?
It tightens and exhausts you, cannot be maintained for long
for the "love" that's just excitement does not leave you deeply strong.
I wanted to float gently in the sunshine of glory
instead excitement stuck me up a blocked-off chimney.
Excitement's just vibration. Children love to feel excited
all that gleeful energy leaves them joyfully ignited.
Good parents can associate excitement with success
understanding where the child is at, ensure there is no mess
"I can tackle this" is trained into the ever-growing child
ensuring that the grown adult never will go wild.
The risk of excitement is to blend into fear
the child without guidance can make that adhere
the "high" of excitement becomes that of "fright"
bad pictures have power to turn day to night
self-destruction pulled in, as they seek more delight
can change to the snake that knows only to bite.
Excitement is sexy, sadism is not
destruction, when added, dismantles the lot
the sadist confuses the hurt with the sex
which defeats enjoyment, it's far too complex.
What goes around comes around, a sadist will find
masochistically brings to self, things most unkind.
Excitement is noisy. It merely vibrates
vibration is trifling when the task's to relate
the other, repelled, and elsewhere now bound
needs love's attraction to turn things around.
Excitement's vibration can heighten awareness
vibration, allowed in will strengthen the bareness.
Depression's mind–body allegiance pollution
suggesting turn-off as the only solution
don't for a moment consider that way
for love is the power that you must obey.

AWARENESS, ESSENTIAL

INTRODUCTION

Awareness, essential. We need to be fully aware. We need others to be fully aware, awake, and listening to us when we speak to them. The person who seems to be going, "Duh, duh, duh," when we speak has an agenda in his head derived from the thinking mind that has nothing to do with you.

Without awareness, we make ourselves irrelevant to life, to what is going on. We can apply a pre-determined attitude to what is before our eyes, but sooner or later this way shows us how we have absented ourselves from the situation.

Agendas quickly age us. To fend that off, the older person, now beyond the time of competitive living, delights in children who are not yet mature enough to preempt joy, full awareness, and spontaneity with mind-derived agendas. Taking back control from the thinking process is a step toward healthy, relevant living.

You will need to build your own awareness as you become ready to do that. No forcing is needed. Meanwhile, you can gather information about some annoying features of unawareness.

Commonly, we pick and choose what we will be aware of. The environment in which we live plays a big part. One of the skills of life is to send out healing messages. Take notice if they are being accepted. You move toward people and environments that will accept your generous offerings, allowing them to be what they choose to be, what they need to be.

It never costs you to pause and listen.

UNAWARENESS

> *Don't it always seem to go*
> *you don't know what you've got 'til it's gone …*
>
> —Joni Mitchell

> *The only imperative that nature utters is "Look. Listen. Attend."*
>
> —C. S. Lewis

A big problem throughout the human race is *un*awareness. People do not see things. People do not see what they are doing. They do not see the effects of their actions. They do not hear instructions or what someone is saying to them. And they don't talk about it.

A traditional image has been three little crouched monkeys, the first with hands over its eyes, the second with hands over its ears, the third with hands over its mouth. The image is called "See no evil, hear no evil, speak no evil." It suggests the false belief that being blind, deaf, and dumb solves problems.

The three little monkeys are of course children. "You little monkey!" a parent says fondly to a mischievous child.

The "evil" is often something the parent has not learned to deal with.

The magical childlike solution is to retreat into unawareness. It is as if not seeing, not hearing, and not speaking are useful responses. The parent passes on, intact, to the next generation a problem learned as a child from the previous generation.

If you find you have such a problem, or if those who know you well say you do, you have a task in front of you. You must make friends—as the mature adult you are—with the three little children, all parts of yourself. Do it gradually. Take it slowly. Take all the time necessary. As you gain the trust of each one, you begin to make a gentle change in direction. You say to each monkey, in turn:

"Your eyes are fine. It is okay to see. It is wonderful to learn how to deal with what you see. You become so powerful as you do that! No more do you have to be blind to what is going on."

"It is okay to hear. Deafness doesn't solve anything. You can take it slowly and listen. You can gently learn to hear more fully. You can un-train a deaf habit."

"It is okay to speak about these things. You have a wonderful mind that can figure things out. You can begin talking with people who are willing to talk. You can solve anything if you will take enough time. You're great!"

Don't see, don't hear, don't speak are all mental programs devised as blanket quick fixes by a thinking mind. All programming leaps forward, blocking awareness as the situation associated with the program arises. Huge quantities of such programming, or intense energies like fear or anger, can accumulate and build upon each other, depleting available awareness down to zero. We are distracted from seeing, hearing, and understanding by internal noise. A life so pruned can lose the ability to delight at something new. Dead-on-your-feet has been substituted for life force.

AWARENESS RETRIEVED

Dealing with novelty
is stimulating:
the essence of aliveness.

Gathering around you
a fog of sameness, so-defined
takes steps to the grave.

Take charge of your mind
appreciate its desire to help
lead it to trust you enough
to let go, relax

Pre-organizing helps
return spontaneity to your life.
Be the good boy scout
be prepared
as best you can

Then you are ready
to be maximally aware
when you get there

AWARENESS, AS YET UNAVAILABLE

You can be unready to open the door to new awareness. For now, it must stay beyond reach. Meanwhile, you can practice moving warm emotions through your experience. Gratitude is the easiest one. It helps you build understanding.

THE DOOR OF AWARENESS

You can bring understanding right up to the door
you can move gratitude more and more
but until you are ready to follow it through
the door of awareness won't open for you.

RIGHT BEFORE YOUR NOSE

When you can't see the very thing
that's right before your nose
a mischief-maker's doing that
Which one do you suppose?
It's mischief mind that cannot stand
your taking of control
It fears you'll take that permanently
so it runs you up the pole.
You can retrieve control it stole
as you regain its trust
It needs to quiet what it does
as you insist it must.
Your mind can never be your friend
it has its job at hand
as you are confident with what it does
it feels you understand.

SELECTIVE AWARENESS

What you see is what you get!

—Flip Wilson

Have you ever wondered why everyone does not have the understanding you have, why they don't see what you see? Part of the answer is your uniqueness. No one else was born with the special combination of awareness, sensitivities, abilities, and interests you have. You are a unique detection device. Combining sensitivity toward and awareness of different people, as they cooperate with one another, can bring great power to bear on any problem.

We see these differences of perception in the courtroom: witnesses to an accident. The car mechanic knows the make and model of the car and details about its performance. The fashion designer notes the clothing the driver was wearing. The police officer measured the length of the skid marks and estimates the cost of repairs for the damage. A video of the event would show something else. Each person selects from the whole picture the ingredients he or she wishes to address.

The awareness we commonly value is visual. "Don't you see!" we exclaim as a common way of saying "don't you understand?" Understanding, the deep grasp of the situation, is more profound than the surface appearances recorded by a camera, the solely visual.

A further intrusion into full awareness comes from editing by the mind. We all know the person whose mind is made up, who refuses to see, refuses to hear, and so deprives herself of the ability to reach understanding.

Feelings have a natural way of extending, boundaryless, into a situation and eliciting a sense of what is going on and how we might respond. We can all do that. With practice, we can improve that ability to sense. Feelings' awareness carries great potential for making choices even before all the facts are in. Such awareness is seen as the feminine part of all of us. Thus, the foreman who commands with no regard for the feelings of his crew will quickly have a riot on his hands. Feelings will not be denied. Even the most masculine of foremen knows this. We all need to use the feminine part of ourselves.

Expanding awareness into deeper sensing is the pathway to a successful life. It lays out the red carpet for your progress; it helps you to stay relevant in your responses. Investigate your editing intrusions and slowly delete them. You have an inbuilt capacity to give humane, balanced, healthy responses. Allow that seed to germinate and blossom.

CRAZY NORMAL

If you are in a crazy situation and you are healthy, open, and in touch, you can expect to be a little bit crazy. This is your membership, your evidence of participation in the crazy situation. You are normal, locally speaking, and acceptable to the group.

If you live in a depressing environment and you are open to it, responsive, you must expect to be depressed. Indeed, if you were feeling fine in a depressive environment, you might be out of touch, feel out-of-it and a little bit crazy, and in need of psychotherapy to normalize you to your environment!

Some people have recognized this and use a protective wall of anger, isolating themselves, to keep sane. They are then seen as "that angry person" or "that strange person" by the group. It can be tricky, even self-destructive to do this for long periods. What we really need is accurate, undistorted feedback. If that is not the accepted norm of a particular group, you would do better by finding other company.

The emotional health of large numbers of people can be positively affected by improving the environment, the community setting in which they live. The environment has to be made not-crazy; i.e., relevant to the needs and wants of its members, not out-of-it or out-of-touch, and not a generator of depression or behaviors with non-productive or destructive aspects.

ASPIRE TO SENSE

Aspire to sense, ever more clearly, ever more sharply, what is going on. Widen your base, expand your awareness. Open the gates that would hold you back. Lower the walls that imprison you. Remove the smoke that obscures and confuses you from seeing deeply and truly. Delve into any irrelevance in what you do. Transform it into relevance, effectiveness.

These efforts on your part will save you lost energy and increase your vitality: a fountain of youth if ever there was one.

As you raise your sensing ability, know that you are doing it *your* way, identical to no one else, enabling you to make your unique contribution to the total pool of awareness that is shared with others.

LISTENING

Listening happens one by one
you listen first; it is begun
hearing what the other's feeling
keeps alive the process healing
walls of anger, frozen fear
allowed to melt, they disappear.
Hearing fully, each understands
the action spreads through many hands.
Safety lying behind a wall?
No longer needed at all, at all.

NOW

Introduction
Be Now. Live Now
School of Hard Knocks
A Life in School
Quotation from Scripture (guru)
Whose Problem?

41

INTRODUCTION

Now. There is something very precious about now. It is all we really have. You can use it to deliberately recreate yesterday. You can use it to plan for tomorrow. But both of these are done now. *Now* can knock us around. Now can strengthen us, if we will allow it.

BE NOW. LIVE NOW

Take now and use it. It's all you have. Yesterday, the past, is gone. Recycling it is questionable. If you've had some great experiences, some wonderful successes in the past, you can recycle them for that boost they give you into now. Then tackle today with gusto. Put on your running shoes, look to the future, and go for it. If the past is full of failures, forget it. Who needs leaden shoes and blinders? Come back to now. Tell the memory (which is only trying to be helpful), "Thanks, but no thanks. I know you have lots of bad examples. They are not the direction I wish to go. I will practice some good examples, some successes. Take those, and when you want to help, present those to me first. Don't bother with the bad ones."

That was the past. You don't have the future either. Taking yourself out of now into the future is questionable also. You may take a moment to set up a future goal. Come quickly back to now and work on the next step toward that goal. *Now* is where the action is!

SCHOOL OF HARD KNOCKS

Life is sometimes described as the School of Hard Knocks. It is a school in the sense that we are here in this life to learn. The hard knocks refers to the way life blocks and jolts us into awareness of the way things are. Some people always have to learn it the hard way.

Within the School of Hard Knocks is a classroom. It is the Room of Present Experience. You sit at your desk. The lesson of the moment is written on the walls. Your job is to learn the lesson. Then you can leave by the exit door, never to return. There will be other lessons. But this one you have under your belt.

There is a window to the outside world. You can leave your desk, go to the window, look out, and see all those other people getting it wrong. You can criticize. You can feel justified. You can seek to gain by comparison. It is easy to see you are right while they are wrong. But none of these are more than distractions. Your task is still to return to your desk and learn your lesson.

Anger and fear, putting up walls, and freezing or running away are non-solutions to life's problems. If life delivers to you a metaphoric blow to the abdomen, followed by an uppercut to your now-exposed jaw, watch for the backing-away errors. There may be something valuable you need to know. If you rigidify everywhere, if you steel yourself into anger at a world that doesn't care, you may be denying yourself the very gift that would be most useful at this point in your life.

Once you have learned that, all else becomes secondary. People and the problems that they have all over you, who suck you effortlessly into their dramas, are mere excuses, prompters for you to master your lesson. That may include the learning of patience, of tolerance, of finding your way back to your loving base when you have been knocked off it. It may include dignity and respect for your own self. With that learned, you can certainly extend it to others. There are many lessons. One lesson learned, another in preparation, in an ever-expanding cycle of empowerment.

There are many moments in a lifetime of learning. We each walk our path. We can help others walk theirs, those who want that help and request it, those who will listen.

A Life in School

I rejected the idea
of the school of hard knocks
"I don't want to be a school child
and I haven't learned a thing."
But life came back to whack me
and in getting my attention
it reduced my stuffy attitude
to manageable proportions.

Quotation from Scripture (Guru)

It is like baking a cake. I stir, I knead, I pound, I twist, I bake you. I drown you in tears; I scorch you in sobs. I make you sweet and crisp, an offering worthy of God.

Bhakti Yoga: Sai Baba[23]

WHOSE PROBLEM?

I thought
it was someone else's problem.
I had all the evidence.
It was obvious
the mistakes they were making
with them so wrong
they clearly weren't right
I had a case against them.
But I was missing
the point.
They were there
for my benefit!
For me to benefit
I would have to take my eyes
off them
in order to see
me.
How was I reacting?
How was I handling the *stress*?
Was it good for me to do that?
If I came out of all this
the better for it
what would I have learned?
Could I come out stronger
for having been through that?
Can I stay with it
a trifle longer
to be certain
I have picked up
every last piece of understanding
the situation has to offer?
Then will I be stronger?
Then I will have drunk in the full experience?
Then will I be wiser?
Then can I let flow the gratitude
for the gifts
I have received
that I stayed to collect
instead of running away?

LIFE AS EXPERIENCED

INTRODUCTION

Life as Experienced. We live life through our experiences. By letting these in, we gather understanding. Computers, robots can collect facts and information. Never does one twit of understanding come to them. They never have the faintest notion of what they are doing.

Life can be turned positive, provided you don't misconstrue it.

LIFE AS EXPERIENCED

Life as experienced is often tragic
Practicing, you can transform that like magic
Building your confidence in what you're doing
surely will guide you through all misconstruing.

PLEASE LET IN THE EXPERIENCE

Please let in the experience
you don't have to agree with it
nor disagree with it
simply allow it to happen.
Allowed in, the experience broadens you
enlarges your base
gives you more understanding
from which you can respond with more wisdom
to the problems that will come your way.

BODY: BREATHING

Introduction
Laughter, Laughter

INTRODUCTION

Body: breathing. The human body is a legitimate subject for discussion. It is *where* we live, in our life on this planet. But before we deal with the body as "Body," we must address two issues that are essential to body functioning. One is breathing, the topic of this section. And the second is heartbeat, the topic of the next section.

Breathing is *the* basic body function. Without breathing going on, the body dies. The brain, the neediest of the body's organs, goes unconscious in three minutes of being denied oxygen, suffocated. Other organs die steadily after that. The entire circulation system is in place to supply rich, red, oxygenated blood to all the far distant parts of the body within only a few heartbeats.

> Breathing you need, so breathe you must
> without that breathing you go bust
> breathe up, breathe in, go slow and deep
> the finest health then you will keep.

But breathing does more than just keep the organs alive. And *restricting our* breathing, just short of not breathing at all, is the main way we shut ourselves down emotionally.

When there is a big interpersonal problem, usually someone, somewhere, somehow is not taking in nearly enough oxygen. Watch for that. Watch for that tragedy. Deliberately breathe in as you watch—to move yourself from part of the problem to part of the solution.

Think about this: Laughter is a key ingredient to breathing. In order to do the hah, hah, hah of laughing, you must breathe in short breaths. That relaxes the diaphragm, even when it has been very tense. Do that. Laugh out loud. Some people who are determined not to laugh have buried themselves in a life-shortening habit of diaphragmatic tension. Every time you turn to something in this book that strikes you as funny, you are being invited to laugh. Breathe yourself silly.

LAUGHTER, LAUGHTER

> Laughter, laughter everywhere
> exhorting you to be aware
> become your melting millionaire
> inviting all to stop and stare
> What miracle is happening there?
> Can I, too, find the thoroughfare
> and no more myself impair?
> And so I say a silent prayer
> for God made laughter for our fare
> inviting each to be the heir
> and no more staying unaware
> (keeping a solitary nightmare
> of a life in disrepair).
> Be bonny, blithe, and debonair
> no more wanting even a hair
> of that frightful lack of care
> for there is beauty everywhere!

BODY: HEART

49

INTRODUCTION

Body: heart. The heartbeat denotes that you have life. The absence of life is signaled by the stopping of the beating of the heart. When you find someone without a pulse, you must quickly begin cardiopulmonary resuscitation (CPR) to attempt to revive him or her. If you wait too long after their heart has stopped beating, your efforts will fail.

The heart is also a symbol for living vitality. When you say, "Have a heart," you imply somebody is not recognizing that a human being is the recipient of their actions. The power in the emotional heart is the title of this book. My use of "Heart" is deeper and broader than the mechanical pump.

THE HEART THAT BEATS

The heart that beats
says you have life
your body lives
there is no strife.
Stop the heartbeat
end that life
all you have
is afterlife.

BODY

INTRODUCTION

Body. The physical body is commonly seen as evidence for our "Self." Many think they are only the physical body. They may not see beyond that in a lifetime. We accept a photo as evidence for the existence of a person—a driver's license or generalized photo ID. The person without the picture—the body, *non habeas corpus*—is unthinkable.

Where you have a body, you have a mind. They work together in a process called double-teaming. The problem of obesity is a common way the mind and body double-team to your detriment. The excess weight itself puts strain on body joints, particularly hips, knees, ankles, and feet to carry the load.

The heart can be likened to the fuel pump used by a car. Obesity is like overloading that car, and it also puts strain on the heart because of how much fuel it requires to move from A to B.

The way out of a downward spiral is to love your body. Heart-drive is high-octane fuel, jet fuel.

MIND TO BODY

If you are not happy with a pattern of responses your body has taken on, you can pay attention to your body, listen, and become responsive to it. As you "gather its trust," it will begin to move toward listening to you and give up its repetitive, automatic responses to the relentless mind.

In a parallel way, you (the truth-seeker at your core) can listen to your thinking mind, hear its concerns and reach out to it with understanding. When you have gained *its* trust, it will similarly begin to let go of old patterns. You then start conducting the new balance you create in your life, as a conductor with full charge of the interdependent orchestra of independent musicians.

The mind can pressure the body. When the body reacts by tensing, the mind can notice the tension and react further to that. Mind and body can bind together and stabilize attitudes, beliefs, and ways of approaching situations by their intertwining actions. If this becomes uncomfortable, you may need to begin a healing.

It is okay to open up channels between mind and body and to begin sending healing messages to your hurting body. *It is important to think well of your body.* See it as your servant. Love it, care for it, and picture it healing. Be patient; it is okay not to rush. The body's speed is slow. It is okay to pause and sense what is happening within you and around as you go about living. Your body can listen and respond, but will do so at its own steady speed—over weeks and months. It is always reacting: tensing in preparation, twitching or perhaps taking on a warm glow in response to what you are experiencing. When you practice something, your body goes through the plan you have chosen, over and over, gradually accustoming itself to your new choice. Once it has it, the body becomes your solid, reliable, and constant companion.

STUFFING FEELINGS

To borrow from computer terminology, if thoughts and feelings make up the software of our functioning, the physical body is the hardware. You cannot see a thought. You *can* see someone deep in thought. You cannot see a feeling. But someone who is blushing has "feeling" written all over her. The body gives firm substance to thoughts and feelings.

"It's chemical," "It's just neurotransmitters in your body," and "It's all in your head," are all examples of common statements we can make or hear from others in daily in our lives. They become *evidence* of the mind intruding, fragmenting, segmenting into *thing-ness* from the larger world of "accepted reality."

Appreciate that. Your body is designed to reflect what you think and what you experience; it punctuates these with tangible physical representations. It always cooperates. It is not designed to let you down. If you have come down with physical illness, always know you can bring relief by using the healing built into love.

MIND HEAVINESS

The mind's heavy horseman
he happily rode
on a body so willing
to carry the load.

STUFFING FEELINGS

The mind doesn't like
the body to return to it
the feelings
that it stuffed into the body
in the first place.
The mind can't handle feelings
they're too complex, too engulfing
so it dumps them in the body
sitting on that barrel of monkeys
hoping they will stay controlled.

OVERWEIGHT REPRESENTS PROBLEMS

Overweight represents problems
the problems are unique to each person
no two people have problems identical to one another
Overweight is there from the problems
Overweight is not the problem
the problems are the problems
the weight was standing in for them
valiantly
unceasingly
punctuating the problems
with its oh-so-obvious physical presence.
Heal the problems
seek out the problems
find out about each one
heal it and move on
In healing the problems
you heal the weight
now the weight has nothing to represent!
You are now happy.

LOVE YOUR BODY

We each own a physical body. It is our gift, to use or abuse as we see fit, for the duration of this lifetime. It is an incredible instrument, constantly repairing itself, adapting itself to what we are thinking and what we are feeling. As you read these words, multi-trillions of chemical reactions, electrical signals, and physiological events are going on automatically, to maintain it. You don't have to do a thing! Not consciously. Yet a much greater you is actually doing all that, as we speak! See also "The Tennis Game."

We are often instructed what to feed the body, how to clothe it, what cosmetics we should use to paint it. By many, often violent popular examples, we are invited to abuse it. We are not usually told how to come to understand the body and then to love what we understand. Look around you. The bodies of so many people are living, walking demonstrations of a lack of caring, a lack of love.

Love is the best support for your body. When you are tired, let your body relax. When you feel energized, you may want to run the energy off. If you are hungry, eat. If your bowels or bladder are full, go to the right place to deal with that. Don't punish your body with holding. Let sadness be a releaser of body tensions. Allow sadness to do that healing job. So loved, your body will serve you well. It is yours for life. You may not trade it in on a different model. Its current state is in many ways a culmination of attitudes and approaches you have been using. Or it may be setting you up for an amazing learning experience. Learn to love it like your family pet. It is with you 24/7, eager to support you, yet disliking abuse.

Let's use the automobile as a metaphor for the body. We can climb inside it, put the pedal to the metal, and see it as an extension of our sexual prowess. But something is missing. The car cannot select what it wants from a menu. It won't fit in easily to a crowded elevator. Its headlights have no ability to see—they merely enhance our perceptions. And it will never conceive or give birth to a toy truck. The metaphor falls short of the real thing. Love is what is alive, what is real.

Most people play favorites with some parts of the body, ignore others, and treat still other parts with disdain. This is a body that is already built and acting as an entire unit!

Love your body. Love it in all its parts. If you put into your body half the care and attention that some people put into their car, it will pay you back a thousandfold. It is common for people to abuse their bodies, often out of ignorance and unawareness of the immaculate instrument they are abusing. Yet a long-abused body can turn forgivingly around the moment the light of love is shed upon it.

As you love your body, sense balance coming in. Ignored parts become more prominent. Disdain disappears, dissolved by your love.

Do it. Do it again. After you have been doing it for a while—to avoid boredom—imagine a little difference in each healing breath you take, comparing it to the last one. Perhaps it is coming from a different angle. Its quality is slightly different. Perhaps it is a different color. Sense the effect of the difference.

Do this five times a day for twenty breaths each time. A month of that should show a change. If you see only 10 percent improvement, notice that improvement. Continue on. Make the sky the limit. Some people can tell something is happening from the first breath. In others, six months may be needed. The body can be slow to change.

Some people experience reluctance, resistance to the process, as if a little guardian were on standby there, keeping the status quo. Send healing into the guardian. See if he or she can stand the heat; healing is warm! You can use gratitude for starters. Gratitude is a great healer. Don't you love it when someone is truly grateful to you for what you did?

When a flare-up of illness occurs at an emotionally provocative time, you may be stuffing feelings into the body. Send healing love into the affected part, loving the body. Visualizing it happening can be useful. Also helpful can be identifying the feeling and sharing it with someone else. Let it out. Reverse the stuffing process.

It is interesting how this process of healing differs from tradition. We talk of fighting illness and look with admiration at someone bravely fighting their condition. Wrong energy. No bash-and-smash is useful. Infusing the region with emotional warmth, being genuinely willing to turn on a flow of love, does the most to support the body's immune system to overcome harmful processes.

You may wish to try your healing power on someone else. Do ask their permission. Some people are undergoing important learning through suffering. They may not welcome your interference in their training. They may prefer to do it for themselves—when they feel ready.

HANDING OUT HEALING LOVE TO YOUR BODY

From laying on of hands to Reiki, it has long been known that there is, within the palm of the human hand, the ability to heal (Boyce 1978). Anything you practice, in time you will improve. Anything an expert can do, any one of us can do a little bit. You can train your hands.

The human body has many sites where suffering can be expressed in undeniable, physical terms. You get headaches often? You have one now? You have arthritis in one or more joint—or at least pain? You have a lump you are scared might be cancer? You have cancer you have been fanning with fear? You would like to see how far you can go fanning it with healing? You are diabetic and would like to help your pancreas? You have asthma or emphysema and want to send healing into that? Your shoulders have been carrying all that weight. Your heart is crying out for help? Or a physical condition involving any part of the body is troubling you?

Place your hand over the part. See your palm as having the ability to glow with healing. Then imagine you are inside the body. This mysterious glow is penetrating through the skin! Breathe it in. Your breath vacuums it. Breathe it in deeply and thoroughly. Feel its warmth. Breathe back gratitude. See your gratitude making a difference. The hand feels validated. It now knows that its healing power is truly wanted. Healing happens in the exchange: the receiving of the heartfelt warmth of love with the sending back of warmth from the emotional heart in your gratitude, that the power of healing lies. You lock in the healing, sandwiching between the love from the hand and the gratitude from the body.

Mind-Meanings:
The Hidden Instigator of
Problems

INTRODUCTION

Mind-meanings: the hidden instigator of problems. Meanings are everything. Differences between people become severe problems when events mean different things to different people. When words with one intended meaning reaches the ears of another, the meaning can change entirely.

The very action of holding on tightly can be your means of defeating yourself; holding onto hatred is particularly self-destructive. Meanings can create problems. You can reverse that. It is my plea that you value your feelings more highly and trust what you feel. Mistrust is based on fear. Much confusion comes from this.

Belief in hatred can imprison you. This holding usually begins with self-suffocation: holding the chest tightly. But you can release it. Just follow the process. Banishing love often starts with a nonsensical fantasy that is not warranted. But it takes practice to learn how to deal with the people who don't have your experience with love.

Worry is a combination of a falsely applied meaning followed by a plan of action (excessive thinking, chagrin). Re-invent your intention to be happy by deliberately creating joy. Using imagery can help you to overcome worry and unhappiness.

The mind is not pure evil. It just creates troublesome meanings. It has a legitimate role to play in your life. Give it its due. There are mixed blessings with the mind that can become frozen with the wrong kind of practice. Meanings can harden into attitudes. Break them with humor.

Humility will also be needed to knock the mind off its high horse. This isn't a new discovery; many scriptural texts point the way.

Indeed, the thinking mind can be the reason we restrict ourselves. The belief in one's own inadequacy can be most inhibiting. You never have been normal! You were always unique. You can do better than confining yourself to some definition of normal!

The mind's process of disconnection is a process we have all used at some time. But you can heal that too.

As you listen to others, watch for the cramping error of your desire to place meaning on what they are saying. You may be preventing yourself—blocking your own awareness—from hearing what they mean. You isolate yourself this way and increase your own loneliness.

DE-MEANING

The meanings of the thinking mind
can leave awareness very blind
the way you take it so confined
it doesn't work.
The other person may then reply
"So rise above your narrowed meaning
see what is that I'm convening
put away your silly screening
Don't be a jerk."

The trumping of previous experience can be clearly described with an image from Walt Disney's *Fantasia*. The "Dance of the Hours" is a beautiful piece of music. Originally composed by Amilcare Ponchielli as a ballet for the opera *La Gioconda*, it has special meaning for music lovers. But in the film, animated elephants and ostriches are dancing to it—original meaning trumped! Forever, there is the risk of bringing to mind that ridiculous image whenever you hear that music again.

If you recognize that the mind is mischievously doing that, adding its own cartoon imagery to otherwise legitimate communiqués, you can overcome it with your inner conductor and return the music to its original purity.

I Didn't Mean That

We can be misinterpreted. We can say, "I didn't mean it the way you took it." Trying to explain the meaning of something spoken or written runs the risk of narrowing it, weighing it down, and running it into the ground. I invite you to loosen and remove the mental loading of meaning and the subsequent reducing of awareness. Free your mind to be more aware, free your eyes to see what is happening and take all of it in, and then you can position yourself to respond as appropriate.

Each word has a dictionary definition, sometimes more than one definition. That gives it a "meaning." Everything then turns on whether the meaning is expansive and can incorporate your own living uniqueness or whether the meaning is restrictive and imprisoning. Your quest must be to go the expansive route, to include yourself in the communication, and not deal yourself out of the game of life by imprisoning yourself in restricted understanding.

> I didn't mean that
> remove all the fat
> the meaning you'll hone
> must be cut to the bone.

Holding and Blocking Out

It is important to hold to what is nourishing and supportive, what enriches your vitality of life. Holding on to something can be a way to be grounded, to stay relevant, coherent, and coordinated in your actions. If you hold on to a goal, you keep it in sight. That holding, like navigating by the stars, keeps you oriented. However, excessive energies invested in holding, particularly through fear, change a simple step toward a goal into a stranglehold that squeezes out life and destroys. It is important to examine the holding that is done from fear and desperation, the holding onto the rock blocking the stream of life, exhausting and drowning you while giving you little in return for your efforts. It is important to notice the changing colors of life, the way people, including yourself, evolve. Stay alert and alive to that. Don't blindly impose a policy of holding that may have been well intentioned and positive initially, but has now become useless and destructive. Don't hold to such attitudes, beliefs, or morbid feelings; they block the flow and stagnate. Don't hold to possessions and power if they stop you from connecting meaningfully with others.

Rage, hatred, terror, and resentment are basic holding actions that extend and distort the raw feelings of anger and fear. Then they normalize—"Doesn't everyone think that way?"—and pull in any leftover bits of friendliness, caring, and emotional warmth like a whirlpool. Even though you would never in a thousand years discard the habits that have long been giving meaning to your life (de-meaning them), you will only evoke ease and a sense of freedom in the long run by *accidentally* using your warm vitality.

59

Holding by someone else can present you with a physical, practical problem. If you are a good swimmer out to save a drowning man, you approach him quietly from behind, take his head between your hands, and invite him to float on his back, while you use your legs to swim backwards to safety. If he turns and grabs you by the neck, you bring your arms up between his hands and bang outwards. His bent wrists are then prevented from being able to grip so hard, and you break his stranglehold. Then you try again, turning him around and inviting him to float. That's how it might work in relationships, if we are aware and truly loving.

A perversion of the word love in common usage refers to holding actions and comfort zones—we talk of how someone loves to do something. We all gain some comfort from doing what is familiar. It feels right, so it is mind-approved—it doesn't invoke a lot of thinking or the self-criticism that occurs when encountering what is defined by the thinking mind as wrong.

Confronted with the threatening storms of life (as they are all too often fearfully experienced), it feels good to stand out of the storm and under the protective awning of a "life lived right." Unfortunately, the relief of mere virtue is as close as some people get to the flowing invigoration of love.

We may say of a person "he loves to …" whatever. In some cases, he is experiencing a genuine flow of love, say engaging in a hobby. In another, we may simply be observing someone enacting a familiar by habit. Maybe there is love in it. But there may be few indications of a genuine basis of love.

Blocking-out strongly resembles holding for the paralyzing effect it has on the flow of life. In a dysfunctional environment that is experienced as traumatic, you may seek to stay alive in the hailstorm by putting a wall up against it. One man, a member of a minority group (aren't we all, in one way or another?), chose to stay in a town hostile to his group. He survived by carrying with him a wall of anger. Anger is a convenient way to block out what is perceived as hostile. The instant-power aspect of it can be reassuring in a self-weakening, unfriendly environment. But a life built around anger is just as debilitating as long-standing holding patterns. Best to move on to a less hostile environment.

In another situation, a different person might choose to express joy instead of anger. The thinking goes "I will not let you dictate what I feel. Joy is much better for my body than anger. I am not going down to your level."

THE BONE–JOINT-MUSCLE UNIT

There are various places where this article could go. It is based on a principle, so it could go in the "Principles" section. It has to do with the physical body, so it could go in the "Body" section. But it has a great deal to do with holding actions, so this is the best section for it. Yet it is not necessarily tied in to the addictive habit pattern that can be a part of holding. The problems arising from it can be an innocent oversight that is easily correctible.

Every bone in the body—including the joints at the end of them and the muscles that span the joints—function as a unit. No muscle starts on one bone and inserts onto the same bone. There would be no point. The joint gives meaning to the action of the muscle. Movement, to do work, to lift things, to move legs in order to progress from here to there, is the purpose of muscle action. The whole combination functions as a unit.

Whenever there is a problem in your life or environment, however large, you do what you can. If the problem is world pollution, you can do what you can not to pollute—even do a little picking up of extraneous garbage, hoping others get the message. If the problem is fast food and obesity, you cannot solve the whole world's problem, but you can switch to nourishing food yourself. You have a better handle on your corner of this problem than you did with pollution. You may find, however, that you have difficulty training yourself to be responsible.

Working on the bone-joint-muscle unit is easier than either of these problems. There is no personal or public addiction problem to be overcome. There is no my-corner-of-the-world aspect, as in the problem of pollution. If you have been misusing muscles, you have probably done it unconsciously. The need is merely to raise your awareness that the problems are there and there is something you can do about it. It's as simple as falling off a log. You are not deeply committed to past muscle action, because you came upon it by accident, not by design. There is no deep-rooted planning to be painfully overcome.

So you can more easily retrain bone-joint-muscle use. There are three key areas for the body—the neck, the lower back, and the shoulders—where your efforts can reap ready rewards. The bones of the whole vertebral column are stacked like bricks. Those bricks can collapse, as in the disease called osteoporosis. The joints in the column are the intervertebral spaces, filled with cushions called discs that give the spinal column its flexibility. You cannot take immediate steps to heal problems in these areas; it takes time to build muscle strength.

Muscles that span those bones give support to bones and joints. That is where you can intercede effectively. For the neck, lock both hands through the fingers and place them behind the head at eye level. Pull forward with the hands, while pushing back with the head. This retrains and strengthens the muscle. (The skull is a bone that sits atop the stack of vertebrae and becomes a bony member of the club.) Hold the push long enough to work the muscle. Then release and do it again. Then repeat and repeat and repeat. You are training strength into the muscles. Turn your head left and do the same. Repeat for the head turned right.

When I once felt a tingling down the outside of my left arm, an x-ray of my neck revealed moderate osteoarthritis. This condition was pressing on nerves that serve the arm, coming out through intervertebral spaces. It had not yet gone on to create muscle weakness. If it had, the process would have taken longer to heal. As I was aware of the bone-joint-muscle unit, a month of strengthening the muscle was enough to remove the tingling. I have kept up working these muscles over three years so far, and the problem has not returned.

In the case of the lower limb, the condition called sciatica can involve pain down the sciatic nerve, which runs down the back of the leg. To strengthen the relevant muscles here, hold the edge of a table for balance, then raise one leg backwards. For balanced retraining, do it on both sides.

Shoulder strengthening is easy. Stand inside a doorframe as if to walk through, touching the frame with the length of one arm. Push the arm against the door frame. That works the deltoid muscle that clasps the shoulder joint as if to protect it. Work that lateral-lift action a number of times. Then turn forty-five degrees forward and do the same. Then forty-five degrees backward and repeat. Move to the opposite side of the doorframe and do the same with your other arm.

HATRED IS THE HOLDER

Hatred is the holder
that hurries you to hell
that "safely"
despite any outward appearances
imprisons you
to a life of deprivation
unknown by others to any deep level
unbefriended by them
in any genuine way
unrecognized
never truly supported
always at risk
generating paranoia
devoid of true joy
deteriorating
on a constant basis
undermined
in all ways.
The merest drop
of the light of love
allowed into that darkness
instantly begins loosening
hate's strangling tightness.

MOVE FROM MISTRUST

Will you move from mistrust
to the life of goodwill?
Leave behind the held steel
use the springboard with skill?
For the frozen, the hardened
is a drain on your life
while limber, free-flowing
leaps away from the strife.

CONFUSION IS

Confusion is the mind
trying hard to find
what it can hold
and then feel bold
although it's still confused.
Confusions had to go
for then you let things flow
no more confined
or left behind
your life can only glow.

BELIEF IN HATRED

Hatred, as a habit, can seem consoling. You always know the wall your back is up against. You can feel justified in your reactions to life's hard knocks. "Who could expect anything more from me?" you can ask. In this way, you can use others' reactions to your wall to prove you still need the wall, keeping you looping around that circle. You can even keep company with others similarly endowed with walls. That can seem to prove it all.

What you may not notice is that the wall is part of a prison you have installed around yourself. Days look bleak, but what else can you expect? There are promises of bright spots, successes, excitement. But they all stay in the context of the comfort zone of darkness that you have built around yourself.

Your body has been a willing cooperator. It carries tensions representing the walls that restrict movement and so encourages arthritic changes in joints, applying pressures that can wear down the parts. The mind, committed to its belief in hatred, can make sure the whole road show continues.

You, as conductor of it all, can at any time let in light. You can breathe slowly and deeply into tight spots, inviting them to relax. You can confer with your mind. It is part of you, not all of you, as it can sometimes insist.

From any point, at any time, you can always make a move toward health.

RELEASING HOLDING

Holding is consoling. Holding can give comfort. Holding can become very familiar. It can be something to do, to fill unstructured time. When you feel your back up against the wall forcing you to do one thing rather than another, it may be hard to recognize that the wall you feel backed into is actually you holding on.

Holding gives the comfort of *something I can do*. We can become so distracted by the activity of doing the task that we don't notice (once again) what the task is doing.

We can feel justified by holding. We can say, "Of course I have to hold. Who wouldn't hold? I'm entitled to hold. It's my right." Anger often drives this perspective, placing you right in the pothole from which the mind is operating. When it's a deep terror driving it, there may be multiple layers of holding carried in the body that together prevent a simple release of the holding. Have you ever tried to stop shaking hands with an octopus?

Holding comes in a variety of guises. Hatred is one. Resentment is another. You can resent right now, resent tomorrow, next week, next year if you still want to. You have heard of someone holding a grudge. If you have ever done that, you may sense the self-strangulation built into the energy it uses up. Holding onto imagery is particularly sticky. The holding involved in the imagery of revenge may seem consoling, until you release the rotting wood you have held so close.

> As I opened up my heart I found
> it didn't need much prying
> 'twas just a case of letting go
> of hard holding I'd been trying.

To let go of a pattern of holding or blocking-out, whether held out of desperation or any other reason, that is no longer useful, do the following exercise.

Reach straight out with both arms in front of you and make each hand a fist. Imagine all of the holding you have been doing inside going out from the body, through the shoulders, the elbows, to the wrists and hands. They become heavier and heavier as the weight of all this long-term holding leaves you. The arms become heavier and heavier as you hold those fists tighter and tighter. But you have been holding hard for a long time, and you can easily do it a little longer.

Gradually the heaviness of the arms takes over. Slowly they begin to drop down until they land in your lap or at your sides. Feel the relaxation, the release from holding. How do you feel in your heart? What is different now in your life?

You may now feel open to being consoled. A friend may now find that her compassion can now get through to you. Your awareness can open up. Things may look clearer. Sounds may seem fresher.

The release of holding energy stops the drain on your life force. Now you can feel lighter. It may seem easier to do things. There is more spring in your step. You have more energy available to you.

QUOTATIONS FROM SCRIPTURE

If men speak evil of you, this must you think: "Our heart shall not waver; and we will abide in compassion, in loving kindness, without resentment. We will think of the man who speaks ill of us with thoughts of love, and in our thoughts of love shall we dwell. And from that abode of love we will fill the whole world with far-reaching, wide-spreading, boundless love."

Moreover, if robbers should attack you and cut you in pieces with a two-handed saw, limb by limb, and one of you should feel hate, such a one is not a follower of my gospel.

BUDDHISM: Majjhima Nikaya

Only by love can men see me, and know me, and come unto me.

HINDUISM: Bhagavad-Gita 11:54

Warren Douglas Phegan

HONEY-DROWNED

I was drowning in a sea of honey
increasingly despairing
until a voice inside me said
"There's something needs an airing."
Then the honey seemed to thin
and I drew in a breath
to my surprise I realized
I'd moved away from death!
The holding I'd been carrying on
that was a source of rancor
I saw my grip, my sinking ship
I won't release the anchor!
The holding I'd been doing
was indeed my way of strife
my efforts were misplaced
for I'd been strangling my life.
My life, it now felt purified
as I admired its beauty
no effort needed to be me
a misplaced sense of duty.

LOVE BANISHED

It has been declared
there is no more love in the world
no longer does anyone care.
It is gone.
You look out.
Nobody cares.
People look dead.
They do things
there is no compassion
Their attitude: Why bother?
All seem isolated.
Children are playing.
You look into their faces.
There is no joy.
Days seem shorter.
You feel yourself shrinking.
All is collapsing.
Ashes to ashes.
Ridiculous!
Love is not banished.
It underpins everything of
value that we do.
It is there.
It can be felt.
We contribute it daily into our lives and the lives of others.
It is the basic thing.
We do have that power.
It is never taken away.
Why is the word "love" not used
with the freedom it deserves?
Why does it not have a more
prominent place in our lives?
The word has been trivialized.
We have made a mistake.
It has gone the way of all words:
Overuse.
The substance of love never was
the word.
We drown in a sea of words.
They can obscure our awareness.
Love is there
deserving a word.
The word is a tool

a handle to bring forth the real
thing
the power
the substance
the endurance
the value
the underpinning
of life.

LOVE DISCOURAGERS

If you spend a long time with someone who does not appear to understand love, who does not acknowledge your love, value your love, and respond to your love, you are invited to do likewise. You are invited not to acknowledge, not value your own love.

If you spend a long time with people in all the situations you enter in your life and they all show little understanding of your love, you are invited to do the same. You are invited not to understand the power, the sustaining power, the healing, nourishing power of your love. They are not familiar with that. They invite you to join the club of non-believers.

Don't accept the invitation. Write on the envelope "Return to Sender/Not at This Address" and put the invitation back in the mail.

It is your business what you do with the love of your life. It is the business of other people what they do with their love. Do not confuse the two. At all times and under all circumstances be prepared to remember that you can love, you have that power, and you know that it is always available to you to do with it what you please. *Then do with it what you please.* Do it effortlessly. You do not have to force your love on those who don't value it. Don't add the foreign energy of strain to your beautiful gift. Just do it. And do it again. Then don't do it—for as long as you like. But don't get out of practice. Keep your ability to love always within reach. Turn on the tap of your love when habits you have not yet mastered are turning it off.

A devotee once said to Mother Theresa, "I love to hear you speak. I feel so inspired by you. I know your next talk is in Mexico. I'll be there."

Mother Theresa replied, "Don't go. Take the money you would have spent on the plane flight and use it to do good. You will learn far more than listening to me speak."

She was talking about her own life. She was a woman of action. She knew full well the value of what she did over words that are merely listened to. She deliberately made a difference. She wanted the devotee to know that truth too.

WORRY

Everybody's talking at me
I don't hear a word they're saying
Only the echoes of my mind …

—Fred Neil
(from the Harry Nilsson hit song "Everybody's Talkin' (Echoes)")

You don't have to worry any more. Worry doesn't help. Worry is your thinking mind revving in neutral.

When something is unresolved (whether a situation, your feelings, or how you feel about a situation), the thinking mind can be given the task of figuring it out. This can be a fruitless task. The resultant worry can be the reductionist mind running in hapless circles, trying to do an impossible task. Noise in the system without results.

If you want to turn off worry, put yourself in gear. Make something happen. Then you can see what you did and adapt as needed. Or turn off your motor and relax as you save energy.

One person said, "But I don't want to *not* care." Herein lies the difference. It is important to care: caring is your aliveness in action, but worry is a cheap substitute. Worry is the mind holding on tightly, burning up energy for little result.

Of course you can care. No one is telling you not to. When the mind steps in, interferes, steals the cookie from the cookie jar and declares that there are none left, then you object.

BOBBY McFERRIN REVISITED

Bobby McFerrin says
"Don't worry. Be happy."
I say
Don't worry. Be joyful.
We all want to be happy.
Strangely, for all the varied
things people are doing
we are each already doing
what we believe will make us happy.
We don't all understand
the best way to make that happen.
Even the embittered person
has a faint hope
that years of creating bitterness
will finally produce a seed of happiness.
Sometimes we pursue a strategy
that is designed to fail
doomed to fail.
Let us look into aspects of failure:
Worry is the mind
valiantly

hopelessly, exhaustingly
burning up your energy
trying in its reductionist way
to solve a problem
beyond its capability
up at the life-as-lived, human level.
Here, at this seamless, invisible, living level
(you can't see a feeling
you can't see a thought)
the mind works hard
thinking, creating thoughts
to contain, confine, control, imprison
the fear
which also drives it
into ever-widening circles
doomed to fail.
Logical string
thoughts strung together in a logical sequence
can't contain invisible fog:
the unbounded nature of feelings,
A different plan
can succeed.
Do your homework.
Think it through.
Do what can be done for now
then let it go.
Now, you can shift up
to life gear.
Count your blessings.
For each one, be grateful.
Then invigorate that gratitude
into full-blooded joy.
Recognize an expanded *NOW*
which you can use mischievously
to revitalize past traumas
as you bring those historic pictures
into full view.
Overcome that.
Use imagery
to travel through time.
Go back before each trauma.
Create for yourself
a protective, armor-plated, hooded
parka
to repel, resist the trauma.

This flips the first card
of a succession of cards
to recreate *NOW*
back-to-the-future style
keeping you safe
as you responsibly take over
for the defenseless, dependent child
you were,
using your matured understanding
and present life experience.
Then the body can slowly catch up
as it adjusts
to your brilliance.
Deliberately evoke joy.
Find things
to be joyful about.
Create the warmth
to organize and so disperse
the invisible fog.
Invigorate your being
with a slice of life's vitality.
We all want to be happy.
We don't all deliberately create it
in this predetermined way.
We set it adrift
in the vain hope
that it will somehow circle back
because we've been "good"
(or constrain ourselves to rebellion,
being "bad"
not noticing
that, that doesn't work either and
there may be other alternatives.)
Take a more vigorous grip
on life.
It's here.
It's yours.
Use it.
Set up
your success.
The guarantee
is at your fingertips.

BEAUTIFUL ROSE

There was a rose
a beautiful rose
that worried itself to ill health
its petals shrank,
its leaves grew thin
and it wilted all over the place.
Then the skies grew dark
and it cowered in fear
of the punishment that was its due.
The rains came down
to beat on the rose
and it knew that its life was through.
Then the earth grew moist
the moisture rose
and suffused all the substance
that made up the rose.
The leaves grew strong
the petals bloomed
and the rose let go
of the worrying thoughts
and the life it had made
that could never support
the beauty within
that beautiful rose.

WORRY: HEALING A LONG-STANDING BAD HABIT

So you've been worrying for a long time. If it's not worry about one thing, it is worry about another. You have come to see that worry drains a lot of your energy, for zero return in results. You are tired from it. You're tired of it. Finally, you feel ready to absorb it, reclaim the errant energy.

You see your worry as a hyperactive child burning up energy uselessly. You want to hold the child, caress the child, console the child, calm the child. You will do it in a special way, with imagery.

Your power is in your emotional heart, in the center of your chest. Reach around your body as far onto your back as you can with both hands. Now, hug yourself in a special way. Imagine releasing from your emotional heart heart-shaped sponges. Imagine them passing, one at a time, out through your shoulders, down through your arms, out the palms of your hands, and back into your back. You are hugging the child, soothing the child in you.

Now see the heart-sponges going first to your stomach, a common place for the body to locate tension. Worry, fear, anxiety and over-excitement tend to join together to make their messes. Imagine each heart-sponge soaking up its share of worry. Their actions are unique. Each one a refinery, weeding out the crud and upgrading it to reveal the sparkling life force buried there.

Visualize more hearts coming from your love center in the chest, loving you, even if you have no feel for that child inside. They go up to your head. Sponging out the headaches. They take their time. Each one absorbing a little more and a little more and a little more headache. Worry's tension is also commonly expressed in neck and shoulders. This is where you can carry the "weight of the world." Feel the heart-sponges going to the back of your neck and out onto your shoulders, cleansing and absorbing all tension as they go.

There's an infinite number of hearts. Let them spread throughout your body, going to all your tense spots: chest, back, abdomen, arms, legs—wherever there is tension, they seek it out, absorb it, refine it, reclaiming your lost energy and discarding the residue of worry.

There is no rush about this. The habit of worrying took along time to develop. It will not heal in one session or even in one day.

Do your self-hug three times a day. If you do it before meals, it will settle your stomach for better digestion when you eat. Do this exercise whenever you can allow yourself to be generous to *you*.

APPRECIATE YOUR THINKING MIND

Say this to yourself in the mirror: "I like your ability to think. I like it when you use it. I like the way you can think clearly. I enjoy your doing that."

Make friends with your thinker. This may seem like a strange suggestion. The reason is that the thinking mind can believe it is all of who you are. It is not. There is a you larger than the thinking mind who will do the appreciating. The thinking mind can then find its proper place at its proper size, becoming the calculator in your hip pocket, ready to punch in new information and make calculations when *you* need it.

The thinking process cannot grasp all of life. It should stay under instruction: a friend to be consulted for the correlation of facts, making lists, etc. You, yourself, are not a fact. You are a total human being, experiencing life smoothly, assessing and reacting, most of the time without bothering the fact processor.

Make friends with your thinker. Make sure also that your good friend, your faithful servant, knows who is boss. No overrides please.

Upsides and Downsides of the Mind

An upside of the mind
is objectivity:
the ability to isolate and define specific elements.

Another upside
is boundaries:
the carving out of a territory
within which
you can live out
the interests, sensitivities, and abilities
you have taken on in this life.

A downside of objectivity
is separation
remoteness
the disconnect
that can make you cold and distant
irrelevant
to the pervading warmth
of people together.

A downside of boundaries
is separation
too often fueled
by anger-protecting fear
the crude-oil feelings
begging to be refined
by friendship.

Another upside of the mind
is getting it right
the way to go that works
with human beings of like mind.

The downside of right
is the narrowing
the confining prison
the gain now for pain later
that excludes you from life
to chew on the all-day sucker
the consolation prize
of being right.

The giving of meaning
to what just happened
is an attribute of the mind
with an upside and a downside.
The upside is the label
the handle with which to carry
the contents within the carrying case.
The downside is the imprisoning
of the butterfly of life
pinned to a board
for the sake of collecting and organizing.

ATTITUDE PROBLEMS

We can use fixed ways of thinking—fixed patterns, fixed attitudes—to try to crowbar our way through life's difficulties. It seems to save time and effort. We just press automatic, and we can almost go to sleep!

Fixed thinking can make you irrelevant. Things are moving along, and there you are: frozen! If you find an attitude that is causing more trouble than it's worth, you can let it go. It has served its purpose. Don't cater to it anymore. Don't be known as someone with attitude. Eat a little humble pie.

Another fixed way of thinking is a belief. A belief is the mind's attempt to step into the gulf between its own narrow thinking and a more open awareness of the true, invisible nature of life.

Mother Teresa was reported to be deeply concerned about whether she believed in God. She had a wonderful feeling-awareness of the nature of invisible love and its power. The *belief* aspect, guarded jealously by the fragmented thinker, involves a separation: I believe this, you believe that. It was her inability to fit a deep awareness of the connected invisible Oneness into the fragmentation, that presented her with problems. The thinking mind is poorly adapted to the separation we readily see before our eyes.

HUMILITY

Changing some attitudes, particularly those we have held close, identified with, can feel like we are being degraded. We want to say "No! No! No! It's impossible!"

But it is possible. The holding was just something we were doing, see "Holding and Blocking-Out." What we are doing at any one time, particularly a holding action, never fully describes who we are. And if the holding involves tightness in the throat, it can feel hard to swallow. Hence the term 'Eating humble pie.'

HOLDING INTENSELY

Holding intensely
creates its own problems.
Energies used
to create all that holding
become the alternatives
too horrible to mention.
Each clinging finger
squeezing so tightly
tells me of terrors
'gainst which it is holding
must hold on tighter
producing a tension
the size of the terror
that it's recreating.

HUMBLE PIE

Humble pie, humble pie,
why should I eat humble pie?
Sometimes it seems pie-in-the-sky
that I should eat humble pie.
Humble pie, humble pie,
can it ever, could it fly?
And why, oh why, oh why should I
eat humble pie?
Humble pie, humble pie,
I'm thinking I should walk on by
on what, on what could I rely
if I ate humble pie?
Humble pie, humble pie,
It happened! I ate humble pie
and now I'm open I see why
I should eat humble pie.
Excessive hardness, it should lie
and as I'm breathing, bye and bye
suppler, more versatile is why
I now eat humble pie.

QUOTATIONS FROM SCRIPTURES

All around I see Nothing pretending to be Something, Emptiness pretending to be Fullness.

CONFUCIANISM: Analects 7:25

Pride goes before destruction, a haughty spirit before a fall.

JUDAISM: Proverbs 16:18

Humility exalteth man to the heaven of glory and power, whilst pride abaseth him to the depths of wretchedness and degradation.

BAHA'I : Epistle to the Son of the Wolf

Do not walk boisterously upon the earth; verily thou wilt not make a hole in the earth, nor yet reach the mountains in stature.

ISLAM: Qur'an 17:39

WHO YOU THINK YOU ARE—ROLE CONFINEMENT

There are no ordinary people

—C. S. Lewis (from "The Weight of Glory"
in *Screwtape Proposes a Toast*)

Each of us goes through many stages during a lifetime. We can identify with the stage we are in. The mind can rejoice at really knowing *who I am*. It pokes us into a container, a category. The ability of the mind to do that expands as we grow up.

At the beginning, we may know the self as the youngest member of the family. With siblings, we are a brother or sister. As we socialize, we become a friend. In school, we are a student. Perhaps we excel at being an athlete. At work, we are an employee; maybe, later, an employer. On the side, we may be an artist, a chess player, a gardener. Any one of these may captivate us. We may be a partner, a spouse, a parent. We can experience joy, find it fulfilling, and say, "Now I know who I really am."

A woman and her husband came with their huge family to a family psychiatrist—thirteen children stood around the office! The problem? Mother was depressed. Her youngest, a daughter, had just turned eight. Mom could see the writing on the wall: her eldest would soon leave home, and eventually, her little girl would too. The only job she had known was to be a mother. Soon, she would be out of a job. Worse, she would be out of an identity.

But was that true? We might settle for one role for a major part of our life, complete with its job description. But this can never describe us completely. At each turn in life, we choose to do this one thing or that one thing. We put aside other choices to immerse ourselves in that experience, to master those skills. A series of such forks in the road, and we soon have chosen one specific path from an enormous number of alternatives. Yet never at any time does the thing we are currently doing tap all of our potential, describe us, in any way, completely. We are always capable of doing other things, different things, more than we have yet done. The mind wants to package us so it can *really know* who we are and dominate us if we will let it. Anything involving a partition will do. So the mind will settle for exclusion: "I'm definitely not …" this and "I'm definitely not …" that.

Beware of the trap, the narrowing, the imprisoning implied. You are a Superbeing, free at all times to breathe in deeply and burst the chains around the chest that would restrict you. You are always greater than anything you do.

MANY PENNIES

I'd like a penny
for each superior, achieving person
who did it from a basic belief
that they were inferior.
I would be rich.
This is incredibly common
as if the advances of the human race
have leaden coattails
trying to hold us all back.
What a shame!
If only they could have used love
sent it into the inferior part
and upgraded it.
That would do nothing
to slow down the achieving person
as achievements
were never truly tied
to negativity.
Achievements are above all, positive.

NOT NORMAL

I am not normal.
I'm not a pureed average
of everyone else.
I am unique.
I revel in my uniqueness.
No longer do I need
to derive consolation
from group membership
by pretending I'm identical.
I am free to join
any group I choose
as an able
full-bodied member
and from my uniqueness
serve that group well.
I can be an active, competent part
of that group, that family.
I can be part of any family
and do that family best service
unique service
from my now-competent position
my freedom
to be fully aware
and respond accurately
as the situation demands.

LOGICAL DISCONNECTION

Found a flaw in your logic
your sequence now broken
I watch feeling safe
as it withers and dies.
Now the life in my mind-set
my sequence of fragments
can last on, supreme
I hope you realize.
With our mind-sets in combat
one must be the winner
survival's the game
and you're the beginner.
The fragments I'm finding
create my conclusion
any life in those pieces
is strictly illusion.
The winning I'm wanting
means I need your losing,
what goes around comes around.

MIND–FILTERING

When all things must be processed
through the filter of the mind
much rich life will be excluded
by the dryness you've designed.
For the mind, by its extracting
to bite sizes it can manage
does not notice that its process
is doing life such damage.
To be balanced, supervise that
do not let the mind run hollow
add back richness to enliven
and your happiness will follow.

It's me I'm abusing.

MIND
AND THE THINGS IT DEALS WITH
WELL

INTRODUCTION

Mind and the Things It Deals with Well. The thinking mind is a superb instrument, well adapted to the physical existence we live out in this lifetime. It does not deal well with what is invisible, the focus of this book, love's power. Physical objects can represent ideas when they are examined closely. The overlap between the unbounded, invisible, and visible physical object can be huge. But always the *idea* behind the object is greater than and carries more meaning for people, than the object itself.

The mind can become overzealous in its quest for control, stealing energy from what should be left over to bring in true living power. Hence the untruths and mistruths in deceptive advertizing, campaigning, and reports. Ultimately, sadness is the ultimate meltdown, bringing feeling back on par with living, having escaped from hardened anger and frozen fear. Look for the sadness. Let it become the silver lining in the darkened clouds.

PHYSICAL OBJECTS AS IDEAS

We talk of a place of worship, a house of ill-repute, a great car, a piece of junk. We attribute qualities to them that a photograph of the hardware might not show. A Martian lands on planet Earth, finds a hammer in a field, and takes it home as an artifact for a museum. He has never seen it in action, does not understand it could have a function beyond its shape. The function is in fact greater than the physical ingredients.

The old farmer is talking proudly about his axe. "I've had it for twenty years," he says. "Three new heads, seven new handles. It has served me well!" That axe was purely an idea.

A sporting club changes location three times, and over the decades, its staff and players many times. Buildings, equipment, personnel are all different. But everyone insists it is the same club. Perhaps it kept its name and its logo. But its name isn't what it is. The name is a label. A logo can be the picture-worth-a-thousand-words that seems more powerful. It is a tool the mind can grasp and apply words to: one word for the name, a thousand for the picture. The club may have the same feeling as it did in its original location. Being there allows you to detect the continuing influence of the founders. The feeling was what was real, what lasted.

With words in operation, the mind gains a sense of control. It can corral and contain slices of life: activities, actions, functions within its territory of definitions, descriptions, and analyses. So worded, the mind settles into its comfort zone. It may object if anyone questions its territory, its control. Certainty is its heaven. Uncertainty—the bailiwick of spontaneity, novelty, and the natural vitality of evolving life, where the idea of control is in question—can cause the mind to whip up more energy, the unrefined energy of fear, in its struggle to regain control. Through it all, the feeling behind it is what is alive.

TWISTING

I lie to you
to make a profit
deceive you
grabbing for control
hide in my group
to prove I'm right
tightening my zone of safety
Sad and lonely
is my plight.
"But I'm not sad and
I'm not lonely
look around. See!
I have friends."
Is it friendship
that connects you?
Fear's mistrust
can stranglehold.
Locked in with
your strange bedfellows
hoping your
impression's bold.
Anger's strikeout
looks impressive
hoping some will
shrink in awe.
Manacled's not
for connecting.
That's what
warm emotion's for.

FEELINGS: FRIENDLY

INTRODUCTION

Feelings: Friendly. There is a great need on this planet for friendliness to be brought forward by each person and extended, as the natural living bridge it is, toward others. Carry that warmth. This is nowhere better expressed than by the apostle Paul when he talked about putting away childish things and getting one thing clear—that love was the key (1 Cor 13). The genuineness of friendliness outreaches and outdistances narrowness of thinking. The warmth in friendliness and love outperforms the meager effects of the thinking process at every turn. Every page in *Love Is Power* points you in this direction. Lap it up.

LOVE AND THE FRIENDLY FEELINGS.

Despite being invisible and immeasurable, love performs a set of feats unmatched by any visible, measureable thing. Love has all the qualities needed to support life, emotionally—where we really live.

Love, practiced, is sustainable; it's the best means to generate endurance. It softens any hardness within endurance, gradually converting it into *joie de vivre*—the joy in just being alive. Love offers a unique support for patience. As love releases tight areas in the body and mind, it opens you to a world of awareness: the ability to be relevant, appropriate, sensitive, and nuanced in your approach to people and situations—without the distractions and discomfort of tight muscles.

Love provides a living, human upgrade to tight situations. It supports and invigorates your determination to embrace them, understand them, and deal with them. Love is an energy saver. It frees you from the bash-and-smash approach. Love gives enlivened, expanded meaning to life. It provides the filling where there was empty, hollow meaninglessness.

Love Is Power. Love provides the support to get it done and carry through to a happy result.

It's no trouble
doing something
for someone you love.
It's less trouble
doing something
when you are already
being loved.
Love kick-starts your effectiveness.
Work becomes fun.
It seems unreal
to be paid
for what you enjoy

When an actor
or other worker says
"I haven't worked
a day in my life"
what he is saying is

he loves his work so much
that love
has drained the effort
out of work
and invigorated him
instead.

Love relaxes the need for excessive thinking and worry. The mind can generate quick fixes, involving mistaken negative interpretations and false meanings. The mind can provide second-rate solutions, often involving anger, a hardening that covers useless fear beneath it. Snacking on gratitude and friendliness can be the penetrating oil that eases tightness apart. Gratitude and friendliness are aspects of love.

Love steadies any excess of excitement, fear, or anger, reducing them to manageable levels. It is a refinery. Love absorbs the crude oils, anger and fear, converting them to warmer, flowing forms, calming body tensions and agitation, and upgrading the life force in a joyful, rewarding way. As you become more afraid, more ruled by fear, love must spend additional time and effort absorbing and refining those feelings. This slows love's effectiveness down. If fear, backed by body tension, succeeds in ousting your love altogether, you need to take stock. Go over to your love. Use love to cream off the fear, mouthful by mouthful, absorbing and digesting it, until it is all gone.

The thinking mind can generate emergency holding actions, attempting to cope with a crisis. In fear at the time, we set it up to do that for us. That leaves us with hang-ups, maintained by the mind, using the crude oil of fear as fuel. These can be maintained as pieces of tightness in the physical body, pieces of negativity, little areas of graveyard in different locations.

My mind proudly lists
the extent of my hang-ups
jealous of territory
it must control.
Working so strongly
to cover all bases
fearing that it will be
left in the hole.

Given the time needed to slowly release these patterns, love can replace them. Love becomes the supportive cushion, the magic carpet to float you out of the dark cave into the sunshine.

Love is dependable. Though we may turn from it to try other methods, in our voyage of discovery, love is never more than a turn away.

Do it for yourself. Go back to your mirror and say to yourself, "I love you." Love is your power and it's in your power to use. Love stays relevant to what is going on. Love watches for the right moment to do something. Love is patient, kind, effective.

QUOTATIONS FROM SCRIPTURES

If I speak in the tongues of men and of angels, but have not love, I am only a resounding gong or a clanging cymbal. If I have the gift of prophecy and have a faith that can move mountains, but have not love, I am nothing. If I can give all I possess to the poor and surrender my body to the flames, but have not love, I gain nothing.

Love is patient, love is kind. It does not envy, it does not boast, it is not proud. It is not rude, it is not self-seeking, it is not easily angered, it keeps no record of wrongs. Love does not delight in evil but rejoices with the truth. It always protects, always trusts, always hopes, always perseveres.

Love never fails. But where there are prophecies, they will cease; where there are tongues, they will be stilled; where there is knowledge, it will pass away. For we know in part and we prophesy in part, but when perfection comes, the imperfect disappears.

When I was a child, I talked like a child, I thought like a child, I reasoned like a child. When I became a man, I put childish ways behind me. Now we see but a poor reflection as in a mirror; then we shall see face to face. Now I know in part; then I shall know fully, even as I am fully known.

And now these three remain: faith, hope, and love. But the greatest of these is love.

CHRISTIANITY: 1 Corinthians 13:1–13 NIV

A disciple having asked for a definition of charity, the Master said, "Love one another."

CONFUCIANISM: Analects

Know thou of a certainty that love is the secret of God's holy dispensation, the manifestation of the All-Merciful, the fountain of spiritual outpourings.

Love is heaven's kindly light, the Holy Spirit's eternal breath that vivifieth the human soul. Love is the cause of God's revelation unto man, the vital bond inherent, in accordance with the divine creation, in the realities of things. Love is the one means that ensureth true felicity both in this world and the next. Love is the light that guideth in darkness, the living link that uniteth God with man, that assureth the progress of every illumined soul.

Baha'i: Selections from the writings of Abudu'l-Baha

CRUDE-OIL FEELINGS

INTRODUCTION

Crude-oil Feelings. The crude-oil feelings are anger, fear, and sadness—sadness being the exit path away from the other two. They are feelings and therefore human. No robot, computer, or machine will ever feel. They will never be afraid, angry, or sad.

Fear is the fundamental crude, full of incompetence. In fear, we run away and hide, freeze on the spot, or collapse entirely. None of these responses is a prescription for effective action. Feelings can feel frozen and out of reach. Fear is a prime example.

Anger adds the supposed advantage of a holding action. But it can freeze in place, a guarantee that the fear will never be healed. When there is physical pain in the body, anger usually worsens it. Anger is a actually cheap exit from life; it's better to absorb the anger with love. You are punished when you choose anger. The Christian bible offers a healing approach, as do most other spiritual traditions.

Fear and anger double-team to grab control. The effect is to increase the hardness of a scab on a boil, merely holding the pus (the fear) inside. Anger and fear fuel ineffective, mess making actions. This is not to say that anger can't be valid. Anger is a feeling and, therefore, human and worthy of recognition. Fear can be held onto in hopes that value can be gained from it. We might try to harvest it for the feeling of being alive that it brings. But both of these feelings tend to lead to mess making instead of solutions. Finding the friendly approach to these feelings can heal the pain that they cover up and do away with them.

Sadness is the way out. It melts frozen fear; it melts anger's holding actions. Two people feeling sad can share their feelings, each recognizing the sadness of the other. In that recognition lies the emotional joining that they seek.

Whether you feel as if you are in some basement swimming pool of sadness or somaticizing it with symptoms like post-nasal drip, you can use imagery to empty the sadness gradually, simply by using a bucket. An exercise that uses imagery and the spirit of meditation follows to show you how.

ANGER

It's good not to be scared of anger. Not your own anger, not someone else's. Expect anger to resolve. Mix with people who also want anger to resolve. Anger, acted out, risks making messes. Avoid people who are always angry, who have an anger habit. Leave childish mess making behind.

ANGER'S PURPOSE

We all feel a sudden blast of energy, often as anger, when the unexpected happens or we feel betrayed or crossed. The energy is a gift. We have a choice: we could turn that anger into fuel and have more energy for effective action or we could lash out, cornering ourselves in the habit of anger. An anger habit has a grinding energy-against-energy effect inside our bodies. That can be harmful.

Occasionally, anger can have value. It can be used as a wall against human contact that is expected to be painful. One man, a member of a minority group living in a town hostile to that group, kept himself psychologically alive by retaining a wall of anger around him. It is a neat balancing act if you can do this without installing a permanent anger habit that will be a problem to you itself—after you leave that hostile town, taking your habit with you.

In the teaching of discipline, the armed forces can use anger or simulated anger to evoke fear (fear of survival). With survival at stake, the recruits can learn the lesson of discipline within a chain of command. Many a recruit, sensing a deep need to develop discipline, willingly undergoes army training to get that teaching. The recruit can emerge with great pride in self and country. With that lesson usefully learned, the question remains: where will he take the associated anger? What will become of it in the next stage of his life?

The risk of mess making lies ahead if the anger–fear modality continues to be the base used. In the case of war (or any violence), the mess is made on physical bodies in response to interpersonal issues (politics and diplomacy are intensely interpersonal, only on the level of nation-states). These issues are embedded with the secondary purpose of gain. In the game of me-up–you-down, genuine relating is lost.

The judge peers over the bench upon the first-offender and says, "Don't you *ever* do that again!" She hopes that the young man's fear will cause him to take the lesson to heart so he never commits a criminal deed again. Fear as motivator. If it turns out he is again before the judge so many offenses later, his lesson was different: he'd installed the anger–fear axis as a lifestyle habit instead.

Living on the anger–fear axis has you switching forever between anger and fear, neither of which allows emotional closeness with others. The need to learn about love—its power, versatility, ease, and effectiveness—has been bypassed. If the first-offender had noticed the glint in the judge's eye, he may more readily have felt some gratitude and gotten it right.

Anger-against is not connection-with. The anger crude needs refining to a higher grade. With refining, it can take on the easing of forgiveness. Forgiveness works best when self-respect is retained—it's not a good apology if it comes from self-loathing; it's not self-loathing if it's offered with love. Actions can speak louder than words. Make eye contact and pause as you make your amends or offer your pardon to see how the gift of forgiveness or apology is being received—show that you mean it. Show respect for yourself and the other. Self-respected action can speak louder than words that seek merely to dominate.

None of these behaviors on your part guarantees a particular response from the person forgiven or apologized to. If that person is cannot maintain eye contact with you, remain relaxed, steady, calm; affirm your goodwill to support both the other and yourself.

ANGER WORSENS PAIN

When you're feeling pain
and you're angry
does the anger ever make the pain better?
You might expect that
anger can feel justifiable
you feel safer when you're right
but the usual experience is that
anger worsens pain.
Upgrade your anger
hold it tight, then let it go
(your will to be angry)
give away that tightness
give away that pain.

ANGER EARNED: THE BOOBY PRIZE

Anger's energy can feel consoling: "See! I'm not a weak little child. I have this anger." It can be saved in secret—into a collection.

A little more anger can be added to the collection after each insult, interpreted from a world seen as hostile. Color the world angry. Such a distorted world will provide you with all the insults you need for your anger collection. The idea of the freebie comes from childhood, when support comes (ideally) from loving parents without your having to do anything for it. An adult child might reenact this expectation with the angry attitude "the world owes me."

Anger can be collected until there is enough for what some of us know to be a payoff (Berne 1980). The only problem with the payoff is the mess. Full of anger, you feel entitled to blast out all that energy, for no reason that will ultimately do you or anyone else any good. It is often a guilt-free booby prize. The judge is supposed to say, "You've collected enough anger. You're no longer guilty. You can do anything you want, guilt-free." A real judge will see it otherwise.

ANGER, I LOVE YOU

I want to be angry
I'm scared to be sad
I must repel others
don't care if I'm bad.

Heal your anger. Mop it up with friendly emotional warmth. Flood yourself with this warm lubricant. Let it soak into you. Let it loose and set adrift the flotsam and jetsam of anger. Their value always was a forgery. Go for the real, enlivened form.

If you are not yet ready to do that, if the anger crud has been around so long you have come to identify it as part of you, you can begin by simply letting yourself relax. Let yourself soak in a warm emotional bath once a month—to get the feel of it. See yourself doing that in your mind's eye.

ANGER RUSHES IN

Anger rushes in to have its way
and with its every effort makes you pay
smashing, bashing, creating disarray
protective walls don't hide the weak display.
Seeking always to make you obey
extra forcing is its résumé
Drops life's colors to a dulling gray
doomed to face its final exposé.

QUOTATION FROM SCRIPTURE

And unto him that smiteth thee on the one cheek offer also the other …

LUKE 6:29, KJV

FROZEN FEELINGS

Do you struggle to feel? Do you find it hard to locate your humanity: a feeling, a living response to the situation before you? Did you decide a long time ago to freeze who you are … for safety reasons? On the grounds that your spontaneous feeling responses were not acceptable to important people around you at the time?

Explore what you feel. Melt a little here, a little there. Let yourself in gradually, let in the moving flow of connections to the world about you—your feelings sense for you what is going on out there and how you feel about it. Feelings are your crucial guide through life. They tell you about each situation and about yourself in that situation before all the facts are in.

They give you a base for going ahead: "I did it because I felt like doing it." And for not going ahead: "I didn't feel like it." Each choice can be modified. But these statements do connect you to what is going on. This is how you stay relevant.

FEAR

You don't have to be afraid. It's okay to re-label the fear as *energy to do something with* and then work out what to do. In the doing, you move on—past the fear. You find it had no worth except as fuel toward something better. It is crude oil that you refine to a better grade.

Start by mixing in courage. Bring the percentage up to the right amount. Use your courage-despite-fear to get something moving. In that way, the fear is made to disappear.

FEAR, FACED

No one faces just one fear
search and you'll find others near
fears, like clouds, can blend together
incompetence creates bad weather
you don't have to be a dunce
you can face it all at once
when you turn and face your fear
you can make that disappear
surprisingly it isn't tall
fear, when faced, becomes so small
fear, when faced, begins to shrink
then faster yet than you can think
it shrivels and becomes quite small
until it isn't there at all.

FEAR IN ACTION

Fear creeps into our lives in the subtlest of ways. How often do you say to yourself, "If I don't do it, I'm afraid that … will happen." The crude-oil fuel of fear gives us a little kick then and makes us do it. It is like skulking in backwards to get the job done.

Turn. Face the job. Understand the positive aspects of doing it. Understand the drawbacks, the downside. Make up your mind. Then if you do it, it is because you *decided* to do it, you *want* to do it. You move forward, under your own steam. Leave your fear at home to cool its heels. No more is fear going to be the fuel you use to drive home a result. Go for the fear-free, squeaky clean existence!

Some common fears are:

Fear of failure

Fear of success: the attention it gains (and the possibility of failing to respond perfectly to that every time)

Fear of intense self-criticism: the ton-of-bricks poised by habit above us to be brutally unleashed at any time, automatically, if we dare to do something less than perfectly. Guilt, blame, shame, and punishment can become a habituated system that attempts to control internally by force

Fear of facing the "real me": indicating underlying self-loathing

Fear of emotional closeness that would necessitate using the "real me" more fully, and so risk uncovering supposed personal deficits that aren't really deficits at all

FEAR REVISITED

Emotions are fuel. Emotions power us to do things. Emotions also rank-order our priorities. "I didn't feel like it" sends an item to the bottom of our priority list: "I had the fuel, but I wasn't going to use it on that!"

Emotional fuels have different qualities. Bottom of the quality list is fear.

Fear is crude oil in your gas tank. You are going nowhere with that stuff. With fear in the driver's seat, you can run away and hide; freeze, shiver on the spot, or fall in a crumpled heap, paralyzed. Neither running away nor being paralyzed or frozen enables you to be effective. They are all prescriptions for incompetence. You need to take courage, and with that courage in tow, lift yourself above the level of acting out of fear.

Fearing to be seen as afraid, fearing even to see your own fear, you can still run away and hide from it. Then you don't see it. "What! Me afraid? Not me." For this reason, fear can be the hardest emotion to identify. Identifying it risks inviting attack from predators looking for evidence of fear—incompetence. Then, they can safely attack. Who needs that?

An escaped tiger turns the corner. You feel instant fear. What you do with it is everything. If you use the fear as fuel to turn and run, game over! The tiger may not even be hungry. He may have walked on by. But the biological signal of fleeing prey may be too much for the tiger to resist.

Do not act out fear. Take a few breaths to loosen tightened muscles. Take time to consider. Gently breathe your way through it.

If you find that something you habitually do is actually done out of fear—that is, fear is fueling the action—don't do it. At least once, simply refrain from doing it. In that way, you move out of the fear realm. You open to other possibilities. If you habitually *don't* do something and you find on examination that it would be simple and useful to do and that the only reason you don't do it is fear, do it anyway. At least once, just do it. That way, you break the fear cycle. You break out into richer realms.

BRINGING FEAR BACK

When you do once more
the same thing you always did
out of fear
you bring back
the fear
that was always there
each time you did
that same thing.
Sometimes, don't do it.
Just say to yourself
"I'm not going to do that!"
Sometimes do it
not out of fear
(catch the fear unawares!).
The very moment you don't feel fear
do it anyway.
Pry the fear loose
by steady stages.
Then you are free to do it
or not do it
neither one determined by fear.

FEAR AND ANGER

Fear can grab for an instant ally: anger, *Go to Hell! Get lost! F___ off! Sh__!* Extra energy of a repulsive nature tries magically to remove the problem. "If I can hurt someone's eardrums with my yelling, maybe they'll go away and take my fear with them." This is another freeze-over, a magical solution that wants to project the fear, relocate it on someone else, and get rid of them! This cannot work. It never was their fear in the first place.

Internally, the mirror image of this becomes "If I can throw enough energy into something else (another thought; another behavior, like making a lot of noise), perhaps less of my life energy will be left over to be involved in imagery and preoccupation with what I am afraid of."

The one-word method is doomed from the start. Words are tools of the thinking mind. The mind has difficulty discriminating between its tools. It operates blindly. Another tool of the mind is imagery. The image is worth a thousand words. When the mind tries to use one word to fight a thousand, even when the one word is spoken loudly, that word is doomed. It cannot win. The picture is larger and paints all over it.

Yet the intensity, the anger, can have a reassuring effect. "See? I'm not weak and powerless. I'm strong after all. I'm not suppressing my energy. I'm letting it fly. Loudly. Noisily. Strongly. And, hopefully, impressively! If I see that someone else is impressed, I can gain momentary relief from my feeling of weakness. See? They are looking at me. I must be important. I must real. I am not a child after all" (you hope!).

This is yet another way anger and fear double-team.

Anger's Scab, the Problem

Strengthening anger's scab all over fear
hoping and hoping it might disappear
I'm forcing the boil to collect and expand
until an explosion takes things out of hand.
Emotional warmth can resolve the problem
loving small hearts take on boils and gobble 'em
noticing anger, I recognize fear
inviting the light of day to reappear.

Fear Retained

One of the commonest (non-)motivators in society is fear. It is so widespread that the media can play to it whenever there is a lull in the news and be sure to draw attention. The public (those interested) are saying, in effect: "What can I do now with the fear I hold so dear? How can I retain my fear-smeared sense of who I am, as I willingly face yet another crisis?" The media are only willing to connect with that human condition.

Fear guarantees our incompetence. Fear makes us run and hide. Fear freezes us (the wild animal in the headlights phenomenon). Fear can paralyze effective action: "Of course I can't do anything about that huge crisis. So I'll just stare. Here I am, useless again."

The seductiveness of fear is its vigor. Little children (all eyes and ears) feel a strong sense of this force when an older child, wanting to grab for a sense of power, does something to scare them. It keeps them incompetent, "in the headlights." A watchful, loving parent can keep this bad behavior to a minimum by reassuring the child with an emphasis on his or her successes.

You can throw away something that is broken: a toy, a worn-out piece of clothing. But how do you throw away your process, your *I have always done it this way*, your *this is who I am*, before you once more abuse your aliveness?

The answer is: you don't throw it away. It never was an object to be discarded. What we are looking at is the invisible spark that is attractive, potentially responsive, an upping-the-stakes to an alive-to-alive encounter. That is what needs enhancing.

You must nourish it. Upgrade it. Allow your sense of self to rise to higher ground. Watch plants. They routinely take mulch and transform it into fruit and beautiful flowers. If the media no longer can play to your fear, they will have to begin playing to something else. Leave them to do their homework. It remains their job to stay in business. They'll find a way, you can be sure of that.

This entire book is based on healing at that level, the level of your life force, at the center of which is love. Scan the pages. Take a bite of each angle on love. Chew over that emotional warmth. Develop by practicing your attitude of gratitude. Enliven your spirit. Arise from the dead—the living dead, that is. Explain to others close to you what you are doing, so they won't play you for the usual payoff (Berne 1980). Keep away from those who refuse to accept the new self you are creating—the original self you are.

MESS MAKERS

Anger and fear are
the mess making siblings
guaranteed useless
in all they achieve.
Fear can do nothing
that's ever effective
leaving the messes
it didn't take care of.
Anger can fix it! Says
"I'll bash and smash it"
creating the chaos
to show off its power.
Anger needs fear
that makes anger feel stronger
so both can make messes
that minimize movement
in healing directions.
Wash them with warmth
the emotional healer
Rinse them with love
to sponge up the dirt
Leave them to dry
supple, they've come alive again
removing the messes
relieving the hurt.

FEAR HARVESTED

I'm so glad that my fear is decreasing
relieving, relaxing, releasing
I'm loving my fear
so it will disappear
as it upgrades, my power's increasing.

REFINING FEAR WITH FRIENDS

Do not forget that your fear's
an expression of your *now*s and *here*s
as in courage you clear it
with friends who can hear it
compassion returns to your ears.
Warm gratitude that you give back
confirms that there was no attack
in the fashion of sharing
both people now wearing
the warmth that fear's coldness did lack.
This refined form of what was earthquakes
does much to relieve pains and aches
your body now better
becomes the trend setter
confirming you have what it takes.

DOING AWAY WITH FEAR

Fear is commonly regarded as an *expectable* emotion from time to time. "Of course I expect to be afraid under certain circumstances." Under these rules, anyone who is not afraid can be regarded as being "in denial." Yet there are some people who show no evidence of fear. How did they train themselves to be free of it?

Fear originates in childhood, a time of immaturity and incompetence. When something new suddenly presents itself, the child's body obligingly floods with energy. The energy is at the ready for any response. An alert parent can show the child quickly how to cope, using experience and maturity to bypass the child's immaturity and incompetence. Such a child can stock its memory with a host of successes, all carrying the message "I have coped before, so I can do it again." This child is training useless fear out of himself or herself. It readily bypasses the incompetence interpretation to get down to the business at hand.

Where do we get such alert parents? Are we doomed if that was not the circumstance of our own childhood? No. But it will take time and patience to build in a solid structure from the house of cards of childhood.

The first stage is to become objective. You cannot fix what you cannot see. Then use that objectivity to develop an understanding of what is going on.

You now observe a part inside that can take center stage, dominate, and take you over from time to time. All it needs not to repeat and repeat that trick is reassurance. It needs to know there is someone older and wiser willing to be available to supply support when needed. That older and wiser person is you.

You are it. You have long since matured beyond those days of incompetence. You might never achieve 24/7 ceaseless support; only a child fearing the worst and intensifying its demands needs 24/7 support. But you have seen the lie given to the worst fears of childhood. You can see and understand how the child could have resorted to the hardness of anger as a protection. You can use the information herein to help you. As you read, you begin to recognize the power available to you. You practice making that warmth flow. You place yourself in a superb position to support the inner child, grow it up away from leaning on fear as fuel for actions—and the thinking that lies behind those actions. As it comes to integrate within you, it brings buckets of beautiful gifts: sensitive awareness, curiosity, creativity, and spontaneity. You can dip into these buckets and use your newfound gifts as you see fit.

Yes, you are losing a friend. Way down deep, we understand the vibrancy of fear. No inanimate object ever gives evidence of feeling fear. Yet lively fear has long been with us. We have felt it there as a companion, constant and reliable. Recognizing that it must go, we prepare ourselves to say good-bye to a friend, a familiar form that our own vitality has absorbed. "Good-bye. I now understand you for what you are. I breathe you in as I renew your energy and upgrade to warmer, more palatable forms."

You don't have to do this all at once. You may take your time. Meanwhile, there are plenty of people in powerful positions, only too willing to use fear in others, take advantage of its incompetence, manipulate it for greed and personal gain, to control the predictable responses of those who are afraid. Unfortunately, they condemn themselves forever to inadequate underachievement in the area of communication and human relationships. As Little Orphan Annie might say, "It's a hard-luck life."

FERRETING OUT THE SADNESS

Behind the frozen ice of fear, behind the hard wall of anger, lies sadness. Sadness represents a melting of the ice, a relaxing of the hardness, a readiness to move on beyond these fixations.

There is no ice. There is no wall. These are images, pictures worth a thousand words, that require a constant drain of life energy to maintain them. The ice, the wall, leave a sense of containment that is supposed to make you feel safe. That sense is driven by the mind, which was given the task of setting it up and so continues to drive it. It is maintained by the body, which represents it physically as armoring (Lowen 1958). "Staying safe" gives the illusion of being imprisoned, feels like a lack of freedom. Readiness to move on is marked by a release of the "prison." The walls come down, the ice melts, allowing you to re-allocate your life energy away from its pre-dedication to such a fixated purpose.

Sadness—both its expression in tears and in speech—is the pathway down the tunnel toward the light at the end. Your sense of release, its freedom, as you regain that missing life energy, feels exhilarating. The relief can be enormous. You sense coming out of darkness into the light. You can breathe again. You can live again! Your constant feeling of agitation, your inexplicable urge to escape is replaced by calm. Gone is the need, the right, the consolation prize of blaming others. You are free to see others as they actually are (warts and all), not through the hazy screen of your projected problems.

Sadness dissolves structure. Structure is maintained in the face. Once "the wall" comes down, all your emotions show in your face. Your face can fall—go limp, cast down. Similarly, the structure of your tone of voice is maintained by your musculature. A person may blubber full out. More likely, however, you may detect someone's difficulty with maintaining an even tone. The bottom seems to have dropped out of it. So sadness comes through both face and voice quality. Bearing in mind the importance of recognizing sadness as a means of making a genuine connection, you are well advised to recognize this potential tool, otherwise you risk leaving someone in your care in a potentially dangerous pool of sadness. (If a fist comes up to give you a black eye, you can always duck.)

SWIMMING POOL OF SADNESS

The swimming pool of sadness
that resides down in my basement
is there for me to empty by the bucket
for it is just a finite pool
requiring new placement
provided there is somewhere you can tuck it
So empty out your swimming pool
however long it takes you
there are times, and times again, when you can do it
and the work that you are doing
will come back to service you
as your understanding lets you see right through it.

SADNESS SHARING

Two people
not in touch
feel the feeling
of not-in-touch.
Each feels sad.
Share the feeling
of not-in-touch
"I feel sad."
"Yes, I'm sad too."
Each now in touch
through sadness shared.
Now in touch
the problem solved
both can go on
to warmer feelings.
Sadness shared
opened that door.
Friendship
acceptance
understanding
all can follow
through the door
opened by
connecting sadness.

POST-NASAL DRIP

Have you ever run into a post-nasal drip
its volume so large as to scuttle six ships
tears that should slow and be blown away
are held deep inside for yet one more day.
Sad tears, please share them
and so get them free
you may have much sadness
you need to let be.
And when it's all shared
and you've cleaned up the past
you may find your dripping
is stopping at last.

THE REJUVENATING FEAR EXERCISE

Fear is crippling. Fear expressed in the body as anxiety can paralyze a person, freeze actions. Fear is the fundamental source of incompetence.

Here is an exercise to deal with fear. Do it many times. It is based on a metaphor: the weak coldness of fear converted to the power of emotional warmth.

Place your wrist in front of your open mouth. Breathe in. Then breathe out. Feel the warmth in the processed air, the air you breathe out. By contrast, the wrist is cold as you are breathing in.

Your body may be racked with fear: tremors, shudders, tensions, pressures and heaviness, racing heart, gurgling bowels, sweating, cold and clammy. When such fear has become familiar, it may be passed off as "normal." Neck tension, shoulder tension, tight stomach can all represent normal fear. *Normal fear?* Who needs that? It can take courage to face this and change it. Take whatever courage you need. It is freely available from the "Universal Store."

THE EXERCISE

Say out loud: "I am slowly, steadily ridding my body of fear. I suck it up. I convert it into compassion." Then breathe in. Draw air and energy up from your body. Breathe out. Feel the warmth in your compassion, on your wrist. It is good. You have great power in your compassion. People love you for it. Feel that your warm compassion lights up the area around you and soaks back into your body. Now picture your warmth going down through your body. Do it again and again.

Now say: "I am slowly, steadily ridding my body of fear. I suck it up. I convert it into empathy." Breathe in. Breathe out. Feel the warmth in your empathy, on your wrist. People will go a long way to find someone capable of genuine empathy. Do it a second and a third time.

Now say: "I am slowly, steadily ridding my body of fear. I suck it up. I convert it into understanding." Feel that on your wrist. Understanding has broad power. Breathe in. Breathe out your warm understanding onto your wrist.

Feel your healing power surging as you continue to convert the raw fuel, the crude oil, the black ooze of fear into this nourishing, lubricating, connecting, enriching marvel of compassion, empathy, and understanding.

MIND: IMAGERY:
PLAYING THE TRUMP CARD

Introduction
Imagery
The Cleansing Meditation
The Self-Hug
Breathe in Warmth

103

INTRODUCTION

Mind-Imagery: Playing the Trump Card. Instant imagery can have devastating effect. It is the thinking mind playing its trump card, the picture worth a thousand words that can beat out love quickly. Love, as the modus operandi of the objective conductor within you, your inner wise sage, needs more time to develop into fully flowered love. Speed beats that. If ever love is out-played, it is by the thinking mind throwing old imagery at you. It aces what was the king. If you intended your generosity to be your best, most effective effort, you can be beaten completely by the mind's throwing out a juicy but negative image is presented at this point. Then, by habit, you retreat into the arms of the self-elected mental problem solver, forever dooming anything but the simplest of actions from being effective.

This section begins with the power of imagery, for good or evil, in the article "Imagery." But a regular bath can offer you advance healing for letting old images go. Breathing and hugging are natural accompaniments. I recommend breathing to all my patients. Breathing adds something special and essential.

IMAGERY

Imagery is a powerful tool. A picture is worth a thousand words. As you construct pictures and talk about the imagery, good or bad, be aware of the ten-ton trucks you are throwing about. Too much energy in powerful negative pictures wreaks havoc.

A positive picture can carry you through unseen difficulties. A negative picture can blight your whole existence. Let go of negative pictures. Take your negative pictures off the wall; face it into the corner and go back to look at the empty space. Begin to assemble the picture of success you need. Use that picture instead.

THE CLEANSING MEDITATION

If you like imagery, you can derive great benefit from this exercise. Do it many times. Do it very, very slowly. Pause a long time (several minutes) between paragraphs. A friend may read it to you. You can make a tape recording that has built-in time breaks.

Do not rush at this. It is not a speed test. Choose a time when you are not under pressure. Pressure can come from the thinking mind driving the pace, probably using fear or a fear-anger mix. You are overcoming this with a more leisurely approach. You postpone fear and anger, wash out their body correlates.

Sit quietly. Close your eyes. Breathe quietly. Relax with both feet on the floor, hands in your lap. You are a sponge—from head to toe an interconnected series of waterways. This should not strain your imagination. Your body is made up of atoms, each one of which is mostly space.

From above, the rain falls, a healing rain that washes and cleanses. It soaks into your head, releasing dirt to drop downwards. "It's all in your head?" No, it isn't. You are washing it out! A moving front of cleansing descends slowly through your head, taking anything that contaminates with it. Breathe it in. Draw it down with your breath. Your face and jaw are similarly purged. Relax several minutes, letting the rain fall.

The healing wave reaches your neck, front, and back, relaxing and soothing them. Let it work for several minutes.

The healing front washes down through your shoulders, easing them of any burden. Let it work for several minutes.

Down, down through your chest moves the healing front, freeing your chest of heaviness, adding sparkle to your breathing, and cleansing your heart. (Several minutes).

Down through your abdomen, the stomach and all the other organs are each in their turn washed and cleansed. The joints of elbows, wrists, and hands hanging at your sides are similarly washed clean. Your spine and all its vertebrae, the powerful muscles that control it, are rinsed and relaxed. (Let it happen over several minutes.)

The healing wave proceeds through your pelvis and behind, removing all tension and disharmony.

Down through your thighs, the cleansing continues. You are scoured, you are scrubbed. Nothing escapes the purifying. (Take several minutes.)

Your knees are blessed with this healing wave. Calves are similarly cared for. No charley-horses will be left here.

Your ankles receive the treatment. Your feet, those long-suffering supporters of your body and your life, are given their just rewards. All the dirt and contamination passes through the soles of your feet, into the ground, where it finds its home.

Now another wave begins. It is still raining. A healing front moves through your prewashed head, finding leftover bits of pollution to remove. Take a breath; let it in and let it out. Down and down, washing over your face, your neck, your shoulders, your arms … all are double-cleansed. Feel the clearing. Breathe it in and out. Now, the liquid warmth washes over your chest and then your abdomen, allowing you to release more and more, the wave carrying the tension on. Take a few releasing breaths. In, out, hold, release. The rinsing continues. Your hips, your behind, your pelvis release much more in this second wash. Notice it, feel it, shake the water through and off. Then, let your thighs, legs, ankles, and feet all succumb to the beautiful cleansing. Take your time and enjoy the water falling and washing out debris, old thoughts, outmoded tensions, caked-on feelings.

With a third wave, the sparkle begins. Can't you almost hear the music? Listen. Sometimes it's thunderous, sometimes delicate; melodies and harmonies join in the celebration of your healing. With dirt removed, your act comes together in marvelous fluidity. Everything you do seems touched with magic. Your power surges. You can be mighty; you can be gentle; by turns all your energies are available to you. Your judgment feels cleansed. All disrespect has been cancelled. Your vision and understanding are enhanced. You rest in a state of readiness as life presents itself.

Repeat this cleansing imagery many times. The healing front can continue in between repeats. Where at first you go from A to B, next time it may be F to G, then L to M. You grow in stature, in awareness, in understanding, between times.

THE SELF-HUG

We are "hugged" for nine months in a warm swimming pool, before we are born. The first language that a newborn understands is to be returned to that warm mother contact, placed on mother's tummy.

Self-appreciation, the focus of this book, can be borne out physically if you are willing to hug yourself. Reach as far across and around your body as you can reach and give yourself a hug. Give with genuine warmth. See the person you are hugging as deserving. Put your heart into it.

Then switch your point of view. Get the feeling someone really nice is giving you a wonderful hug. Be hugged. Enjoy it. Soak it in.

If we consider the muscles all together as one organ, then this organ is the largest of all the body organs. Muscles drape the bones, connect them, and move them toward or away from one another by acting across joints. Muscles carry a rich blood supply to do this work. This warm blood from deeper within the body contributes to their warmth.

Muscles can—under the direction of the mind to harden or put up a wall—go into a chronic state of tension. They become always-on-guard protectors. This is body armoring (Lowen 1958). But it can be felt as a strange form of "hugging," at the bone level. As a body part, muscles are restricted in their communicating to tensing and relaxing. Always-tense muscles weaken under the stress. This is the opposite of the stretching and limbering workout they require to be in good physical health.

As you hug yourself, feel through what may have become layers of armor. Give mercy to such a long-standing body commitment to mental attitudes. Sense your healing power, your ability to leaven and release tensions, as you use both physical and emotional warmth on a deserving person: yourself.

BREATHE IN WARMTH

The universe is loving you. Warmth is coming into you. Compassion is coming into you: the same compassion you sent out, before. It is the same universally available healing energy. You are deserving of it. You choose that. Feel how wonderful it is to receive compassion. Your life is upgraded as you do that.

Is there something for which you need forgiveness? Is your self-critic willing to let you forgive yourself? If not, you may need first to quiet that noisemaker. Once that issue has settled, breathe in forgiveness. It is the unforgiving state that is the problem. Let the forgiveness suffuse throughout your body. Feel the relief build.

Let yourself breathe in any other warm emotion you desire. Take your fill. These emotions are available to all—to be used as we see fit.

Finally, it's time for the overall healer: love. Be loved. Breathe in love. Take it to your heart. Let it spread from there to all places. Feel loved. Resolve to recreate this wonderful feeling. Often!

Notice an interesting feeling: excitement. You may feel excited about the power you were just using. You may want to use it again. You may be excited, thinking about that. Excitement is a fast-paced emotion. It revs you back up to thinking speed. Leavened by healing warmth, excitement blends in and is validated by the warmth. Thinking elements are best supported by a foundation of warm emotion. Without that, they are like houses built on sand: they quickly crumble.

If you cannot contain high-speed energies, if you cannot control the excitement down to a level capable of healing, tag it with a meaning. Say out loud to yourself, "This I do in the name of doing it too quickly." The speed you could not contain before, you now act out deliberately. This brings it back under control. That is the first of a series of lead weights you add to the saddle. This runaway horse needs the handicap you steadily, repeatedly give it.

RUSHING

107

INTRODUCTION

Rushing. Rushing can plague us. "I must get it done yesterday" is an attitude full of doom. The article "Rushing" lays this out, as well as the poems "Rushing through a Sea Of Honey" and "Too Much."

When rushing combines with excitement, you have two foxes in charge of the chicken coop. Excitement is a naturally high-speed vibration. When it is not leavened with love, there is hell to pay.

Imagery is another mind-related problem that can outfox you. The picture worth a thousand words can guarantee that the mind territory (words and images) is in charge. Control, restriction, and imprisonment in a fixed attitude can quickly follow.

The thinking process can work against itself. When one quick fix, frozen in by the mind, doesn't work, another freeze occurs. You can send out the subconscious mental command "Block that!" superimposing it on the previous freeze-over. By so doing, you stop the solution that never did deal with the fully operating human being in the first place. Add rushing to that and you put a bang-bang sequence in place before the slower loving process has gained awareness. This can be most annoying when a mind-originated line of thinking, now practiced into a habit as a personal attitude, runs into the realization, That didn't work." The mind uses its primitive capacity to block the defeating action. But when the action was the thinking process itself, then suddenly you can't think! Thinking is blocked. It might be a word that you cannot retrieve: "It's on the tip of my tongue." It might become an incapacity to make a decision: "I'm sorry. I can't consider that now. Will you give me a moment to collect my thoughts?"

The mind does not realize it is fighting itself. The pattern begins in childhood. We all know the specific instructions children need to learn success and not defeat themselves. Layering upon layers of "I must block that" thought sequences can end up with a human being paralyzed into inaction.

RUSHING

Nearly everyone seems to be in a hurry: "C'mon! Hurry up. Got to go. Get moving!" The slower pace of the agrarian lifestyle of yesteryear has been replaced by city traffic, road rage, deadlines, and looming failure if you can't go even faster.

> Act in haste, repent at leisure
> sets a path with little pleasure
> go for "easy," take your time
> that sets you for a life sublime.
> You can pause and think it through
> that's always something you can do.
> When you see where you must go
> you will get there steady, slow.

All this speed is actually self-abusive. You reduce your awareness at high speeds; things go by too fast to fix on them. This increases the risk of making mistakes. Then, at speed, you have much less time to correct the errors. You end up carrying extra energy in reserve, similar to anger, which you use to "whack the fix" into place—just in time. Such harmful pressure!

Take your time to smell the rose
lest the thorns should slash your nose.

Rushing is reminiscent of the high energy of childhood. Watch children at play, at school lunch break. Running, jumping, yelling, screaming, pushing, shoving: energy to burn! Grownups, told to emulate every movement of a child in a kindergarten class, quickly become exhausted. The urge to pour all that energy into a developing body, perhaps to explore what it can do today that it couldn't do yesterday, perhaps to give newly growing tissue its first workout, all this has receded into the past by the time you are an adult.

Yet habits can remain. Just as some children, labeled hyperactive, can have trouble sitting still, so, too, can adults be hyperactive.

When the habit begins in the cradle, a deep unrest can be forged that seems out of reach. For the first six months of life, a child is discovering who he or she is. By six months, she realizes, "Oh, that foot down there stays with me in the cradle, but the face that appears above, belongs to someone else!" And it is twelve months before any words can be used to describe experience. An adult with a problem that began before she developed language can be speechless to explain it. There was no speech to store along with her memories. A deep-driving urge from a dysfunctional beginning can underlie an entire life.

Every baby needs to be held and enveloped in love coming from a loving heart. A global policy to ensure that that happens to every child might eliminate many problems that face and overpower human beings.

Love the vestiges of infancy still left inside you. Swamp that infant with love. Love and hug yourself to quiet all agitation inside. Again, reach around to your back with both arms. Send the love from your heart right through the palms of your hands. Now be the one receiving the hug; feel those arms around you sending love through those palms, as you think, "Someone wonderful is loving me!"

Love the older child still inside of you. Send your goodwill back to that time, to that little deserving person still active inside you. Be accepting. We all, to the end of our days, seek acceptance. We yearn to be understood, even after we have long given up on its ever happening. With this deep shuddering inside you healed, you can move ahead as a more effective adult.

Beam ahead your calming love to any situation of agitation that you are expecting. Then, when you arrive, soak in the love. Imagine little hearts sitting around waiting for you. When you arrive, they light up with smiles and rush to be absorbed into you, breathed in by you. It will help steady you to be alert, calm, and appropriate, ahead of those who don't know what you are doing.

Whether or not you sense the origin of your rushing in infancy or early childhood, you can change the habit with a few simple and practical activities.. When you are out walking, walk so as to pass the person *behind* you. If you are doing a task that you always speed through, break the task down into five parts. Then slow each part down by remaining fully aware of every movement, every change. Do it in slow motion. Do the second part even slower than the first. See how slow you can go by the time you get to part five. Every bit of practice tells the body, "This is the way I want to go."

RUSHING THROUGH A SEA OF HONEY

Rushing through a sea of honey
trying to go fast, not slow
I get exhausted from the efforts—
honey is the way to go.

Sometimes having headaches can signal that the mind is in charge, holding the fort. Thinking at high speed and trying to be perfect are two habits that can also clue you in. Getting real, becoming alive, means moving up to the level of *feelings*. It is sad that we would ever be far from this level.

TOO MUCH

Going faster to be perfect
double-tasks the thinking mind
look behind excessive effort
hidden sadness you will find.

THE CHILD WITHIN

Child Sections. Many qualities of children, such as spontaneity, creativity, and the capacity for fun are highly desirable. Adults who can recreate these childhood states can add immeasurably to the societies they inhabit. The word "childlike" is often used for such fine qualities.

There is a downside. It is generally covered by the word "childish." We have all behaved many times in ways that, in retrospect, we can look upon as childish. Democracies have many problems. It is in the nature of a democracy to seek out problems on a continuing basis and solve them. But when the way of seeking out the problems is a problem in itself, the whole thing is compounded. The article "The Stage" spotlights this.

This happens when the citizens of the democracy behave in childish ways. They underachieve. They do not reach their matured potential. When the child is hurt or injured, the power of mother to "kiss it better" is very clear. To the child, it is a miracle, part of the reality of a world it does not yet understand. Fortunately, counterbalancing this is the capacity of adults to act maturely.

The whistleblower is a prime example. The organization is acting childishly—as all organizations do occasionally or regularly depending on their commitment to the property we might call organizational stupidity, a case of the whole being *less* than the sum of its parts. But when the whistleblower sees the process reaching catastrophic proportions, his conscience dictates that he must call outside attention to the problem. He does this at the risk of severe retaliation from the organization's entities who are willing to behave in less than humane ways.

At the group level, people coming together to draw attention to such problems, complaining and insisting that something must be done, can counterbalance the childish actions of an organization or democracy. The World Wide Web has contributed enormously to this function. With the ability of individuals to take group action, the problems of organizational stupidity or childish selfishness can be solved. Soldiers with cell phones that can make movies have the ability to intervene on the insanities of war, ensuring these cannot continue to go unrecognized. It is human equivalent of the natural self-correcting built into Newton's Third Law of Motion: for every action there is an equal and opposite reaction.

CHILD: AWARE

INTRODUCTION

Child: Aware. A child is naturally fully aware. Part of the fascination grown-ups feel toward young children is their capacity for that full awareness. Unfortunately, and sometimes amusingly, it is a quality adults seem so often to have lost. "Delight and Other Replaceables" describes the thinking-driven way that this quality can be lost. Retrieve the lost awareness by taking deliberate steps; learn to laugh at yourself. These pages are designed to gently raise your awareness.

QUOTATION FROM SCRIPTURE

> *Unless you change and become as little children, you will never enter the kingdom of heaven.*

> Matthew 18:3 NIV

AWARE

Without awareness, you are dead. A corpse has lost all awareness. People can act like that too. The child does not start out that way. Curiosity and full awareness may well start in the womb: nine months of feeling comfortable, protected, listening to Mother's heartbeat and other sounds that mysteriously filter through.

The newborn infant has full awareness. All is one, at least for the first six months following birth, after which awareness dawns on the child that the foot down there stays with him, while the faces over the crib appear and disappear. He also is fully aware that it is very comforting to be picked up and held near to Mama's heartbeat, again.

Awareness tends to dwindle after that. Habits of thinking move in. Habits of behavior give us to imagining that there is only advantage in running on automatic. Much of this book invites you to upgrade that idea and return to full awareness, away from the fixed automatic response. Delight becomes possible again. Your best prescription for a long life is not some pill. You can guarantee for yourself extended years by attending to the needs of the child inside, nourishing him with attention.

DELIGHT AND OTHER REPLACEABLES

"Listen to the pretty bird!" says the small child, delight written all over her face. "That's a robin," replies the grown-up, naming the bird. The grown-up knows more, has more facts, more information than the child. The grown-up is proud of the knowledge, feels superior to the child, and praises himself at his ability to increase the child's education.

The child has two choices at this point. The one is to stay with the delight and continue to observe and experience the bird, to take in the full spontaneous offering. If the child feels free and safe to do that, this will likely be her choice. The experience beats the name-word hands down. On the other hand, if the child values the grown-up's approval over the delight experience, or if she feels insecure in her surroundings, she may leave behind the experience in order to focus on the acquisition of a new word for her mental dictionary.

A third option is that the child can do both. But the introduction of the name takes on the weight of an agenda item that tends to recur, and depletes the child's access to her awareness for the experience of the bird. A succession of such agenda associations, over the period of a lifetime, can become like an accumulation of impurities that choke off awareness, deadening the wholeness of the living human being.

Grown-ups can become used to substituting words for experiences. We do it automatically—so fast that we can obliterate the process of experiencing almost completely. The occasional intense incident may blast at us, trying to force us to see afresh. Unfortunately, this is often in the form of a threat. We use fear to wake us up to experiencing again. We do it only when our very survival is threatened.

Some people are highly planned and organized into a routine of beliefs and expectations, opinions, and attitudes, repeatedly thinking "been there, done that." It is tragic that the only fresh feeling they are allowing, that will make them lift up their heads and pay attention, is the cruddy feeling of fear.

Children can bring freshness into a life gone stale. We can use their example—the light in their eyes, the wonder at life's mysteries in their voices—to leap back into living. A child can be the source of heaven on earth.

Quotation from Scripture

Unless you change and become like little children, you will never enter the kingdom of heaven.

CHRISTIANITY: Matthew 18:3 NIV

The Spelling of Weight

The spelling of wait is simple and straight
it could have been *wate*, but it isn't
but what about weight, that's not simple and straight
it could have been that, but it sure isn't.
Americanize looks around, simplifies
and reaches a logical spelling
but to weight *weight* for wate or even wait
brings in results far from compelling.

CHILD: CURIOUS

117

INTRODUCTION

Child: Curious. The capacity of a child to be curious can be a wonder to behold. But there is so much pressure to shut it down, that by adulthood, you may have imprisoned it.

CURIOUS

Curiosity is a gift present in all children, too often scrubbed out of us by a maturing process. This gift, the gift of curiosity is a marvelous return to full aliveness, that many a child can show us, to our delight.

Say this in support of yourself: "I like your curiosity, your way of seeking growth and understanding. Your curiosity will take you far, expand you, open you to the riches life can offer. You escape from your prison."

IMPRISONED CURIOSITY

When fear
drives your mind
to put four walls
around your curiosity
you live life in a prison
of your own making.
Tell your fear
that its incompetence
is no longer worthy
to drive your life.
Tell your body
that its tightness
which expresses the fear
and backs it up
is nonsense
that you will no longer put up with.
Make fear listen.
Make body listen.
When you have those in control
your mind is free to collapse the walls
releasing you from prison
once more free to be curious.

CHILD: SPONTANEOUS

INTRODUCTION

Child: Spontaneous. The capacity of a child to be spontaneous can be a wonder for an adult to behold. Sometimes it can bring embarrassment; we can wish away childhood if we focus on that embarrassment. Don't do that. Accept the child for what she is. Then provide the support and protective love the child will need through the dependent years, without the weight of criticism to crush her. Instead, revel in it!

SPONTANEITY

Spontaneity! Such joy!
It's good for every girl and boy
It is good for grown-ups too
Good for me and good for you.
Switch yourself to being spontaneous
don't leave it to be just extraneous
live it full, no grunge remain-eous
no more you being abstain-eous.

SPONTANEOUS

Spontaneity. What a beautiful gift! How many of us feel completely free to be spontaneous? Not many. We carry our load of mind-chatter, driven by fear and anger. "I mustn't say this … I could never say that … Don't even think it …" The driving fear and anger are crude oils to be upgraded to compassion, understanding, and love through deliberate stages. Every step along that path is a move toward the joy of spontaneity. Take those steps.

CHILD: CREATIVITY

INTRODUCTION

Child: Creativity. The natural creativity that comes with childhood is a source of fascination. As a psychiatrist who sees families, often with little children, I can watch how they play with colored, sponge-foam bricks. Never have I seen two children approach them exactly the same way. Do they simply stack them? No! They create roadways, bridges, enclosures, forts, the list goes on and on. Fortunately, we can retrieve this creativity with a little practice—playing!

CREATIVITY

What a joy to be creative, to let your creativity flow again! Creativity is the first step toward making life fun. The most free-flowing fun in life comes through basing life on love. With the fun-loving person, you never know what is coming up next. Such a person is an entertainment show all by himself. Yet the sensitive awareness made available through basing it all on love minimizes over-the-top offensiveness. You are not going to get it too wrong. Your flowing warmth, when you did indeed say too much, is a solid invitation for the other to forgive. Then life's party can continue. You won't win them all. But you'll come close.

LOST CREATIVITY

Creativity is intimately associated with breathing. We talk of a creation as being inspired! At times where breathing is restricted, we cannot expect to be creative. Giving living vitality to our efforts in this physical life by breathing slowly and deeply is a best first move to regenerate the creative impulse.

Some people have lost their creativity and despair of ever getting it back. If this is you, recognize the unfriendliness you have been perpetuating. Personify your creativity with a personal Muse and open your heart to it. Encouragement works wonders. Encouraged, it may come back to play with you. Play is where creativity is most alive.

CREATIVITY LOST, CREATIVITY REGAINED

Me: Where is my Muse, my lovely Muse
   pray, why have you abandoned me?

Muse: I'm here, right here, inside of you
   except that you would strangle me.

Me: I can't create. My efforts lately
   have shrunk down to zero.
   Come back and my companion be
   I need you for my hero.

Muse: I like your invitation. P'raps
   we both could work together.
   As you must see, you'd frozen me
   changed daylight to bad weather.

Me: Creation's where I love to be
          I grew afraid you'd leave me.

Muse: You grew afraid. You grew the weeds
          that strangled and bereaved me.
          But I'm not gone. You can create
          the wonders you desire.
          Just stop the strangulation.
          Watch our teamwork building higher.

Me: I tried too hard. My trying was
          the effort that deceived me.
          So I'll lie low and welcome you
          as you come back to greet me.

CHILD: FUN

Introduction
Fun

INTRODUCTION

Child: Fun. If you want to have genuine, enjoyable, invigorating fun, spend time with a child. Or you may find a grown-up who embodies the spirit of this book. Natural fun is free of anger, free of anger's expression as aggressive behavior. It is that anger, and the fear that it may show up, that inhibits us from having fun: "No, no ... You go ahead; I'll watch."

FUN

So many lives! So little fun! If the whole world could open progressively (through love) to more and more fun, we could return life to being worthwhile. There are so many ways to cull fun from life, it isn't funny.

When a child is having fun, he is playing. When the child within you is having the fun that spreads out all over your face as a smile, you are having fun. Play invites fun. That can mean a relaxation of body tightness. The child who is invited to play when she feels tight and tense in her body, may decline. However, her curiosity is powerful. As she watches the others playing, the overall effect can be relaxing. Then she can move slowly in and begin to take part. The play-scene is an enormous magnet, drawing the child in. The adult who is tense, can allow awareness in too, allow in curiosity, and allow relaxation. Then he can join in.

Laughter is present when we are having fun. *Readers Digest* has a section called "Laughter: The Best Medicine." Laughter can relax long-tightened diaphragms. But it does nothing to remove the forces driving the tension, so it is at risk to tighten again. As the author of this book, I am dedicated to removing all forms of tension.

CHILD: NEGATIVE

INTRODUCTION

Child: Negative. So-called "evil" behavior is childish behavior. Within all evil lies the seeds of its destruction—what goes around comes around. As such, evil behavior is woefully misguided. Yet a child, be it a young person or one now fully grown, can hold onto patterns they might otherwise have let go as a lost cause.

The belief was rampant up to the nineteenth century that children had no particular personality, needs, thoughts, or wants. Some people continue to act under that assumption, those seeking control above all. And there is little defense against the resulting dehumanization while remaining in the child state: the discriminating powers of the inner child can be overestimated and so misread and misunderstood.

But there is hope. We grow to full maturity by recognizing the child we have been and can still be at times. The child basically wants and needs to survive. With self-recognition comes self-knowledge. The poem "The Child Matures" captures the entire spirit of this book. It may take several readings to absorb it all.

CHILD: NEGATIVE

The supposed negative aspects of childish behavior, be it in a young person or in a fully-grown adult, all spring from a belief or hope that "what I am doing will be most likely to get my needs met." Even the most abominable behavior has a link of thinking behind it that has set the behavior up. People are set upon getting their needs met, however misguided their needs and methods are.

Being rebellious is the most obvious annoying behavior to see in someone else. As well, the person who constantly wants to be center stage can be annoying. Less obvious is the compliant person, who is always agreeable to anything you say. Even this can be a trap. If all you are looking for is an obedient servant, and all they say is "Yes," the two of you may totally ignore the greater human to human connection, where the power to be effective lies. Likely, the compliant person has been using agreeableness as a "best choice" ever since they felt misunderstood as a child. It can be so easy to continue the insult of not noticing the person behind the behavior.

Yet all experiences can be turned to good effect. Use the range of responses that come in, reactions to what you are doing. Milk them for the invitation they give you to heal. Do that healing. Don't fall prey to the trap of diagnosing the other person's problem. That was just a red herring to distract you from your task.

CHILDHOOD REPEATED

No one ever asked me
what I wanted of my life
so how could I believe that
there'd be anything but strife?
The very same insult
that my parents had endured
passed on faithfully to me
insult's future was secured.
My parents didn't know
how to ask me what I wanted
they'd never heard that question
so its absence stayed undaunted.
I could only conclude
that my life could have no meaning:
a useless, pointless tragedy
that's ultimately demeaning.
Now grown up I choose to say
"The buck stops here,"
I want dialogue to rule
words that everyone can hear.
So I'll assume my personhood
become a human being
start with "I forgive my parents"
(for their pattern of not seeing).
For I can understand
that they saw nowhere to go
that they loved as best they could
hoping problems wouldn't show.
My unforgiving habit
merely tied me to their knee
in such a shrunken posture
what good could become of me?
Now I'm free and walking tall
making choices as I'm learning
the right to full maturity's
the pathway I am earning.

THE DISCRIMINATING POWER OF THE INNER CHILD

You want to nurture the child inside. So you do. You have read "How Much Self-Nurturing Should You Do?" You have paid attention to the details. You have begun practicing toward the seven to ten days needed to install the habit.

Then something happens. The mischievous mind speaks up. "If you can't say it sincerely, it won't work." Say it sincerely? You were being sincere. You have read "Building Storm-Water Channels" in "Principles." You know that practice is needed before the penny drops. Yet in other contexts, you have been nurturing and loving. You are no stranger to it. So why the mind's cheeky intervention?

Perhaps you were tired. At the end of a busy day, we can all feel tried. Yet you reach beyond to a much more fundamental question: What is the power of a small child (such as the inner child, when we feel that way) to discriminate?

Certain basics must be seen. You need to say the words. A lack of words is most unimpressive to a child. It merely thinks, "This topic is unspeakable." When the topic is your very love for that child, that topic *must be speakable.* The words themselves have much greater significance than the nuances of their pronunciation. The child cannot discriminate that well. He or she is not mature yet. Sure, if you throw "I love you" over your shoulder in a disinterested voice as you walk away, the child will not be impressed. But you didn't do that! You would never do that. Your interest in the child is sincere. You want to get through to the child.

Take confidence in your capacity to get through. And tell that bamboozling mind where to get off. Its comments, you don't need. Its interference, you will not tolerate. Say it with sincerity and with certainty. See the mind cower and shrink as you show it you mean it.

EXPANDING FROM A CROOKED PAST

A crooked past
can be a mast
misguiding your adventures.
It holds a sail
that makes you wail
and blow apart your dentures.
But don't give in
through thick and thin
you can be in charge
A greater you
can see you through
while watching you enlarge.

CHILD

Grown-ups can sometimes behave in habitual ways that date from childhood. Grownups can behave childishly. When this is pointed out, they can feel like a child. We all can do that.

CHILD SHENANIGANS

Don't get off your high horse
I'll pick up your rattle
everyone can see the child
going into battle
winners, losers everywhere
the game is called survival
how can we turn catastrophe
to everybody's thrival?

Sense the part inside yourself that is a small child in need of patient understanding and a listening ear. Extend a friendly hand and be open to it as days turn into weeks turn into months. With such practice, you can only improve. You may have to practice patience until you are ready to have it happen.

Feed her; *nutrify* that child. Stuff him with such extending love and understanding that, over time, he comes to see he need never again feel alone and unwanted.

If you have children of your own, recognize that how you treat them may parallel the way you treat the child within yourself. If you are mean to the child within, she may react to make sure you are not nicer to any rival child outside. You cause meanness in your internal infant. Coincidence? Surprise? Not at all. You will not have a double standard.

Just like your family pet, each child needs limits. The humanity you employ as you set those limits can parallel desirable treatment of your cat or dog. Recognize that your growing infant can, for a while, be a pet of far more ultimate sophistication then your family pet.

SELF-UNDERSTANDING

Understand your Inner Child
When you learn how to make him mild
you have your nature reconciled
you'll no longer feel defiled.

THE CHILD MATURES

I was a child and sometimes good
all children try that on for size
I'm now grown up and sometimes good
but doing that's not always wise.
I was a child and sometimes bad
all children try that on for size
I'm now grown up and sometimes bad
but doing that's not always wise.
I was a child and got it right
each time I did I made things work
I had to learn to get things right
just screwing up leaves me a jerk.
I rise above my childhood ways
in full awareness of each scene
see fighting it or seeking praise
agendas that can dim my gaze.
My learning's grown beyond what's right
for right is always narrow.
In situations too complex
discernment aims my arrow.
When I don't yet know the facts
and feel I'm shooting blind
my sensing guides my arrow so
the target it can find.
Each situation is unique
my specialness, my presence there
brings answers as I learn to seek
to grow and to be more aware.
Relevance is what I need
appropriateness follows
and as results come rolling in
I'm flying with the swallows.

SELF: BROAD-EXPERIENCING

Conducting the Me-Orchestra
Distinguishing Conductor from Mischievous Mind
Relationship-Balancing: Conducting an Orchestra Well
Conducting Extraordinaire
Healing Warmth from the Conductor to His Own Beleaguered Soul
The Tennis Game
Obstructing Mind
The Tennis Game Expands You
Knowledge and Understanding
Seek Love
Love: The High Road
Caring for Self
Okay, Tops
Flow
In the Flow of Life

INTRODUCTION

Self: Broad-Experiencing. To understand fully what we are doing in this life, one way to look at it that makes sense is to read "God's Task." We can wear a mask in hopes of protecting ourselves. But it won't work. You might as well discard it. Trying to help others change doesn't work either. Instead, try picturing a self that is not rigidly contained, but is a more limber, functioning self. These are not new ideas; Jesus talked about these things to his disciples over two thousand years ago.

In this life, our experience of time becomes a useful tool provided we are willing to get in sync with the natural flow of life and wait for the right moment. Strangely, time can be upgraded, if we are willing to rearrange the dead straight line on which it is usually graphed. Rather than retreat into a comfort zone, let your little light shine. Withstand your frustration, overcome your despair. Overcome growth jitters and create your own surroundings in which to live—physically and emotionally. Change can raise anxiety, it's true. In our keenness to change for the better, it becomes clearer and clearer how well geared the thinking process is to prevent changing at all.

Above all, this life is here to experience. You can turn any experience to your advantage. Experience the low points as well as the high points. Release your stranglehold on the low points in order to allow in the highs, which naturally follow. Raise everything to the living level.

Experience can trap us. When we have long become used to recycling bad memories and the feelings we had when we got them, we can feel trapped. Divining meanings and diagnosing "right" (and by exclusion, what is "wrong"), we fall prey to a variety of skills the mind has to maintain the status quo. Interrupt your life and get out of the rut.

All of this becomes simpler if we develop the skills of objectifying. It can most readily be developed in the naturally separated nature of this physical life we live out. There is a level of broadened brilliance to which we can aspire. Being fully you is so important. Knowledge (facts, information, bits, and bytes) is totally outclassed by a steadily developed understanding of what life is about.

Love can carry all … when it is allowed to do so. With love you can best care for yourself. You are fine. Get with it, and get with the flow of your life.

GOD'S TASK

Menu item: *Raisins d'être*

Whether you believe or you don't believe, here is a useful way to look at life:

God says to each of us, "I have a task for you to do. You will find it at the far corner of my property. There will be tools for you to use to complete your task."

So off you go. When you get there, you find the task is to live the life that is your life. The tools? These are your talents—the skills and abilities you have—combined with the special way you have of looking at things, the unique sensitivity that is yours. One person has always been good with his hands. Another is naturally attracted to math. Another likes hair and is destined to be a hair stylist. Another likes to interact with people. All of these people have variety in their awareness, their sensitivity. These are your assets, the "white light" you take wherever you go, the special "me" you always present whenever you approach something. The light is your presence that you carry everywhere.

We also take on a quantity of problems, negativity, "darkness." Always make sure the amount of light you bring is far greater than the darkness you are going to tackle … today. Don't rush at the whole lot of negativity and then find it won't immediately heal, only to give up in disgust. When a driller strikes oil, he is delighted. He calls it black gold. He sees the potential in it. Use *your* power to gradually digest the problems you face, one or a part of one at a time. You can be a refinery.

At first glance, it may seem that the tools are not enough for the job. But you start in. As you work on it, you find the tools seem to expand. Not only can you do the job, you may be able to add a little extra: yourself.

We, like the trees and animals of the forest, are part of creation. But unlike the other life forms, we have the capacity to do some creating of our own. We are extensions of God. You are the wave of which God is the ocean.

You are a unique experiment in the art of living. It is as if you are announcing to the world, "See if it can be done from this point of view, in this way, with this approach."

You have just been given the gift of a sports car. You sit there looking at the dashboard: all those dials and knobs yearning to be used and understood. Your life in your body is that sports car: a magnificent gift begging to be touched, felt, experienced. There is a learning curve. It is well worth the effort. Take it in your hands and run with it. Waste no more time. It is yours!

In this life, we enter the school of hard knocks, where life pummels and jolts us, trying to knock some sense into us. This book seeks to turn those hard knocks into gentle taps, reminders that life doesn't work that way. Always with balance, seek to incorporate the power of love into your life.

Do not try to force it into someone else's life. They may not be ready. There are many people who spend a lifetime retaining holding patterns, as supposed protection against the hard knocks that seek to release the holding. When they are ready, they will release the holding. When they are ready, they will relax. But not before. They are here to show us the contrast between what we seek to do and what they are doing. Can you approach them with love? Will you learn patience, tolerance? Can you reach out with a genuine desire to understand them? These are the warm, supportive penetrating oils that can ultimately release the holding patterns. But it is on their time schedule, not yours.

DISCARD YOUR MASK—REVEAL THE REAL YOU

God has given you a task
you truly have the right to ask
do not stay around to bask
straight away discard your mask
you have come with God-given tools
do not pause. Don't be a fool
you'll find it cool to overrule
restrictions that can tend to pool.
You have many talents, skills.
You will find they'll fill the bill.
If you settle down to drill
explore, indeed I know you will
expand your power to be aware
you can make it anywhere
show the world just how you care
you'll be happy everywhere
Be unafraid to shed your light
for you own the copyright
you can lead with your delight
disbelievers? Fly a kite!
As you see your skills expand
your desire to self-command
you will grow to understand
it's your life you take in hand
for you're part of all creation
do it all with inspiration
you will find much stimulation
understanding information
for you're God's experiment
born to handle discontent
be your own advertisement
to everyone's bewilderment
for you have a point of view
you can take your cue anew
much good action will ensue.
This effort has been overdue
for you now are good and ready
taking on a task that's heady
no more will you stay unready
you can plot a course that's steady
for you have become a sports car
you can now cavort-star
it's your passport caviar

for they may be holding on
out of fear that you're a con
believe they've naught to draw upon
it's artificial silicone.
Fear can drive some crazy actions
causing more dissatisfactions
this is all one big abstraction
tied to one alarmed reaction.
You need tolerance and patience
need to work from different stations
if you are to build relations
without causing indignations
If you're using your goodwill
you will be no imbecile
quickly you will fill the bill
new understanding you'll distill.
Pure desire to contact's
determining the way you act
Because it is, you're using tact
a living bonding you'll attract.

DON'T CHANGE OTHERS—THEY DO IT BETTER

You mustn't force another's life
for you may only create strife
cutting down as with a knife
delaying any afterlife.

TRUE TO SELF: A BALANCING ACT, A WORK IN PROGRESS.

This above all: to thine own self be true,
And it must follow, as the night the day
Thou canst not then be false to any man.

—William Shakespeare (*Hamlet* I: iii:75,
Polonius's advice to his son Laertes)

What is this self to which we must be true? There is a point of convergence of a number of factors,[2] where self is being reworked constantly. The huge potential that will go largely unexplored in a lifetime is dipped into as we rise to new challenges. Self, how we define ourselves, enlarges with each new rise. Courage increases as we do that; it becomes part of a moving, less stagnated view of who we are.

Experience (what we have gone through up until now) has been the field we have harvested. Beliefs we use come from experiences we had and the choices we made around dealing with those experiences. We decided, sometimes under duress when we were small, to set up those beliefs as the most understandable, acceptable way to interpret the world and ourselves in it. Any heaviness or tension we have about that is expressed in the body, which anchors tension and heaviness as its contribution to (quasi-) stability.

Memory stores all these experiences and decisions. Mind dips into memory for examples in order to play its repetitive part. If experience has been traumatic, fear and its inefficiency may be the fuel used by the thinking, worrying mind. If experience has seemed punishing, we can set up an internal Self-Critic to incorporate ongoing punishment (blame and guilt). This gives to the self a sense of control over the experience, in an internal monologue that is part of the self we believe we are, the self we hold to.

The optimal evolution of the true self is to shed the shell, let go of the fears and the thinking accretions, the dried mud that attempts to exert control, often by anger. The butterfly then emerges in its full beauty.

QUOTATIONS FROM SCRIPTURES

[Jesus said], I tell you the truth, anyone who has faith in me will do what I have been doing. He will do even greater things than these, because I am going to the Father.

CHRISTIANITY: John 14:12 NIV

The kingdom of God is within you.

CHRISTIANITY: Luke 17:21 NIV

---

2   The factors being reworked are: the thinking, chattering from the mind; the self as experienced in the physical body where solidity and the language of tensions, pressures, heaviness, and pain, are used; the feelings' self, poorly understood by the mind, that is seeking to control what it cannot grasp, that is limited to serving up what it has in it (in hopes of resolution of any problems); and the inner child, a collection of all of the above, that intrudes when we are "being childish." You can make contact with mind, with body, with feelings, and with the inner child. You can build trust with each and allow the living relationship to develop, to be there for you when you need it. If a friend suddenly needs you, you can be there. Likewise, you can expect good support, when you need it. Such is the reciprocity of trust. The life process stays invisibly in touch, without effort. It reaches around, supports, contains and nourishes all possibilities, all the eventualities in advance.

TIMES AND CHOICES.

> *There is a tide in the affairs of men*
> *Which, taken at the flood, leads on to fortune.*

—William Shakespeare (Brutus in *Julius Caesar* IV iii)

There is a time for action and a time for rest. There's a time to move in and a time to back off. There is a time for planning with care. Then it is time to put down the planning and enjoy a diversion, to replenish. There can be a time to push hard and keep pushing to get a result. There will be a time when pushing is counterproductive, building resistance against the push, as well as blinding the pusher to what is really happening. That is time to stop, to relax, re-open your eyes, and see the *untimeliness*. Learn to wait.

There is a time to take a deep breath and say, "Here goes nothing," and plunge into what you know is going to be an experience where you determine to come out on top. You seek the joy of overcoming a challenge.

There is a time to confront what is going on. There is a time not to confront at all, but to take a deep breath and roll with it.

There's a time to tighten the controls a little bit and a time to loosen the controls.

There is a time to get it wrong once again, if only to prove you can still do it. There is a time to get it exactly right. There is a third time to vary right by being true to yourself, how you feel, and what your choice is right now. You know right. There may be freedom to do it however you want.

There is a time for pushing a little bit harder, for just a little bit longer, in the name of expanding your capacity, extending your boundaries.

There is a time when you can't see; you don't yet have a full understanding of what is going on, yet you must do something. These are times to tread softly, not to react too intensely, because you lack true understanding.

You can use your soft reaction to gain understanding. You recognize that your response is part of the scene; it does make a difference. You give thanks that your response was not too great. You use the improved understanding you now have to make a stronger, wiser reaction next time.

There is a time to say, "I recognize I am a little addicted to this. I will delay doing it by one day [or one hour, ten minutes, one minute, or even ten seconds] in the name of breaching the stranglehold of my addiction. I am inserting my own control, the thin edge of the wedge toward my ultimate goal of gaining total control of my life.

"Today is a day for me to rejoice and be thankful for my successes and the good things in my life, no matter how small or infrequent. I set my sights right by practicing that, rejoicing.

"Today is a day for me to feel despair and let it penetrate deeply into the holding patterns I have been maintaining and loosen them some more." (This is the true healing built into despair).

"I am practicing being nice to myself. To do it this time would represent overworking myself. That would not be being nice to myself. So I choose not to do it.

"This time around, not to do it would represent to me a shirking of my responsibilities. This would be based on fear: a fear of change. So I choose to take courage and do it anyway.

"This time I will see it all the way through.

"This time around, because of my frame of mind, to do it would be rebellious. Because I don't want to practice being a child, I will not do it this time."

There is a time for seeing with fully opened eyes. There is a time for sensing more widely what is really going on, beyond what the eyes can see.

There is a time to go it alone. There is a further time to work it out with others.

The overall purpose of each of these times is to achieve a balance in all things, a balance between all things. Each new day requires a new balancing.

WAITING

What am I waiting for
no sense debating more
not worth the hate before
I move on my life.

WAITING

A most annoying problem, particularly if it is a partner, can be another's habit of making you wait. They can do it over and over and over again. Your anger, you may observe, does not deal with the problem. No matter how many times you are angry, the problem continues.

Take a step back. Reconsider. The most likely reason for the problem is emotional under-nourishment. Is he overweight? If so, this may be due to his confusing physical nutrition with emotional nutrition. If you, yourself, are overweight, you have both been compounding the problem. Do you both get angry at one another? Such a useless waste of energy!

Begin a program designed for effectiveness. Begin to nourish the other emotionally. Come from the heart. Tell your partner what you truly appreciate about her, why you love her, the reasons you chose her originally as a partner. If you are in the habit of talking a lot to one another, your change of style will quickly draw attention. You will be able to talk it over. You may both like to read this article.

If you don't have a habit of talking, you may have a style of dominance and submission. This is always shared. It may seem to others that one is the dominant one. But there will be times and situations, however small, where the pattern is reversed. That keeps things in a crazy sort of balance, which you both have been tolerating.

Whether or not you have a dominance–submission style, begin a habit of coming from the heart. Give heartfelt emotional nourishment to the other. Do it for weeks. Let the weeks expand into months. If you are truly coming from the heart, it may become obvious to you how lacking in strain this is. It proves unexpectedly easy to do. You may have already learned something.

If your diagnosis of the problem has been correct, you may slowly see a change in your partner. Your partner may relax. He may begin to smile more often. If he becomes depressed, inattentive, or forgetful, it may help if you read "Two Energy Misuses in Depression."

If you continue for weeks and months, emotionally nourishing your partner, you set the stage for a discussion between the two of you. Such a discussion can be a revelation for you both. Only if either of you is completely unready will such a discussion not work. At this point, you may have to look at whether you want to continue the relationship.

All relationships are learning opportunities. You will not, in fact, separate from your partner before you have gleaned the maximum learning he has to offer. "They should have split up long ago," others may say. But "long ago" can expand into six months or even years before it actually happens.

If you are a loving, supportive person, dedicated to your partner, your love will support you as well as nourishing the other. In my psychiatric, relation-oriented practice, I have seen a number of such dedicated relationships. There is something deeply spiritual in what is going on.

QUOTATIONS FROM SCRIPTURES

To every thing there is a season, and a time to every purpose under the heaven:

A time to be born, and a time to die; a time to plant, and a time to pluck up that which is planted; a time to kill, and a time to heal; a time to break down, and a time to dance; a time to cast away stones, and a time to gather stones together; a time to embrace, and a time to refrain from embracing; a time to get, and a time to lose; a time to keep, and a time to cast away; a time to rend, and a time to lose; a time to keep silence, and a time to speak; a time to love, and a time to hate; a time of war, and a time of peace.

JUDAISM: Ecclesiastes 3:1–8 KJV

The Master said, "At fifteen I set my heart upon learning. At thirty, I had planted my feet upon firm ground. At forty, I no longer suffered from perplexities. At fifty, I knew what were the biddings of Heaven. At sixty, I heard them with a docile ear. At seventy, I no longer overstepped the boundaries of right."

CONFUCIANISM: Analects 2:4

MEASURING TIME.

Graphed against a vertical achievement, time is traditionally a horizontal line that is dead and straight. Add to that, enliven that to the life we actually live, and you add the real-life element of opportunity. Suddenly you have added chances to do what you want. The dead straight line develops a wiggle of peaks and valleys. The valleys are times we all experience when it is wrong to do anything. Best to wait patiently. The peaks are times and moments when you can touch the sky. With a minimum of effort, you achieve what was difficult before. Add to the wiggle a moment-to-moment wobble and you have an even closer approximation to real life. This moment may have become right where the moment before was not. That didn't take much waiting.

It is amazing: A simple straight line with a measurable height above it to the line graph can be totally outclassed by a multidimensional varying, moving position above a wobbly base. The reason is the sophistication you truly have if you let it show. Of course, the thinking mind is not keen to lose control and its rigidity by letting that happen. The difference lies in the class of fuel you use. Fear is the inferior fuel. You merely choose to sponge it up with love. Love takes fear power and upgrades it to move useful level.

Science, traditionally based on dead straight timelines, has been stolen for its own selfish territory by the thinking mind. Expanding that to more realistically approximate life, you note that human beings, even scientists, make things relevant to human life. It was not exact at all. Not really.

MY LIGHT

You seek out the most enormous church you can find. You enter it in the dead of night and place a tiny candle in the center. You light that candle. Then you go to the farthest corner, all the far corners. You discover something. No matter where you are, unless you deliberately hide behind a pillar, you can see the candle! All that huge darkness? It is nothing. It has no power. All you had to do was light that tiny candle. Your action made all the difference. Size meant nothing.

You can choose to be afraid of the darkness. As long as you fail to light that candle, you can maintain the fear. It is your choice. Light the candle and the fear vanishes. If you watch "Night on Bald Mountain" from the movie *Fantasia*, you see the "forces of evil" doing scary things. There is fire. There are eating evil forms. There is a false form of enjoyment. But the moment the light of dawn appears, all scurry away: in fear of the light! Fear, darkness, not seeing, evil—all are equivalents. Watch the movie fifty times and it has long since become boring. Repetitive. Useless. So can repetition grow stale.

You have learned something. You can light your candle any time. You can not-light your candle. The light is a metaphor for your presence. You can dim it if you want to, ignore it, discount it. Vision and size are metaphors for a greater reality that is not physical, not visual, not bound by size. It is looking inside at who you are, finding courage (freely available, at no cost, invisible), and setting in living motion the invisible but oh-so-freeing sense of who you are. It is yours to do with it as you choose on this planet you have chosen to inhabit.

QUOTATION FROM SCRIPTURE .

The light of a good character surpasseth the light of the sun and the radiance thereof. Who so attaineth unto it is accounted as a jewel among men.

BAHA'I FAITH: Tablets of Baha'u'llah

COMFORT ZONES/SAFETY ZONES

The life which is unexamined is not worth living

—Plato in *Dialogues: Apology*

We all have our own style. It includes our skill sets: the natural blend of thinking, feeling, and action (our way of doing things) that gives us our individuality, the inborn qualities in our approaches to life. We develop a routine—a sequence of things we do and the underlying meanings they give to our lives. This includes obligations to the outside world. On the inside, we carry varying proportions of a sense of freedom and of limitations. They form a comfort zone. When we use our comfort zone to ward off other people, we turn it into a safety zone, implying the feeling of threat and fear involved.

Children, unable to cope with the big world, need loving adults to set limits for them. Then they can feel safe within those limits. An adult's safety zone is a continuation from childhood and its fears.

Your mind is the self-selected guardian of your comfort zone. This is the zone that defines the ways you like to think about things—yourself, the world, people, the feelings you usually have as you do that thinking—as well as the way your body reacts, and the things you like to do. Fear seems magically to be excluded.

Within your comfort zone, you can feel safe. It is home for you. You can relax your on-guard tension. You can be right. "Right" is written on the inside of the walls of your comfort zone. You can see it. Others may not be able to read it as well, being on the other side of the wall. But since some of the purpose was to exclude them (they might attack), you will be already approving of the walls.

If overused, however, a comfort zone can become a source of self-abuse. You are at risk in there. The risk is loneliness. People with similar comfort zones may mill around you. You may form a group, with the consolation prize called safety-in-numbers. But the connection between these people is not heartfelt warmth, but a limiting barrier, a wall that surrounds all. The situation is ripe for the appearance of strange bedfellows, as elements of repulsion are revealed within the club. People who could be companions and friends are on the other side of your wall. If your aloofness offends them, they may become angry. If they show that, you may feel justified: "See! They were going to attack me!" Your comfort zone creates the problem for which it is the solution!

Your comfort zone is a home you carry with you. Like the turtle, you carry it on your back. You can retreat in there any time. You may become aware you are carrying problems. Have you tension in your back that mirrors this stance? The more unresolved feelings (fear, anger, sadness) you have, the stronger, thicker, and higher are the walls of your comfort zone. High, protective, defensive walls in someone suggests they may have fears they are not identifying.

Be brave. Take courage. Resolve unresolved emotions. Use the ideas in this book to become more versatile, more effective. Breathe deep. Walk tall. Break out of your cage, your comfort zone. Pick your company. Come to see that you are better off free than in a cage at the zoo. Explore your freedom and revel in it.

FRUSTRATION AND DESPAIR

Protect your frustration
value despair
stay with them
milk them for value in there.
They are your life force
trapped in your safety-zone
awaiting its melting
to get out of there.
With your life force earth-quaking
the walls of your safety-zone
braced by your fear
that's afraid it will crumble
holding on tighter
despair joins the battle
while sharing the weakness
fear's freezing subsists with.
Pour *love* to the problem
melt fear with its warming
love strengthens frustration
and eases despair.
When love storms the fortress
the fortress relaxes
no more fear, frustration
releasing despair.

QUOTATIONS FROM SCRIPTURES

By degrees, little by little, from time to time, a wise person should remove his own impurities as a smith removes the dross from silver.

BUDDHISM: Dhammapada 239

Man makes a harness for his beast; all the more should he make one for the beast within himself, his evil desire.

JUDAISM: Talmud

GENERATING MY ENVIRONMENT

Through our habits (what we do) and our expectations (what we think about and look for), we create our environment. We reach out into the infinite mix of possibilities and use our interests and our habits of thinking to pull into the foreground those elements to which we give importance. We selectively say, "This is important. That is not."

Hopefully, many of these prioritized pieces will be warm, supportive cushions to live on, bridges for us to cross into new, exciting terrains of possibility and opportunity. Also present will be the rough stones, things that do not comfort us, but irritate and challenge us. Be thankful for these too. They keep life interesting, keep us alive, oblige us to dig a little deeper into our unused stockpile of resources, to come up with a response that works or at least keeps us afloat.

Be grateful for the whole mix: the supports and the challenges. See the value in that. If life was all supports and no challenges, it could quickly become a bore. If life is, for you, all challenges and no supports, waste no time in moving in some supports. Take every possibility to express gratitude. Use your heart to drive that. Let it flow fully. No simpering thank-yous here. Then take the rest of the book to heart for all the invitations to start your love flowing.

It is no crime to be interested in what interests you. Take responsibility for prioritizing, bringing to the foreground what you value and leaving other things to recede or stay back. Begin to recognize the active role you have in life as it comes to you.

GROWTH JITTERS

The joke goes like this: A man is feeling terrible. He goes to the psychotherapist for help. He has some sessions. Then he phones the therapist saying he can't come. He's feeling too terrible.

The same reason for going to the therapist in the first place has now become the reason he doesn't want to come!

If the therapy was truly helping, there may be a good reason for the switch: growth jitters. The terrible feeling he had at the start had a lot to do with some lifestyle errors. They were familiar. But he recognized that they were causing pain. He no longer wanted that pain.

Then, as change began to follow, the sense of unfamiliarity took over. "This is not normal. This is not me," became his thinking. His mind moved into overdrive. Fear of change appeared. The *fear* felt terrible. He exchanged one terrible for another.

Fear pours out a lot of energy that is not needed. It cannot help. There is no need for it. So it comes predefined as useless. Then, seeking to find a reason for this flood of life energy, this "me" in action, all we can find is uselessness, incompetence, ineffectiveness.

145

"But, it's me!" we say, meaning *my* energy, *my* life! If we put two and two together, we can easily assume "I am useless." Then there is the dive for familiarity, the grab for something we know, something we are familiar with, comfortable with. We might even seek to retrieve the lifestyle errors together with their pain.

Many situations in life can become like our psychotherapy. Learn to breathe in deeply, take it very slowly, and be sure, above all else, that you conserve, not waste, your precious life energy. And certainly don't misinterpret it.

I WANT TO CHANGE

The patient
said to the psychiatrist
"I want to change."
The psychiatrist
gave him a few sessions.
Then the patient said
"What I really want
is to stay the same
but feel better."
The psychiatrist said
"But what if
the way you have been doing
things
makes it impossible
to feel better?
Your request for change
was fine.
What you must understand
is that change
makes things feel different.
It will not be the same.
It will feel strange
uncomfortable
unfamiliar.
Your job
is to allow in the experience
familiarize yourself
with the difference
and from your expanded
understanding
your greater wisdom
make fresh choices
that no longer
cramp your style."

HIGHS AND LOWS

Life has its funny little ups and downs. It is not even. If life were even, if there were never any changes, it would be a turnoff. Everything always the same would be like death. "Why bother to pay attention? It's all going to be the same, anyway."

So it isn't. Life has its high moments and its low moments. And with that go our feelings. One person (a therapist) once said "I value my lows. It is because of them I can tell how high my ups are."

Low feelings are normal. Don't fret them. There's a better feeling to follow. The cycle will swing. Don't do a heavy on it. You may be able to gain control by keeping it down. But who needs that? Play with it. If you push the beach ball deeper into the swimming pool, it may rebound higher when you let it go.

THE EXPERIENCE

Central to our lives, the basis on which we construct the way we face the world, is the experience. We are alive. We feel things. We can endeavor to suppress our feelings with preprogramming. But we have a spontaneous reaction to things that is never, no matter how much we suppress it, fully preprogrammed. We do feel something, if only for a moment. So predetermining can never fully destroy spontaneity. The experience is the unit on which the entire concept of *Love Is Power* is based.

Each person is different. The uniqueness with which we were each born, combined with the individuality, developed from our own history of experiences, reactions, choices, and solutions to life's problems, can lead us to look at things one way and approach them from the opposite direction. No harm done. If we notice this accident of our journey to this point, we can more easily offer understanding and generosity to others.

We may. We may not. But either way, we are light years ahead of the trivial level of facts, of information, of the programming of computers and robots, of the construction of machines, built to do one job and one job only.

The fact is necessarily a reduction from experience. The thinking mind, incapable of grasping the flowing, swirling complexities of life, chooses one piece, defines it, contains it, and feels pride of possession at the completed task. But life continues, always moving, always evolving away from this snapshot captured by the mind.

We have a mind. We need it. It handles very well such aspects of life that come under the heading of *thingness*. But where understanding human interactions is concerned, it needs to retire, to allow our natural awareness and sensitivity, including our "gut reactions," tell us unencumbered what is happening. After that, the thinking mind may make a decision, perhaps based on a longer-term goal, or other considerations. It is important to distinguish the role of observer—what I call the conductor—from the thinking mind. The mind is bent on defining, containing, and controlling our responses, based on automatic reactions from the conclusions it has drawn from memories of experiences. The observer self, the conductor, however, desires to maintain a balanced response between all the inputs; it's about total awareness but is often interrupted by the thinking mind.

147

EXPERIENCES: ALL GOOD

We all strive to get what we want. When we get it, we are pleased. We call that good. When we don't get what we wanted, we are disappointed. We call that bad. Struggling with the bad, we gain experience. We come out the long-haul winner, stronger for a lifetime! It wasn't bad at all. It was just one more experience.

We are not all good "wanters." Sometimes the very thing we wanted, were we to succeed at getting it, would prove to be the worst thing to happen to us. One mischief-maker knew this so well he wished all his enemies to get everything they wanted. Then they would be punished!

It is fine to want something. Reach for it and succeed. Then you are happy. But there is a downside to that. When we succeed, we learn nothing. Everything we know at the end we knew before we started. When we don't succeed, we can pick ourselves up, dust ourselves off, and go meticulously over exactly what happened. "What went wrong?" we ask. Therein lies the learning. Therein lies the power. From such an examined failure can come knowledge, understanding, strength that lasts for life. The non-learning that was no advance from the good result is replaced by good learning. This becomes strength for a hundred more positive experiences, all gained from a result previously considered bad.

All experiences can be made good. There is no bad. It is a deepening of your understanding that you seek. Enjoy when you succeed. Call that good. When you fail (an irrelevant word), move as fast as you can to turn that lemon into lemonade. Make that good too. If any experience is related to a habit of holding, you only stand to gain by the release of that pent-up energy.

It can be a difficult test to turn severe, intense, negative experiences into something useful, something nourishing, even refreshing. From the teachings through the ages, we can assume that whatever life hands us, there is an elevating way to deal with it. One prayer reads, "Dear God, help me to see that no matter what comes my way today, that between the two of us we can deal with it." Look at yourself as a strong horse; you can get through this leg of your life's relay.

In the Adam Sandler vehicle *Click,* the hero is given a device like a TV remote that allows him to fast-forward through bad times. Which he does. Again and again. Until he discovers, to his dismay, that he has no recollection of being with his wife and children when they went through, survived, and were melded into a closer, stronger family by these same difficult times.

YOU CANNOT *UN-HAVE* AN EXPERIENCE

You cannot un-have an experience
it was there, you went through it, you felt it
it occurred even when you deny it
it happened, so you can return to it.
You can build on what was your experience
it is there to retrieve from your memory
don't let mind's denial restrain you from that
building on good while discarding the bad
you selectively strengthen your life.

QUOTATIONS FROM SCRIPTURES

The Master said, "Even when walking in a party of no more than three I can always be certain of learning from those I am with. There will be good qualities that I can select for imitation and bad ones that will teach me what requires correction in myself."

CONFUCIANISM: Analects 7:21

In all things God works for the good of those who love him.

CHRISTIANITY: Romans 8:28 NIV

Do not rebuke a mocker or he will hate you; rebuke a wise man and he will love you.

JUDAISM: Proverbs 9:8 NIV

RAISING EVERYTHING TO THE LIVING LEVEL

We live and rise above machines and computers by our ability to be curious, have experiences, and develop understanding; by taking ourselves through a series of experiences, our awareness opens. As we do this, we each live out our own unique design. We do best operating at that level. We see the importance of caretaking and maintenance, even when the object of our affections *is* inanimate, for example, our car, our computer, our hobby.

We can lift ourselves to the power of being alive, by choice. You do that as you read these words. You reach out to the alphabetical characters, water their dryness like watering a garden, to create flourishing enlivening. Your brilliance is instantaneous.

"Choose your weapons" is a phrase from dueling. When you enter a situation, you can experience it. You are *in there like a dirty shirt*, as alive as you can be. You don't have to settle for less.

Choose your weapons in life. Raise things, situations to your level. Notice the people. See the effects that events are having on them. Feel it all to the full. Keep yourself sensitively aware of the emotional state of each person in order to read them personally, so you can respond accurately. You do not have to get tangled and involved in their issues. You can balance your involvement in a way that works for you. Not so much that you are overwhelmed. Not so little that you shrivel yourself to the mechanical level of uncaring.

Practice interacting with people, making emotional contact with them. Don't cringe from that (in fear) or use repulsive smash-and-bash (anger), both of which avoid genuine interaction.

Raise everything you do to the living level.

EXPERIENCE: THE TRAP

We have all had experiences. We began having them soon after we were conceived. We experience life intimately with Mother carrying us for the first nine months of our existence.

Experiences teach us. They are so designed. Forever and a day after we have a key experience, we rely on the learning we took from that experience, the meaning we gave to it.

Experiences begin at the immature end of our life. There is none born so immature as the newborn human being, incapable of walking for twelve months, or of feeding itself for years later. Every other animal does it faster. So the human child is in a unique position to be able to take on immature learning, from experiences. This can become "stuff" to be re-worked later in life.

When experiences match our capacity to cope with them, we can learn. If a loving, watchful parent keeps away savage dogs and makes sure the child is not excessively challenged, the child learns that life is good and rewarding, and curiosity stays active. If a brutalizing, dysfunctional environment over-stresses the coping power of the small person, another form of learning takes over: being self-protective. "I can't cope. I must protect myself from all this stress. Decision: I will forever be not-open-to-it." From that moment, learning can be minimal, and the planet has one more unresponsive person.

Experience, from then on, can stay superficial. The experience has been a trap. Many a been-there-done-that person relegates the freshness available in each new scenario to the rubbish heap. These people can be on their way out, living a deadness that can only be life-shortening.

A mature person, seeing all this, can dip a rudder in the water and slowly, over time, turn an entire death around toward life. Pinocchio, the wooden puppet, comes alive! Sleeping Beauty wakes up!

The best use of this book is like that. You want to feel warm emotions. So you do warm things. Using warm emotion is a matter of practice. Sometimes it can seem difficult. You may be surprised to find forgiveness to be part of the necessary letting-go. Even caring can offer a turnaround opportunity, as awkward as caring can be for some people. The easiest entry to warm emotions is to practice gratitude. You want to feel gratitude more easily. So you count your blessings. Counting has nothing to do with feelings. But by focusing on each blessing, you encourage the sludge inside to soften and start moving.

You want to feel more loving? Do loving things! Sooner or later the power built into love will be yours for the taking. You move yourself in to a different realm of understanding.

MISTAKES

It makes sense to rethink your "mistakes." A mistake is simply a result; do not call it failure. Let that go. We must do things. We must see what happens. If it didn't work, we do it better next time. Or the time after that. This is natural self-correcting. Then we can go on.

Make a successes book. Buy a blank book you can keep in your pocket. In it, write down your successes. Even small successes help, especially at first. Write down any successes. "I succeeded at making a shopping list. I succeeded at telling someone something. I succeeded at completing this task, that task." Build the list.

Then, when you are feeling down, open your book. Drink in the encouragement you have written. Recycle your successes.

"Mistake" is an irrelevant word. All experiences are good. We can turn around any so-called mistake we want merely by taking on the attitude promoted in "Experiences: All Good." This lifts it to a higher level, love, where simple words become irrelevant except as labels for where the power truly lies.

We can learn not only from what we first saw as our mistakes, but we can reach out to others and farm them for their experiences, capitalize on everybody's mistakes. The media present us with many examples to make use of. In one lifetime, packing it all in, we don't have time to make all the mistakes ourselves!

Learn from the mistakes of others. You don't have time to make them all yourself.

—Eleanor Roosevelt

RIGHT

It is okay to recognize when you are right and to celebrate the success of that with others who can also appreciate its truth. It is important to be able to get it right. Once you have mastered that, you are free to do it exactly the same next time, or any other way you choose, depending on how you feel and what would be a welcome change, or whatever is appropriate for the occasion or a bit of fun. With this variety, you stay alive to the task.

It is okay to appreciate when others are right and to celebrate along with them the successes in their lives. It is important to distinguish our differences, that each one of us is unique and each moment is a fresh experience, not identical to any other. It becomes possible to see that what is right for you, now, is good for you but may be totally inappropriate for someone else at this moment in his or her life. It is important to deflate your need to prove your rightness by insisting someone else behave identically. You are not in danger of being wrong and so not in need of proving anything. Your ups and your downs are part of a normal cycle. You are already doing fine. Relax. Your shoe may not fit another's foot, either. Both feet are fine.

IT'S NOT WRONG TO BE WRONG

It is wonderful to be able to get it right.

It's not wrong to be wrong. An opinion is as good as the prejudices and biases of its sources. Mistakes are for learning. It is essential to be free to explore, discover, and correct. Errors are the means whereby we increase our understanding. Knowledge, our collection of "facts," is undergoing constant revision, even as the frontier of science advances. It is not static, frozen, or still.

The attitude of "I'm wrong; you're wrong" can only come from the mischief mind seeking to imprison us in mind-sets, controlling at all costs. And what a price that exacts! The classroom that puts a priority on being right is a hotbed for nervousness and silence, for quelling discussion, a training ground for cheating and lying to make an impression; it's a short-term stall for the long-term fall.

The mind, housed in the brain, is a legitimate part of our total constitution. It functions to steady us through difficult times. What can pass unnoticed is that steadying needs a balance if it is not to become constricting. You reach maturity and become an observer. You draw upon a brilliance that outshines the simplicity of the mind. You note that a life lived to the full is a life kept in balance, and that "unbalanced" is another name for insane.

It is human nature to be curious, explore, gain understanding, and through that, power and mastery. This living reality must not be stifled by mental fragmentation.

It is not wrong to be wrong.

A brain is as strong as its weakest think.

SCIENTIFIC INEXACTNESS

Every good scientist takes copious notes. This takes the pressure off memory, which can fail when you are tired.

The good scientist does an experiment. Suppose it takes thirty-nine steps. The experiment goes perfectly. Is that good? Not necessarily. Because everything he or she knows at the end he or she also knew at the beginning.

Now suppose the scientist does the experiment and something goes terribly wrong at step #23. Then the scientist can go over the notes carefully. This can lead him or her to design other experiments to elucidate the "error." From that may come an advancement of the frontier of science!

Not only was the "perfect" experiment useless, the "error" was absolutely essential to the process of genuine discovery. Advancement can happen in no other way. The same applies to a life lived to the full.

WHAT IT MEANS

Two people are arguing about the meaning of something that just happened. The one is saying what it really means, and "Why won't you understand?" The other is saying: "No! You got it all wrong. What it really means is …" and this one goes on about how right that opinion is.

You listen. The event didn't mean a lot to you. You feel strangely free to be generous. You say to them, "I hear what you are saying, and I hear what you are saying too. Each one of you has a valid viewpoint. You are each seeing it slightly differently. Could you allow room for both of you to be right? Each one of you is giving what happened the meaning that has most value to you."

You leave. But you think further about it. Your feeling of generosity made you far more free and versatile than either of the two combatants. You could move in, see it all, move out, with ease. Not so the arguers. They were tight. It felt like they had squeezed the toothpaste tube empty with their intensities. Your generosity was far more desirable: a plenty-for-all approach.

Yet you acknowledge your own tendency to have strong opinions, your need to give a particular meaning to something. You wonder if you might add some warmth, some generosity to the next time you found yourself coldly pushing an opinion. You would like to repeat some of the delicious freedom that came with it.

GIVING HEALING MEANINGS TO SITUATIONS

We all know about people who consistently take things the wrong way. They get upset over what seems like nothing to others. We look at them and wonder how they can do that.

You can do better. You can observe that there are useless, destructive ways to take what is going on. There are also healthy, healing ways to react.

Make a commitment. Decide for yourself that you are going to do yourself a favor. You are going to upgrade your meanings. You are going, at every possible opportunity, to examine the first-impulse meaning you gave to what just happened. Then you are going to give it the biggest, best upgrade you can find. In this way, you ensure you don't take things the wrong way and drive yourself into the ditch as you walk life's path. Rather, you feed, strengthen, enliven your life.

A few examples:

Change This:	Into This:
I can't get what I want.	I can get what I want, but I need to practice patience. OR I'll think this through; is that what I really want?
I am powerless.	I have power. I'll have to find out how to use it.
I'm stupid.	My intelligence and sensitivity are a unique combination. I will find out how to value and use them.
You are stupid. He/she is stupid. They are stupid.	If I take some extra time to understand you, I won't have to box you (and me too) into a useless, imprisoning category.
I said the wrong thing.	I spoke up, with good intentions. I cannot expect to get it right the first time, every time. I can again speak up, this time with the intention of making myself absolutely clear.

There are many situations to which we can give an advance healthy meaning, before we start. Here's one:

"I will go into this with a positive attitude. I will interpret any setbacks as meaning I need to back off momentarily, before beginning to move forward again. I will keep my vision clear, to see what is possible. I will carry with me an overall picture of success, in whatever (renewed) form that success takes."

CONDUCTING THE ME [YOUR NAME HERE]– ORCHESTRA

You can be proud to own an orchestra with three distinct sections—mind, body, heart—each capable of magnificent contributions to the beautiful music of your life.

Your job is to open up to them and listen. Each speaks its own language. Only the mind uses the word-language of the conductor, who must be fluent in all three. This can lead to confusion until you, as conductor, step outside the habits of the mind and begin your unique task. There is a difference between the objective conductor, always seeking growth through understanding and building experience upon experience, and the fragmenting, thinking mind. The mind always seeks to separate, looks for reasons to be more microscopic. One such story involves Mother Teresa. She was asked "Why don't you take part in the pro-life/pro-choice debate?" Her answer was "Because I don't want to seem to be against the other side." She was aware of the for/against fighting aspect of humanity (the thinking mind creating problems), while also understanding the human capacity to be objective (the conductor).

She could feel for the human beings in the two points of view. She had compassion for both. She deeply wished for each side to see that there were people involved and let that awareness override their differences. In the long run, no two people are identical, let alone in agreement on two sides of an argument. They were just living out interpretations of their very different experiences of life. What hell can be created by two people, each attempting to *prove* that he or she is *right*. "I am right. So you are wrong," is the division designed to make *me* feel *safe*. The fanatic who seeks the primitive *kill* approach is doing the opposite of the message in the article "Love Your

Body." Kill-in-order-not-to-kill does not hang together. In what-goes-around-comes-around style, those who do pursue that approach do hang together. They seek safety in numbers. Anger acted out achieves only crude results. By listening, you give mind, body, and heart the opportunity to begin trusting you. When they do that, you have them at your fingertips. Then you can tap your baton on the podium, wait until you have their full attention, and announce:

> *We are going to play the beautiful music of my life. I will tell each of you when you may come in. There will be no prima donnas, no spontaneous outbursts. You each have something valuable to contribute. It is my job to bring you harmoniously together. Please let me know if you are having problems.*

You have a thinking mind, using words and images to help you adapt to life as we live it. It filters and extracts from life.

You have a physical body that often echoes what the mind is saying, the feelings that the mind cannot grasp, that it stuffs into the body. Love your body. It speaks and reacts in its own way—pains, tensions, heartache, heaviness, as well as the positive encouragers of calm, relaxation, relief, and an all-encompassing sense of peace.

You have also the emotional heart, capable of reaching out invisibly into situations to give you sensing information about what is going on and how you are fitting into it … or not. This sensitivity can alert you way ahead of when all the facts are in, and you can become able to discuss it, with mind-derived words.

At least one seat in each section of the orchestra is occupied by the child in you. This historic person may have, at a tender age, given the thinking mind the task of freezing body, feelings, and mind into a desperate holding action. This has been the source of unwelcome earthquakes ever since. Gaining the trust of this tiny person can bring a releasing that is long overdue.

DISTINGUISHING CONDUCTOR FROM MISCHIEVOUS MIND

Distinguish conductor from mischievous mind
by noting the quality of what you find
conductor's expansive and freeing and eased
mind is restrictive, imprisoned, and freezed.
Take a quick look at the way that you feel
that in itself can quickly reveal
the one that is functioning, conductor or mind
armed with those facts, you're no more in a bind.
Use this great tool to position you clearly
then with this tool you will function sincerely
always enabled to clarify meaning
a headstart is what you will find yourself gleaning.

RELATIONSHIP BALANCING: CONDUCTING AN ORCHESTRA WELL

When a real conductor leads an orchestra, each section trusts the conductor. Trust is alive. No machine, no robot can achieve trust. Trust allows each section to relax, to focus on doing its own job with confidence in the conductor. The conductor listens carefully. He then powerfully blends each section into a magnificent, living sound.

Conducting mind, body, and emotional heart into a coordinated whole requires patience in building the trust connection. Each section, unique in what it has to say, requires a specific approach designed to bring out the best. In this way, you harmonize your approach to life as you live it.

Feelings are not logical. If you feel a certain way, that is how you feel. You cannot prove you feel that way. You simply do. You cannot induce the feeling in someone else through a logical process. Others will feel the way they feel. There is a continuum of feelings and sensing that is full of information.

Conflict between feelings and thoughts can present interesting dilemmas for the conductor. If logic has indicated that you should take a particular course of action, but you feel strongly that you don't want to, that may decide it. One can lead a horse to water; thousands cannot make him drink.

If you feel strongly that you *do* want to do something, the conductor may check out the body for tensions. Body tensions and pains are the ultimate hardware. They can be very insistent compared to the software of thoughts and feelings. Relief of tensions by taking action, such as having a good fight, may bring temporary relief, but does nothing to change a habitual pattern of creating more tension. Is there a habitual pattern involved? *Do I always do this? Do I want to retain that pattern? Why?* Is it vainly seeking relief from an insistent mind that never shuts up? Is the mind driving the body repeatedly into tension? *Should I, as conductor, deal more directly with the mind?*

If you feel strongly that you want to do something and that action would be destructive, actually carrying out destruction is rarely the solution. Damage does not solve problems of communication between people who show evidence of childish thinking. Some adults should know better. A small boy is complaining about a classmate" "Jonni bugs me. I wish he was dead." Mother says, "You don't kill someone because you don't like them. Why don't you invite him to your birthday party? He can bring a present, and maybe you can be friends." Such retraining needs to start at an early age. Some people learn the hard way, and for some, tragically, the lesson is never learned. Interestingly, the metaphor enables the conductor to switch the focus from one form of destruction to another. The metaphor can be allowed to have symbolic meaning. You can do it in your head with imagery; that can be just as impressive to the mind, avoiding physical destruction of any sort. You just imagine the villain in diapers, or whatever picture you choose.

CONDUCTING EXTRAORDINAIRE

Conducting the Me-Orchestra
means learning languages extreme
you can show you have the patience
build a balance from your dream.
Without the interference of the
thinking mind
a wondrous full awareness is
what you will find
there is no need for error in this
glorious state
mistakes are merely history. Life's
what you create.

HEALING WARMTH FROM THE CONDUCTOR TO HIS OWN BELEAGUERED SOUL

The conductor addresses each of his charges—mind, body, and the inner child—in turn.

To the mind:

"I know what you're thinking. I understand you. You work so hard trying to make happen what you want to have happen. You are mystified why it doesn't always work. But you valiantly carry on despite fears of failure. You are even willing to try harder when evidence that it doesn't work is coming clearer. You override your fears in your determination.

"I have the greatest admiration for you, my thinking mind. Without you I would not have survived to this point. I will always be grateful to you for that. I love you. You can gradually release tightly holding attitudes."

To the body:

"I know what you are feeling in your body. I admire how faithfully you have imitated and emphasized the meandering of the mind. You made it all real! I thank you for your faithfulness to the cause. I want you well. You can trust as I take over and insert a balance, that I will listen to you, the comments you make in body language. To your cries for help, I will become ever more sensitive. I love you."

To the child inside:

"Thank you for your sensing awareness, your spontaneity, your creativity, your curiosity. You have always been the base of life from which I work. I also acknowledge your immaturity, the freezes you put on life based on fear that became habits. I will help you gradually to remove those restrictive clothes, the shoes that were always too small for the magnificent destiny you had inside. I will protect and love you as you come gradually to trust me and respond to me."

The child inside requires sensitive handling. It can present itself as different ages, one after another. Just as you would use a different approach for a babe in arms than you would a toddler, and different again for a youth, you must stay alert and listen for what age is now presenting itself for healing.

Becoming an effective conductor generates for you a life of delight. A long-standing pattern of mistrust or disconnection from a possibly well-meaning mind, or from a body long ignored, can be leavened, lightened, and let go. This will not happen in a twinkling. The conductor sits back and reflects. The mind is often the primary mischief-maker. Its actions can have a driven quality.

Drivenness can come from fear or anger or a combination of both. The mind then applies an agenda which tends to blind you to what is going on, deafen you to genuine listening. Instant confusion can be the mind throwing in a monkey wrench to ongoing awareness. A series of questions and answers can be a way of the mind reducing everything to words, staking out its territory, and claiming squatter's rights. All of these can be in the name of the mind's attempting to regain control of its right to make fragments and install a holding pattern. Balancing mind, body, and emotional heart can be like taking care of a bunch of unruly kids. With a knee problem here, a chest problem there, a worrier here, a self-critic there, a tightness here, a heaviness there, or fear of too many feelings taking over, you pay attention to each one in turn, and then tuck them lovingly into bed. It becomes an ongoing, involving role that keeps you alive and well as you extend your life and enrich it. Patience is essential. Forgiving yourself also helps. The conductor is your inner genius.

THE TENNIS GAME

You are playing a game of tennis. You say, "The ball is coming at an angle of fifty-two degrees from the north-northwest. If I hold the racquet with a grip of nineteen pounds per square inch at an angle of …"

No. You don't. If you went through all that you would have already lost the point. You are far more brilliant than that! Your mind wants to be in charge, wants to think it is in control, wants to be appreciated for its efforts. But your greatness swamps it.

You track on the path of the ball using multibillions of signals from the eyes. You run to the right spot using multitrillions of signals from all the muscles of the body to maintain balance as you go. You play the shot. You watch where the ball lands. You integrate all of the above information instantaneously, to play a better shot next time. You are incredible!

Your mind likes to believe it is all of you. It likes to stake out its territory, cookie-cutting its extracts of facts from the totality that it cannot understand: the complex flow of life.

You are not a fact. You are not a string of facts hung together in a sequence called logic, coming to a conclusion. The freezing-in of an attitude like this cannot begin to deal with the situation. You are far beyond that triviality.

You are you: a being of far greater presence, far greater creative potential than you will ever reach in a lifetime. Or a string of lifetimes. The lyrics of "On A Clear Day You Can See Forever" from the 1965 Broadway musical,[3] spell it out exactly. You have within you the capacity to sense the infinite.

On a clear day
Rise and look around you
And you'll see who you are
On a clear day
How it will astound you
That the glow of your being
Outshines every star
You'll feel part of
Every mountain, sea and shore
You can hear from far and near
A world you've never heard before
And on a clear day
On that clear day
You can see forever, and ever more …
—Alan Jay Lerner

The thinking mind likes to, needs to, has to make extracts, reduce life to bites it can manage. From your enormity, address the thinking mind with understanding. Appreciate it for what it does. Then practice returning this calculator to your pocket, where it belongs; available at all times, but not to dominate and imprison you. Cultivate, practice being your genius. Take that on to be a fully functioning, fully alive conductor.

---

3   Words by Alan Jay Lerner, music by Burton Lane, book by Alan Jay Lerner. *On a Clear Day You Can See Forever* opened at the Mark Hellinger Theatre on October 17, 1965, and ran for 280 performances. It was subsequently made into a movie.

The composer George Gershwin admired the orchestrations of composer Maurice Ravel. He asked Ravel to give him lessons. Ravel refused. Implied was the comment, "Why should I teach you to be a second-rate Maurice Ravel when you are already a first-rate George Gershwin?"

OBSTRUCTING MIND
(THE CENTIPEDE'S DILEMMA)

A centipede was happy, quite
until a toad in fun
said "Pray, which leg goes after which?"
which set his mind to such a pitch
he fell exhausted in the ditch
not knowing how to run.
—Anon.

TENNIS GAME EXPANDS YOU

The Tennis Game reveals your truth
it demonstrates what you can show.
The thinking mind says "I can't stand it."
You can tell that where to go.
Conducting the Me-Orchestra with flair
becomes a balancing act
you can do it ever stronger
you don't have to be exact.

KNOWLEDGE AND UNDERSTANDING

Knowledge and understanding are worlds apart. Knowledge, information, facts, data, the bits and bytes that computers interchange at amazing speeds, are far away from the rich lushness of human understanding.

Computers share data in enormous quantities. Never once do they develop any understanding of what they are doing. They are inanimate, totally unaware. We have awareness that allows us to have experiences and, through the collecting of those experiences, to compile an ever-deepening base of understanding and wisdom. No automatic device, forever tied to the rules of its construction, could ever achieve any of this.

As you read these pages, you water the words. The black-and-white letters are dry as dust. As you scan along, you raise up a lush garden. You bring the warmth of your unique sensitivities and interests to give rich meaning as you associate what you read with remembered experiences. No inanimate object and no other animal can approach your brilliance.

SEEK LOVE

Some people have been hurt when they wanted love and have learned not to look for it anymore. At the same time, they can constipate their own giving of love. Say to yourself, "We can beat that, you and I. I love you. We can create new and better experiences out of love. We can practice it with good loving people."

LOVE—THE HIGH ROAD

Love rises higher than problems that trouble you
lifts you above what was getting you down
reaches inside, elevates the low levels
you take the high road, enjoying the ride.

CARING FOR SELF

"I love you very much." Say this "I love you" to yourself as often as possible. That will quickly bring out of the woodwork any "I hate myself" statements. You can examine these rotten fruit and discard them as unworthy. They have no nutrition in them.

"But isn't that being selfish?", you might ask. Children receive gifts, what they need, from grown-ups. Children can be motivated by fear of not getting enough, or by a wish to explore what power they have. If a child sees how far he can go and tries to take what belongs rightfully to another child, he may be called "selfish."

Grown-ups rise above that. It is a put-down to be treated like a child. Yet we all have needs. The grown-up can take care of her own needs. Once you have done that, you are satisfied and no longer needy. You have loved yourself. This form of planned "selfishness" is vital to your functioning.

If instead you choose the mind's reduced version of solving the problem and focus on material things to be selfish about, you can easily enter the runaway state called greed. In this state, there can be an endless accumulation of the material things that can never rise to the level of being satisfying. Instead, find the balance point. Then, with your needs met, you are in a position to invoke human warmth.

You are now open to the love of others. You are also open to assuming the power within your state of love in the presence of others—your power to be present, alert, and undistracted—listen and respond with relevance and relaxed assurance.

OKAY, TOPS

You are Okay just the way you are. You were Okay yesterday even if today you're not happy with something you did yesterday. (That is just today's head-tripping.) You will be OK tomorrow no matter what comes. A top-of-the-line computer does not change its basic quality because it runs an inferior program for a while. You are tops. Drop inferior programs.

FLOW

It is vital to sense the flow of life and to get with it. Some people seem always to paddle upstream, punishing themselves with the extra drain on their efforts for which they get little in return. It is okay to go with the flow. You can take opportunities as they come, easier because you are more alert, less exhausted. You can paddle to the side, get out of your canoe and take stock, make plans, or simply take a break. But do get back into the stream. That is where the life is.

IN THE FLOW OF LIFE

Things in sync they bounce in rhythm.
Living life you dance along.
Ski those moguls. Ride those horses.
In the flow you'll sing your song.
But sometimes it seems the rhythm isn't flowing.
It may be time to pause, have a look, take stock.
It's no crime to lose the rhythm for a while.
Looking for it, praying for it, you can smooth off edges,
drop a load you may no longer need to carry, and
find your way back into the flow.
Back in the rhythm you find a new flowing
Living a life that has come through the storm
Gaining from having gone through what you went through
Stronger, experienced, feeling your form.

SELF: NARROW

INTRODUCTION

Self: Narrow. Narrow ways of looking at ourselves, such as self-criticism, restrict us. We can beat ourselves to a pulp, not realizing two points: (a) it is exhausting, draining of our energies to do that, and (b) it doesn't work. Thinking, *failure,* is a way to self-criticize. In truth, failure is merely a stage on the path to success. Being self-critical is one favorite way to be your own worst enemy. Destructive fantasies pack the power punch of not only of being the picture-worth-a-thousand-words that lord it all over verbal self-criticism, they are also movies in your head, for they are more attractive than the still image.

Think about your experiences. Be objective. Don't leave yourself hung-up. You can readily attend to them and heal them. The thinking process is the way you achieve these failures. As part of healing, you may need to confront the self-critic. This is a composite of the thinking mind using anger to invoke guilt and punishment. Guilt is a tool the mind uses to achieve its restricted goal.

Long practiced, these become old bad habits. Counting down is a technique mentioned in "Old Bad Habits." These habits can be dealt with.

A move up to the healing level is available in the following pages. This can be hard work, taking focused, patient attention. Then you can rest.

HEALING THE SELF-CRITIC

The self-critic is just the thinking mind trying to make extra energy (anger) bring about some goal. Your object is to pull the plug on that and allow your natural self to flower up between the noisy brambles.

On your journey through life with this traveling companion (your willingness to self-criticize with words like "Stupid! … Idiot! …It's all my fault …"), you will pass through three stages:

Not Enough
Enough
Too Much

At the earlier stage, you will have made statements like "Life is not a bowl of cherries" and "You can't win them all." During this entire process, you have been undergoing a gathering of understanding, a deep learning about the nature of punishment—through experiencing it, from you to you. You are in charge. You have been making it happen.

Then, bingo! You hit the jackpot. You have learned all you needed to learn. That stage of your life is over. You can move on.

FAILURES FOR LEARNING

You need to have some failures
then you learn from your mistakes
that sharpens your awareness
so that you'll have what it takes.
To help heal the critic in your head, humanize it. If the self-critic could speak, it might say:

I am your self-selected punisher. I represent your continuing belief that punishment is a useful way to solve problems. With my every move on you, I confirm for you a belief you have about yourself: you deserve to be punished. You set me up that way. No one else is responsible for what is in your head. You may have used examples from other people, when you set me up, of how to do it. But it was you who made the final choice.

As I see you there receiving my punishments, if I allow myself to have a feeling for you, that feeling is compassion. I see you for what you are believing and what you are doing to yourself. If I truly open my heart to you, all I can find in there is compassion for your plight.

Seeing the self-critic as compassionate lifts the whole mechanical process of self-beating to the human level. Now you have a real person who is relating, having a natural response, rather than the boring, repetitive, forced anger. Can you feel grateful? Or friendly? Or any form of warmth? Is your rage, your commitment to the path you are walking, so intense, that all you want to do is destroy, destroy the critic? This would mean you are still at the earlier Not Enough stage, and you are still committed to the anger that went with that stage. You will need to continue with this until you understand it fully. You are still working toward understanding.

A human reaction to that can only be more compassion, combined with a deep understanding of the predicament some people can reach on their path through life.

MY OWN WORST ENEMY

Has anyone ever said to you, "You are your own worst enemy"? Would you like to try for "second worst"? You could give that a go. Is a change impossible? How about being friendly to yourself? Could you be a little bit friendly? No? How about the teensiest tiny bit of friendliness to yourself, to sneak in when no one is looking?

It is okay to see what you do, to know its effectiveness, and to shape what you do until you have it right. This becomes a part of the pattern of success in your life. It overflows out, affects others in positive ways, and brings back to you evidence of yourself in action. That is being friendly to yourself.

> The little things I do to me
> are not things that are true to me
> I worry and self-criticize
> trying to cut me down to size
> believing that self-punishment
> can be my best self-management.
> As I so burn up energy
> I fail to see discrepancy
> that all this noise cannot be healing
> anger's such a cramping feeling.
> I'll expand my operation
> healing warmth's incorporation
> was the item that was missing
> loving me I'd been dismissing.

Remembered errors I'll recall
prefer successes to install
picture-power I will use
healing me must not abuse.

DESTRUCTIVE FANTASIES

Are you bothered by destructive fantasies? Do you sometimes fear that you will carry them out, trying to relieve the pressure? What you need is a change of focus.

At present, you are focused on words and their expansion: pictures. Words are reduced fragments from your experience of life: a function performed by the thinking mind. Bunch words together and you create descriptions, *facts*, which can be strung together in logical sequences to create a *conclusion*. But you are not a conclusion. You are more alive than that. When you have an image, a picture worth a thousand words, the thinking mind is playing its trump card, putting out its best effort to retain control, to do a job you gave it to do.

But what drives all this? You can change focus to be far more effective in dealing with the problem. The fantasy (the movie with pictures worth a thousand words) is destructive. Is anger involved? That would make sense. Destruction is often the result of anger acted out. But look a little closer. Is there something you are afraid of? Anger can be a magical attempt to protect fear with a shower of force to repel all threats. But that leaves the fear festering and not dealt with behind a wall of anger.

Go beyond these trivia. You can take charge. You are more powerful than you may have allowed yourself to see. You can befriend anger even if the anger is your own. More important, you can reach behind the anger to the fear it is protecting. See all these pieces as childlike in their naïveté, compared to the power you can use, the power into which you have matured.

THINKING ABOUT EXPERIENCES .

Life is lived at the level of experiences. Thinking about an experience is a process of reduction. Words, laid out in sequences that obey rules of grammar, are fragments applied to the reduction process. They talk of facts, details extracted from the whole. They may expand into interpretations, beliefs, opinions, and attitudes. These can be collected in sequences of logic, leading to a conclusion. Beliefs, attitudes, opinions, and conclusions are often consistent with a predetermined mind-set.

But the actual experience was none of these. The experience was the experience, unreduced. The experience is not the word fragment. The experience is not the facts. Five minutes of experience may take an hour to talk about. And still there may be more that could be said. The words, at a simpler level, can never fully explain the experience or recreate it. Two people experiencing the same event may have completely different ways of describing it. And still there are more ways it could be described.

The experience is not the interpretation of it or any belief about it or attitude extracted from it or applied to it. It is simply the experience, larger than that. The move into words created the shortfall.

The experience will not fit into a mind-set, a comfort zone or a safety zone. It is too full of nuances, the complex overlapping of life aspects, for the thinking mind ever to fully grasp. The mind wants to, needs to, work with its extracts, takes mental snapshots of it, and draws its conclusions. It wants to be sure, to turn openness into closure. The experience continues gaily on into the next experience, seamlessly, without regard for any process of reduction.

Come to value openness, the lack of closure. Value uncertainty. See the fun potential in it. Say "What do we have here?" with a genuine joy of expectancy. Use the turned-on approach to life rather than the turned-off.

Most experience is not so reduced. Only a tiny fraction of the total waking hours we spend each day ever reaches the reduced-to-words status. We continue living our aliveness, experiencing the ongoing continuum of life. When we do use words, the words say as much about the person speaking them as they do about the event. Such speaking is important. It brings the thinking mind and its baggage up to speed.

The mind, seeking to dominate, perhaps driven by fear of threat to its comfort zone, can speak up. The logical sequence, populated by those items we deem important, reaches its conclusion, what we may have constructed as our safe place against life seen as confusion, as threat. We may identify (also a mind-construct) with the conclusion. We may believe we are the conclusion. (We dutifully shrink ourselves and *worship* the mind as we do that.) We can use fear to justify, prove, and defend our position, against others who would choose different extracts for their logical sequence and so reach a different conclusion. Fearing being weak, we may add anger and noise in an effort to dominate. We may believe *might is right* as we seek to establish our comfort zone over someone else's *wrong* one.

Yet life continues. You are not a conclusion, never have been, never will be. The ongoing experience never comprises the extracts, never is right or wrong, never requires fear or anger to play any part. It simply is what it is, an infinite canvas on which we can write whatever we choose and delight in our ever more creative ways of taking it, interpreting the richness of life.

> When I have gained insight
> because of adversity
> I thank the adversity
> for the insight I've gained.
> Adversity helped me
> to reach understanding
> though its methods felt hurtful
> it was my friend.

Some extremely bad experiences can make us dig deep. They open us up to levels of healing that could have been achieved in no other way. If the experience has been traumatic and severe, creating a fishing-line tangle of thoughts and body tensions, it may take time and a supportive environment for you to slowly unravel the tangles.

The best experiences prove to be the ones that involve learning. Permanent personal improvement surpasses momentary gratification, leaving it way behind at the starting gate. The only bad is the non-experience: the person who gets it wrong fifty times and never once learns from it. Yet even with those, the penny will eventually drop, even if it is not in this lifetime.

With this clear, it becomes possible to take the thinking mind off the case. Worry is going over and over it, repetitively, which often merely drains energy. Be grateful to the mind, for the trouble it took. Then give the mind its walking papers. Take back control. Don't worry. Be happy.

HANG-UPS

You don't have to work hard to dump a hang-up. It is okay to let it go. It was always something you were holding on to. Do this: with arms outstretched make two fists; let the grip of those fists be the power of the holding. Hold that hang-up tight, so tight your hands almost fall off. Now let go. Let the hang-up go too. It went with the fists!

A hang-up includes a body-tension component, a holding action that is done physically. Behind that, often driving it, forcing it, insisting on it, is a mind component, a piece of thinking. By repetition, this can become congealed into an attitude, something that is believed, held tightly, squeezed, as if to gain a drop of life from it that it never had in the first place. Some examples:

"I'll never succeed. But I'll show them. They'll never get the best of me. I'm so angry!"

"I'm useless. I can't do it. Forever I'll remain a child, crestfallen, and incompetent."

"I'm terrified and untrusting. But I must never show it, or I'd be hurt. So, I'll disguise it behind so much anger no one will ever know, not even me! I'll be the terror of the block."

See life as a climb up a mountain. That gives you the right to let go of the idea of *failure* while keeping your sights on the view from the top as your light-at the end of the tunnel.

GUILT, BLAME, SHAME, AND PUNISHMENT

So much of guilt is self-punishment, internal beating on yourself. Some people do it to themselves mercilessly, endlessly. But for others, fault is pain that can be automatically off-loaded. Blaming someone else becomes a magical attempt to gain a moment's respite from the incessant habit of self-punishing out of shame. The punishment lifestyle continues, reliably. Now you do it to someone else.

If I attribute my slightest discomfort to you, I attribute power to you, hemorrhaging my own power as I do. I grab for the false power of blaming and throwing guilt, while discarding my right to the true power in love.

Beating doesn't help. Enormous effort can be put into finding fault. Once you have found it, the only option is to rain terror on the one at fault. It can be your own self. Label it. Instead of saying "I feel guilty," just say, "I am choosing to punish myself. I am choosing angry mess making as the way to go."

Stop it. Say out loud, "Stop that! I don't need it. So stop!" Then let it go. Be free to see beyond the noise, the beating. It was only something you were holding onto.

This is not to say that people don't commit crimes for which they can be called guilty. The difficulty with the person with a long-standing problem of being guilt-ridden is that she can stand in the witness box and be so tongue-tied that, in the absence of clear evidence, it is easy to follow her invitation: "I already punish myself on the inside; please validate my worldview by punishing me on the outside as well (even though I didn't do it)." The kick-me game can be almost irresistible to those of us with a long-standing anger, or kicking, habit.

Guilt is a desiccated, dried-up version of a natural awareness we are all gifted with: conscience. Conscience is that innate sense of the rightness and wrongness of what people do to one another. The mind, often acting out of fear, wants control and believes in the value of punishment ("at least it is something I can do"). It takes its extracted, cut-down version of conscience and proceeds with its plan for a cure. It beats and beats and beats on the elephant of awareness. It can sap the life force, providing such a distracting interruption that it is hard to be aware of anything, over all the noise. It tries to squeeze the enormity of your total being into the pigeonhole of punishment.

Neither Kicker nor a Kickee be.

—wise saying

POLICED TO MEET YOU

When you talk to some people
what you do not know
is that they have a small policeman
standing on their shoulder,
(or so they imagine him)
truncheon in hand,
ready to whack them hard
if they say something
the policeman doesn't like.
If you have ever tried
to carry on two conversations
at the same time
you will know
how difficult it can become.
What trouble they must have
talking to you
and to their policeman
at the same time!
These people
may seem strangely confused.
They may have trouble
staying on topic.
They can be so hard to talk to
you may wish you had a truncheon
so you could beat them over the head
and knock some sense into them!
Thank heavens you don't.
One punishment
is more than enough.

OLD BAD HABITS

Old bad habits can be hard to break. They can become so automatic that trying to stop one can feel like trying to stop an express train. From the time you start thinking about a particular bad habit, you may have to get it wrong fifty more times before you can stop that and do it right just once. Learn from that experience. You may need to do it twenty-five more times before you can make another correction. Then fifteen times. Then ten, five, two until you are getting it right just as often as you are making the error.

When you get it right twice in a row, then five times, ten times, twenty times, you have regained the power. Count it down. Bring it slowly down, steadily down, inevitably down. It has to go. Because you are gently, persistently insisting. You may waiver. But you can always return to the task again.

COUNTING DOWN

Counting down retrieves your power
takes it back to build your tower
you can break your habit-pattern
you don't have to go to Saturn.

CONFRONTING A BAD HABIT

Habits can be consoling. Like the child who grabs a blanket or a favorite stuffed animal, we can gain the comfort of familiarity and control, from doing that holding.

Where a habit no longer carries us through life, but has become destructive, we label it *bad*. Mental overactivity can be part of the problem. Unraveling has been mentioned. Guilt, the belief in internal self-punishment as a cure-all, can become a crippler.

When a habit is being destructive to your life, take charge. Address it directly. Say the following:

"Stop that. Stop what you are doing. You are no longer welcome to interfere with my life."

The habit has been a part of your life. As such, it supported you through to the present. There is room for gratitude for that. Never miss a chance to place a river of gratitude under your canoe:

> *I am grateful for the part you have played in my life. You helped get me here. I couldn't have done it without you. There will always be thanks in my heart for that.*

> *But I need to practice some changes. You are draining my energies and creating noise in the system. I need my energies. I have much to do. I don't need the interruption.*

> *There is some good news and some bad news. The good news is: you can relax. Your work is done. Here is your pink slip. The bad news is: things will be different. It will not be familiar. You may become afraid. You many want to jump in and take over.*

> *Don't be worried. I'm in charge now. I know you are there. I can always find you if I need you. Relax and sit back.*

OLD HABIT REGROUPED

Your friend is saying to you, "Stop. You can't do that any more. I am grateful for the help you have been. But stop that."

Drink that in. Breathe it in fully to every pore of your body. Take in the gratitude. You wouldn't want to miss out on that. But also the message: times are changing.

The healing miracle comes when this message is received and responded to in kind. A friend is the one who does this. Enter the Kingdom of Miracles by doing this. Be a friend. Always a friend. A friend gets it right. A friend is open to fully receive. Be that friend. Switch to being the habit, upgraded to become responsive.

What do you feel? Can you relax? Are you relieved? Do you feel scared? Are you grateful? Whatever you're feeling, send it back. That helps seal the deal.

OLD HABIT REGROUPED

I've been misusing my energy needlessly
spreading it 'round in a thousand odd ways.
I'll bring it back to me
under my leadership
retrain it until it is *me* it obeys!

CHANGING AN OLD HABIT USING HEALING EMOTIONS

We can feel trapped by an old habit, locked into it, frozen hard and hopeless ever to change. We can feel like an ancient fish frozen forever in a glacier.

The freeze suspends the natural flow of life with great ice blocks of fear and anger. We have all seen people frozen by their own fear. They are scared to make a move. We have all experienced the hardness of someone's anger. Often protecting a deep fear they have, they seek to be repulsive, to push you back with their anger. They are locked into a belief that *you* are hostile, that you are one of them, one of those who would be hurtful.

That any of this could ever be true is simply sad. Herein lies the healing. Sadness brings a melting. The tears of sadness are symbolic of the melting of a glacier. People feel feelings. Glaciers do not.

The trick is to personify the habit. Upgrade the freezing of it by imagining it could be human. Something—someone, a part of you—with whom you can actually connect. The warmth needed is human emotional warmth.

The first step is gratitude. If you can find a way to feel grateful in any situation, you practice your humanity, your quality of being alive. True thankfulness is emotionally warm. We are not talking here of the person who mutters "Thanks" as they turn their back and walk away. You are braver than that. You look at your habit and say, "Thank you. Thanks for all you have been to me. You got me this far in my life. I might not have made it without you. Whatever happens, I will always be grateful to you for that."

Then, *be* the habit. You look at this person, you, who is doing something tragic. She is locked into a pattern she cannot control. Be a friend. A friend can be warm. See your friend, trapped!

How do you feel? Can you feel compassion? That is not hard. It is the warmth in your compassion that has melting power, the ability to melt the glacier.

But the healing is coming from both sides. Your friend is already grateful. You soak in the gratitude. Gratitude says you got it right. There has all along been something you have been doing that was right. You are being validated. Breathe that in. If you weren't warm before, you are now!

But you were already warm. You have compassion in you. Send your compassion into your friend. Compassion's warmth. Gratitude's warmth. There is a profusion of warmth! Watch the first trickling, as the glacier begins an inexorable, inevitable warming, melting. The fish will swim again!

Ha. There never was any glacier. There never were any trapped fish. It was all something you were doing—an alive person doing a strange thing out of the belief that it was necessary. So, it was not. You will discover more and more about that as time passes.

Moving these feelings around is like doing a workout. It can be exhausting. The best thing to follow a workout with is rest. Just as in a workout, new muscle builds when you recuperate.

In changing an old habit, it's is best to use intermittent reinforcement. But it should not be regular. If you do it every second time, if you say, "Stop that," every other time the habit occurs, you invite the habit to think, *I know when the* stop *is coming. I can work around that.*

But if you do it on the second time the habit happens; then wait five times and say, "Stop that"; then wait two more times and then do it twice in a row, you are asking the habit to pay attention. Now it may think, *I can't tell when the interruption is coming. I need to pay attention.* It is as if you are waking the habit up from a deep sleep. Now it is watching you. It may not happen instantaneously. The habit may be long-standing. You may have to wait patiently over days, weeks, or even months, repeating the intermittent reinforcement.

Once you have its attention, you can take charge. Your adversary, the habit, previously repeating itself boringly, now is in a dialogue with you. You can begin to dictate the terms. In the terms of the article "Spiral Mountain," you are well up the mountain, well on your way to rising above the problem, above the slab.

Some nations have a bad habit of self-defining by establishing who their enemies are. As for the nation, so for the individual citizens. You do not find your own uniqueness, your history, or your habit patterns by looking at those of someone else.

REST

Now rest is best
I am confessed
I won't contest
That ruling.
I must lie down
not go to town
don't count me down
no fooling.

MEMORY

Introduction
Memory
Enlivening Memory
The Past
Fighting Old Battles
Memories Debunked

INTRODUCTION

Memory. Memory is deserving of your respect and understanding for the purpose it serves. You can use imagery and humor to overcome forgetfulness. The moment you know you have something to remember, it already lies in the past. We can pour a lot of wasted energy into that. Memory isn't all it's cracked up to be; it's more than that … and less.

MEMORY

It is important to respect your memory. It serves you on a constant basis. Some people are ready to pour dismay on their memory's failures when they have never once shown gratitude for its successes. Memory is part of your aliveness. When aliveness is involved, you need to invoke warm healing emotions to gain improvement. I can't say it enough: gratitude is the simplest warm emotion to evoke.

It is important to acknowledge the limitations of your memory and not be restricted by them. It is your library, presenting to you your past experiences together with your reactions to them. If your experiences have been mostly negative, it may be important to ignore memory, to focus on placing fresh new positive books on the shelves and start letting the old dusty ones pass.

Working with positive emotions, such as gratitude, love, compassion, and empathy, improves your memory in a natural healing way. These feelings lend internal support, smooth and lubricate your internal processes, reducing the friction of worries, fears, rage, and anger—which perhaps surprisingly, disrupt memory. For example, intense anger so pulls on your energies, it is hard to see over the top to what is really going on, and so to remember that.

You can clear your way to being simply there for whatever is going on. Your later recall of what happened—your memory—is then free of the chaff and gravel that not only makes your memory inaccurate, but can ruin your ability to remember at all!

If you're enjoying a holiday, you're involved in the holiday. But you might not remember the holiday in every detail. This is normal. The mind, good at focusing, grabbing details, is not fully engaged, as it cannot fully grasp the experience of a vacation. You have a greater ability to have experiences; be there.

Appreciate your memory. Use memory as an excuse to practice moving the warm life force of gratitude. Kill two birds with one stone.

Focus on your memory's successes. Bring those to the fore. Create an increasing pile of memory successes. Take them for a ride! Develop a preference for recalling them over failures.

If you show as much delight and enthusiasm as you can muster every time your memory serves you well, you send it a clear message: This is the way to go! Your memories will slowly move in that direction.

ENLIVENING MEMORY

So you forget things. And you may get mad at your memory. But there's also some fear that your memory may be deteriorating. Your memory needs enlivening.

Your memory is a recording of the events in your life. So enliven your life. You can't remember where you put your keys. Or your glasses. Or where you put a book.

At least five times a day, for a minimum of five minutes, do one thing, anything, in a highly exaggerated, colorful, imaginative, flamboyant, comical, stimulating, obvious way. Make a color cartoon in your imagination of the thing you select.

You put your keys down. See exactly the place you put them. Not slightly to the right. Exactly there. Before you take your hand away, squeeze them slightly. Enough to make a mark on your thumb, even cause a little pain. If you place them on a tabletop, imagine that just after you leave other objects on the tabletop conspire to rush the keys and slide them off onto the floor. They want you to have trouble finding the keys when you return. Silly? Of course. Memorable? Yes. That is the point.

Or that book. You place it on a chair. Pick it up again. Put it down. *See* the process. Pick it up. Turn it over. Put it down that way. Look at it. Decide you prefer it the other way. So you pick it up again. Finally you leave. The book immediately sprouts a thousand centipede legs and walks out of the chair across the room and relocates in an entirely different place!

Or perhaps the book opens and closes because it is actually the mute on a trumpet and you are followed by trumpet tones as you walk away from the book. It is mocking you!

Or the leaves fly out and form a magic carpet to waft you away. Later they return to bring you back to where the book is.

Do you still think you will forget where you placed the book or the keys? Keep the practice going—five times a day. Your life will be stimulated, your awareness raised. No arguments that you can't do it. Do it. Your memory can only improve. And so will your creativity!

THE PAST

The past is a collection of memories about what worked before—or how you tried to make something work before. Take from your collection what works now and use it. Let the rest go. Don't blindly repeat the past. Stop memories from falling all over you, like books off a dusty old shelf. Don't tolerate that. Say to your memory, "Stop! I don't need the whole library! I will tell you when I want something. Meanwhile, remember you are my servant, not my master!"

If a particular memory keeps popping into your head and will not be quiet, it may be saying, "Pay attention. I am hurting. I need understanding. I need acceptance. Please will you accept me?" Your solution may be to become the kindly mother, the understanding grandfather to the poor little thing. Take it under your wing. Be patient with it. Love it. Take the power that being loving gives to you and use it. Care for it until it really feels listened to, until it can feel it trusts you. Then it will settle down and release its pain (as much of it as it is able to at the present time), leaving you free and unencumbered to get on with your life.

Some memories have been severe and repetitive. Perhaps at the time you were struck with a physical reaction; your body took on the memory and your mind tried to overcome it, but you were struck down again and again. The mind may lose hope, settle for a decision of hopelessness, which fixates an image of no-future. The layered nature of the down and up again … down again and up … down-up-down … may require slow reversal over time with a professional psychotherapist, movement therapist, or body worker who you feel you can trust. The body releases slowly.

FIGHTING OLD BATTLES

I'm fighting old battles
that come from the past.
My input of energy
makes sure they last.
Recycling frightening
scenes of abuse
bringing them back here
as if they had use
reliving, fighting them,
thinking things bleak
depletes present energy
renders me weak,
makes noise in the system
just when I need quiet
to see what is happening
not make a riot.

MEMORIES DEBUNKED

Memories
are wonderful
joyous memories
of happy times
with people we love
stored
in great detail
with all of the feelings
for happy recycling
whenever we choose.
Memories
are terrible
bad experiences
we'd rather forget
loaded
with negative feelings
that insist
on recycling
and destroying
our lives.
Memories
are terrible
fantasy ways
of transporting us
out of reality,
stealing
the vitality
that we need
to be alive,
distracting us away
from the *NOW*
which is there
which is an opportunity
which is all we truly have
which we need
to be
who we are.
Memories
are memories
simple memories
they happened
good and bad.
We can steal away

from our life
to play with them.
We can invest
in a past
that was there
to show us how
to be now
not
to just invest
in a past
that is passed
and so choose
to lose
where we are
what we have to give
that's alive
as we strive
to express
what is best
from our store
that is the more
as we explore
who we are.

UPDATING AND UPGRADING CRUDE FEELINGS

Warren Douglas Phegan

INTRODUCTION

Updating and Upgrading Crude Feelings. Crude feelings—anger, fear, and their softened form, sadness—are ripe for upgrading. If your true friend feels anger, fear, or sadness, you only have to extend the slightest amount of compassion to begin the healing process. Being friends, your true friend is safe to begin breathing in the compassion.

A steady determination to practice the necessary steps will help a great deal.

People with different backgrounds and different experiences of life can face difficulties understanding one another and showing compassion. But warm emotions have many healing qualities.

Create a warm support around yourself. You can use your entire life to do that. Gratitude is a readily available warm emotion on which to practice. There are so many aspects to gratitude that it's no surprise that I touch on it in each section. It is particularly pertinent when focusing on your upgrade practice.

The interpersonal environment is where the healing works best.

DETERMINED

I breathe in love
to heal my ills
dissolve fixed attitudes
I no more need
to smooth my words
as I reach out
connect to others
with healing speech.
I breathe in oxygen
to fuel my fires
warm my body
all conspires
to benefit me.
I breathe out clutching
horrid hatred's holding prison
that I am no longer needing
releasing me to freedom found
no more restricted and held down.
Carbon dioxide I breathe out
rid my body of pollution
freeing it, now cleaned and freshened
physically it functions fully
oxygen was what I needed.
Determined to do it you'll find that you've made
a life in the sunshine, no longer in shade
determined continues to reap for my health
for I am creating emotional warmth.

178

LOVE ARGUMENT

Two men are arguing about love. One had been very much a wanted child. His every milestone was looked at with delight. He was appreciated. His family reveled in his successes.

The other man came from a dysfunctional family. Father had been an alcoholic. Mother was withdrawn and depressed. Neither had been loved by their own parents, and they hadn't found out about it before having their son.

So now these two men are arguing about love. They are not talking about the same thing! Love is above all an experience. It is far too nuanced and complex to ever be categorized, pigeon-holed, defined and confined to some simple formula. If these two are ever to agree, they must first have the experience of love. One way to do that is to start being loving. With practice, only improvement can happen.

Each child born into a dysfunctional family reacts differently to the situation. One child, feeling abandoned in a loveless family, reaches out into the darkness for the love he wants, fearing it will never be there, and angry about it. For this poor man love comes as a combination of deprivation (scarcity), anger, and fear. Another child, born into the same deprived situation, attempts to fill the gap. She behaves in a loving manner to the other children and to the parents—at times when it is safe to do that. How does this child know to do that?

We cannot know for sure. Research cannot yet fathom the depths of our souls. Yet this young woman may have learned that love is a state of being stretched to the limit. She may still combine a belief that her needs will never be met along with some deeply held anger about that. Both of these people may later, in a loving situation, actively resist taking in love, not fully allowing themselves to *be* loved. It wouldn't be consistent. It wouldn't fit their comfort zones, the uncomfortable state, the shoe that never fits, which has become their familiar way of living. Releasing the past is part of regaining the present.

Sometimes two people who do love one another are arguing. By listening to the music of the other's intonations, each can gain far more information about the other's emotional state at the moment, than ever they would gain by trading facts and information.

This book is about love. You could read it from cover to cover and not experience one drop of love. That would be a fruitless exercise. Don't do that. Don't waste your time. A book cannot love you. It is only a collection of words. But you can improve on that. You can flood in between the lines your own love. You can use the words to expand your experience. If you cannot do that, it would be best to put the book down. Find someone, lots of people, who know about love. Watch how they do it. See if you can gather a sense of what is going on in them and from them. That will do you far more good than forcing yourself to read a lot of words that you have reduced to the trivial meaning of someone else's opinion.

If you find you know more about loving than someone else, you may have to tread softly; even loving guidance can feel shaming to someone who does not trust the world of love.

Unloving states are sad. Acknowledging the sadness can be the first step in a pathway of willingness to feel, which leads on eventually to happiness.

As you seek the company of loving people, you may run into those who seek to make a big impression about how loving they are. There is a hardness to this display that is not at all the nature of love. Turn, look at another person, and you may find love simply there. This person is already living in the Garden of Eden, already familiar with nirvana. You are free to bask in his warmth.

THE VERSATILITY OF WARM EMOTIONS

Love is the all-inclusive word for a number of warm emotions—such as compassion, understanding, gratitude, and caring—that emphasize different parts of love.

All the warm emotions have a number of characteristics in common. Here are three:

They are like cushions on which we can rest and relax. If someone openly sends us caring, friendship, or another warm emotion, and if we open our hearts and freely breathe it in, we settle, relax, and become at ease, even rest back into their beautiful gift as if it were a warm cushion.

Warm feelings have an inbuilt wisdom. They are natural healers. We can sometimes be concerned how the warm feelings we risk sharing will be taken. We want to follow up and make them work. Don't bother. When a gardener waters a dry plant, he does not instruct each droplet where to go. They get it right automatically. Your warmth has its own capacity to relax and heal. If someone else wants to self-protectively block himself from receiving your warmth, that is his problem. But your job is done merely by genuinely sending the warmth or sympathy or other warm feeling. Leave it to do its own work.

There is a gentle washing, cleansing action in all the warm emotions. It is as if we feel internally "dirtied" by worrisome problems, fears, and other unresolved emotions. Compassion, sympathy, empathy, caring can beautifully alleviate that stress—if we will breathe them in. They can hopefully come from others, whose company we have cultivated. Meanwhile, we can inhale, saying to ourselves, "I am choosing to breathe in compassion and caring." Then watch the metaphor of oxygen do its enlivening work.

ENVIRONMENT OF LOVE

Say often to yourself, "I love you." Despite frictions, despite experiences that obscure it and vie for your attention, you live in an environment of love. It is available to be tapped for the power it contains, the joy that it brings. Learn to use love for your own strengthening and for the benefit of others.

If you are loving what you are doing as you do it, your love will sustain you, float your canoe on its river through irksome times, boring times, times when you are tired. Don't dry up that river.

To feel this love is to be blessed. If you are not loving what you are doing, find a way to love it. Or change to doing something else. No matter what you are doing, you will find there is someone who loves to do it. Pick up some clues from him or her. If you cannot find a way to feel blessed, you can switch to doing something else. But it may be important to ask why it is that you cannot feel blessed, at every moment of your life.

THE WORLD IS MY RORSCHACH TEST

The Rorschach test consists of a series of inkblots of no particular shape on cards. You look at the cards. Since they are not clearly anything, you tend to invest them with meaning from the filter, the screen through which you see the world and by which you edit what is going on to fit the requirements of that filter. When you report on what you see, the tester sees that as a "projection" onto the cards of your preset view of the world, your slant on what it is you see.

Your mind reaches out, stakes out territory for itself by giving meaning to events. No longer did an event simply happen: "What that really means is …" The mind delights how it has now fitted the event into (or imprisoned the event in) its zone of comfort.

Meaning gathers its greatest power, for good or ill, when it is interpersonal, what it means between you and me. Meanings then move you *toward* contact with others, or *away from* that contact.

Life invites us to confront this process. If you belong to a group given to a jointly agreed upon style of projecting, you may be criticized or punished until you adjust your filter, your editing process, to what the group feels comfortable with. But life is not restricted by the requirements of a group. It continues. Outside of that group, any dysfunctionality you continue to act upon tends to be reacted to with hard knocks. In this way, life can move you toward functionality.

Merely to be alive and to do things brings reactions that give you feedback. Particularly immediate and accurate can be the feedback you get from your family pet. Your dog, in vigorous ways, and your cat more subtly, are capable of instantaneously mirroring back to you how you are doing. When you take your pet to the veterinarian, staff quickly notice how your agitation becomes the animal's agitation. Animals, like children, are reliable mirrors.

You can learn even from your projections. That becomes your job as you put a positive spin on what you is in your view, and so gain, strengthen, and mature. Life becomes its own form of psychotherapy. The world is the projection card, your own living Rorschach test.

A diamond is piece of coal that made good under pressure.

—Anon.

GRATEFUL

Perhaps the biggest lesson on the path of love is that it is self-healing to be grateful. Gratitude is one of the versatile, warm emotions. Be grateful many times for many things. Focus on these flowers. Energize these beauties in your garden in preference to the depressive weeds of negativity. Give weeds no time. Be grateful for many small things: a blessing here, a smile there, a color that makes a difference, a positive in what may seem to be a sea of negativity. Do this many times a day. Be grateful for the large things: the oxygen you breathe that lights your fires and your warmth and energizes your actions. Be grateful for your life, full of opportunities to get it right, to grow, and to strengthen from that the process. Give more warmth out than you get. Develop a credit at the bank. Don't operate on overdraft. Find a positive angle to anything that happens. Package it in a flood of your gratitude. Gratitude begins a healing for you of any negative aspects to events. You polish your activity, groom the way you do things on the go, as you install an attitude of gratitude.

Gratitude is a releaser. You can feel the process of thanksgiving untying little knots inside of you, knots you didn't need. As you begin to enthuse about being grateful, you become eager to untie as many knots as you can find. This opens your sense of freedom and the glory of your being to the light of day.

Beam your gratitude to others. Some will receive it and be energized by it. You will feel your power as they do that. When someone is grateful to you, they truly recognize the gift you gave them. Others, with their own agendas, may freeze your gift out of their awareness. That is their problem, not yours.

The recognition built into gratitude is nourishing. When someone is grateful to you, they truly recognize what you did for them. Some gratitude seekers vainly try to earn gratitude without (a) giving it out themselves or (b) recognizing who are the ones truly interested in warm exchanges.

From time to time, we all have to do what we might call thankless tasks. As you do, think of what you are grateful for and let that energy flow. That way, you permeate your environment with the love-as-power that you need.

Turn a few drops of gratitude sent out into a trickle, to a flood, to a river of gratitude that carries, absorbs, discards (as flotsam and jetsam) the accretions of resentment, fear-driven holding actions, and worries. The little bits of gratitude you keep putting out are fishes. Enough fishes and the river begins flowing around them.

Your life and your life force are vital. They are worthy, worthy of recording. Buy a blank book. Call it *My Thankfulness*. In it, record anything and everything you are grateful for. Then, whenever you feel blocked or inhibited by events, open the book. It will show for you your vitality in action.

GRATITUDE

Gratitude says what you
did was so wonderful
gratitude strengthens
it works like a charm.
Gratitude taken, it
makes us feel wonderful
"I really did something
I am so great!"
Grateful, when given
it strengthens the other
you know that *you* did it
you had an effect.
Gratitude joins you
to those who would help you.
It turns on their helping
so both of you win.

GRATITUDE FOR LOVE

I wanted the gratitude, needed the gratitude
opened my doors to take in the gratitude.
But my house was full of the love I'd not given
jammed to the walls with no room for the gratitude.
So I opened my heart to the love I'd not given
let it pour out, freeing up my insides
in came the gratitude, wanting to be there
grateful for getting the love I'd not given.

GRATITUDE GLOWS

Gratitude the Great Connector
Gratitude the Strengthener
Gratitude the Healing Pathway
Gratitude the True Response.
Grateful says, "You did it well.
Grateful as I am to know you
Thankful you can be my friend."
Grateful opens me no end.

COUPLING: COMMUNICATION

Introduction
Empathy's the Way to Go
Masculine and Feminine Principles in Communication
Feeling *into* the Problem Person
Contact
Jumping Lightly
"I Hear What You Are Saying"
I Am a Refinery
You Come to My Refinery
Couple Connections
Incomplete Communication Replaced by Behavior
The Rule of Three in Communication
Child Communication
Schizophrenogenic Communication
How Can I Say to You "You Are Worthwhile"?
Threats
Rampant Love
What Is the Feeling?
Love: Water to the Dry Creek Bed
Patience Wins
Watering Can
Violence Wins
Physical Nutrition Mistaken for Emotional Nutrition
Marital Love Base
Feed Your Primary Relationship
Reaching for Reciprocity
Richness for Connecting or Dryness of Details
Coupling by Communicating
Maude and Herb
Feelings as Colors for Connecting
Enriching by Empathy
Empathy, the Connector: "I Don't Know What to Say"

INTRODUCTION

Coupling: Communication. Communications—spoken or non-verbal facial expressions and body language—make up the way we connect to one another. There are in each one of us, male or female, both feminine and masculine ways of communicating. If someone presents a problem, know in advance that your openness to feeling into that person may be the key to saving time and trouble. This is a dexterous way to solve these problems. We all want to be listened to, heard, and understood. If, knowing that, you take the initiative, then you begin the bridge building to the other person. You set your path toward effectiveness, modeling that for the other, whether he or she clues in or doesn't.

All too often, communication is incomplete.

There is something fundamental about the third time around of doing something. As if we all have an inner three-strikes rule, we endow it with additional reality when something happens a third time.

We have already seen in the sections on "Child" how childishness can infect adult (supposedly) mature communication. Understanding what any child copes with helps us understand the dynamic in ourselves as adults. Some even think these dynamics can expand into schizophrenia.

It can be frustrating when a person, perhaps someone close, repeatedly translates what is going on into ways of beating uselessly on himself.

Feeling threatened, misinterpreting a threat when none was intended, can be a habit with some people, but again, love offers a solution to that. It is always useful to seek out the human element amongst a profusion of facts and information. It may take patience to deal with some situations, but that's all part of the path. Violence, while espoused by many the world over, doesn't work, of course, even when it wins. But neither does stuffing ourselves or each other with food, readily confused with the power of emotions.

Marriages and all committed relationships need a base of love if they are to last and thrive. They need ongoing nourishment. Both partners must strive for that. Indeed, we have a constant choice: whether to prioritize inanimate objects or living, breathing human beings. We couple as we communicate— with everyone. There is enormous potential for making emotional contact. It is a creative process. Creativity itself is a vessel for full human expression. Some of the time we need to laugh at it.

The way we connect with one another is through the sharing of emotions. If all else fails, empathize. Indeed make empathy your priority at all times, so as not to be caught out. Empathy has a wonderful inbuilt quality of reaching out to make human contact.

EMPATHY'S THE WAY TO GO

As we blame, we shrink our own personal power. We can truly believe that putting lots of effort into controlling other people is a worthwhile endeavor. It isn't. What goes around comes around. The control we aspire to comes back to haunt us, as we become the *controlee*, controlled by others. Blaming is a loser thing to do. Jealousy is another self-crippler. Living in a fantasy world of your own glory makes you irrelevant.

Heartfelt contact is a far better way to go. Closeness and separation follow one after the other and then back again in a natural sequence. A friendly approach to each person you meet can work wonders, especially when it is not expected. But we need to pay attention to the responses we get. Watch for when your attention or connection is not appreciated.

Empathy is not the same as people pleasing or coming from an attitude of trying to be a perfect saint. There are many people whose basic approach to life is to please others. But authentic connection, being real in your empathy, can make a pleaser uncomfortable.

When we communicate, we have a pulling effect on other people. The uniqueness of this experience for each of us enables us to create a narrowed, inadequate representation in our head of each person.

MASCULINE AND FEMININE PRINCIPLES IN COMMUNICATION

Each one of us is alive. This gives us all the capacity to feel and to think, two very different skills that beg to be more completely understood. Then you can balance them, using your experience, wisdom, and skill.

In teaching couples to communicate, I find that both men and women are capable of using masculine and feminine ways of communicating. Sometimes it is the man who is using the feminine way far more than the woman is! In general, women use communication to make emotional contact. The average woman wants empathy, support to feel she is not crazy, and the company of someone to walk the mile with her in her moccasins. A man will typically reach out for that contact. He takes what she says, divides it into pieces, rearranges them, and hands it all back. Problem solved.

She didn't want to be a problem to be solved. So what he did irks her. He in turn notices that his magnificent problem-solving ability went for nothing. He becomes angry at her for the insult.

Where the problem involves adding up figures, simple decisions about mechanical things, the thinking mind is the best tool. The tax department will not appreciate a statement that you do not feel like paying taxes this year. Where people are involved, both processes are necessary. But they need to happen in sequence. It happens that emotional connectedness should precede problem solving. The two may have different requirements how that can be done. Mutual respect and active listening can ensure that all needs are met. Once that is done, there may be little need to solve problems. She has a brain. He may be able to avoid all that hard work (doing his problem-solving duty). He can just rest and enjoy.

FEELING INTO THE PROBLEM PERSON

If you can feel into and momentarily *become* the person you are having trouble with (walk in their shoes), you give *to yourself* understanding. From there, anything is possible. Method actors do that. They get inside the skin of the character they are portraying. For the duration of the show, they eat, think, feel, and breathe that character. They *are* the person. They *live* that person. They give themselves an in-depth understanding of the character, which gives their performance an astonishingly convincing realism. This is a tremendous skill to cultivate. Your ability to do this, while keeping yourself grounded, will serve you through difficult times and help you mature.

In my view, supposedly evil people are actually confused kids (grown up). Some things they say make sense and are consistent within their way of being. Other things that they hold to make no sense at all.

We are here to help one another. There may be a time and a place when you could talk to such an "enemy." Your talk will come more easily based on the river of understanding you have placed under your canoe. Not theirs. Yours. The initiative, the timing is up to you.

Succeed or fail at such talk, or even if the talk never happens, you have gained by your understanding, your empathy. That was your doing, your contribution to your life.

CONTACT!

If you continue
to use your loving empathy
for your own support, but also
to think the way he thinks
sooner or later
he may begin to return the compliment
and show a willingness
to think how you think
and empathize with you.
Emotional bridge achieved!

JUMPING LIGHTLY

Jumping lightly from peak to peak
finding what's good when others speak
seeing the best of what they say
letting the rest just float away.
What other people find destroying
I find room to feel enjoying
seeking out the stimulation
using all for inspiration.
The swamps of life are beneath concern
I rise above where they would churn
lightness, fleetness, where I stomp
keeps me from the stalling swamp.

"I HEAR WHAT YOU ARE SAYING"

The one thing that can be music to our ears and bring joy to our hearts is to be carrying on a conversation and hear these words, "I hear what you're saying." To be truly heard is a beautiful gift to receive. We can feel understood. We can feel a new lease on life. The words validate us. They say "I care." They say, "I see you there. You matter to me. You make a difference." They are evidence of someone reaching for the highest level—the level of interpersonal contact—and rising above *things*.

Be the source of this generous gift. Create for yourself an environment of warmth by your words, "I hear what you are saying." Don't blow them out like hot air, or follow them with "but ..." Do your homework. Reach out with your emotion sensors to find out who it is you are dealing with. Your own path forward will be smoothed by your efforts.

I Am a Refinery

I am a refinery.
It is my job
as a friend
to take in your crude oil:
to hear your pain and frustration
receive your fear
listen to your anger
absorb them
and from the depths of my heart
upgrade and refine your crude feelings
producing healing
sending back compassion
responding with warmth and sympathy
giving respect and understanding
all of which are healers
when truly received.
My love
is the river I canoe
that supports me
to be your friend
to serve you so well
unconditionally.
It is my delight
and my strengthener
to do that.

You Come to My Refinery

Your frozen fear and hardened anger
melt to tears of sadness.
I respond with empathy
as you share your badness.
The understanding you receive
rewards your risk in sharing.
The tattered clothes you handed off
replaced by warmth you're wearing.

Couple Connections

If you take two bar magnets and try to push their north poles together, they repel one another. If you take a board as thick as the magnets and cut a hole in it, the length of both magnets, it is possible to imprison both magnets in that hole (with boards above and below to stop them from popping out).

Some human relationships are like that. Two people trying to repel one another with punishing behavior, nevertheless stay together. Frequently imprisoning the two of them are the boards of their fear. They have so long been together that they each fear they would not survive if they parted. Or they have never practiced positive ways of being together.

Anger at the injustice of it all is natural. The repulsiveness of the anger would normally separate them, were it not for the fear forcing them together. Unfortunately, anger and fear frequently work together in this weird way.

There is a solution. Turning just one of the magnets around, so its north pole contacts the other's south pole, connects them beautifully. Find what each person loves to do. Fan the glowing embers of that love within the two. Then bring them around to face the love toward one another and you can develop a beautiful, living, intimate relationship, far more nuanced and nutritiously rewarding than any two magnets could ever achieve. The combination of anger and fear trying to lock them up is no substitute for love.

> If you'd fully be together
> can't be scared to be apart.
> Not a lasso 'round repulsion
> but connections from the heart.
> Seek out fear, identify it.
> Find that cancer, root it out.
> Then you're free to feel life fully
> find what living's all about.

INCOMPLETE COMMUNICATION REPLACED BY BEHAVIOR

As human beings, we are the privileged possessors of a magnificent method of communication: language. With language, we can infinitely define and refine what we wish to communicate. Communication has enabled civilization to advance to levels of sophistication and productivity never before seen on the planet. The closest, deepest relationships are achieved through open, complete communication. To trash language is to reduce us to the level of barking dogs, or cows bumping one another in the field.

Verbal communication always occurs in a context. That context includes the behaviors of the people involved.

The legal phrase "the truth, the whole truth, and nothing but the truth" covers the requirements. We need to know, we need to know it all, and to not have it contaminated by falsehoods and distortions for momentary gain and personal advantage. As habits, these contaminations cripple us.

People can render words useless. Grown people can continue childhood patterns. Childhood fears can force the child to grab some power and control at any cost. The child creates a habit, a boil with a hard scab of power and control covering the putrid fear that underlies it. The habit can be lying or merely saying words that are meaningless: a word-crowbar to manipulate a situation.

The child grows up. Unless the adult edits out the habit, the childhood pattern continues.

Language trashing is momentary gain for long-term disaster. The person who routinely throws in lies to her communication reduces her speech to the level of noise. There is nothing there to be relied on. Anyone else walking that bridge risks falling off at any time. So people back off. Such a person is self-imprisoned for life in superficial relationships without deep personal meaning or reward. The person who uses words as a crowbar to manipulate people runs the same risk. It is the method of a small child without power desperately trying to save himself or herself and get some power. So many grown "children"!

A man working at a company was asked by his superior to lie for him. He said no, "because then I could lie to *you*." He stayed with the company for forty years.

Behavior necessarily replaces communication. When an abusing spouse says to his partner, "Alright. I won't abuse you any more," and three days later does it again, words have been made irrelevant. Behavior has replaced them. The abused one needs to notice the shift. No longer do they have a joint agreement to use words. One has trashed that; so it is trashed.

The one on the receiving end, the victim, needs to see that her behavior is what is being read, for its truth. Staying under the same roof, continuing to live with such a partner, is a behavior too. That staying makes the statement, "I want to be with you. Don't pay attention to my complaints. I approve of what you are doing."

If the victim does not approve of what the other is doing, that message must not be sent. Words, having no value, must stop. No discussion. No complaining. No objecting. As quick an exit as possible (moving out) may be the best way of ensuring that the abusive behavior does not continue. Such a move balances the level that communication has descended to: behavior. It recognizes the level the other is using and validates (disappointingly) that choice.

Truth and the child state are inextricably intertwined. If you give someone the truth, knowing it is highly likely they will immediately kill themselves or someone else, you are again a child underachieving well below your potential. "Look at what I made him do. See! I'm not a weak child after all (but I really am)." Use your wisdom and maturity to govern your mouth.

Truth always has a context. My truth and your truth are rarely identical. We are constantly required to build bridges across truths. The bridge is a friendly lateral move from the way I live to the way you live, from the path I am walking to the path you are walking. Love has the capacity to surround and join these isolates, these truths. Love invites you both to walk the bridge in friendship, comparing and contrasting truths.

Compassion, love, and understanding create the best foundation on which to build the magnificence of language. With that base, you can then speak accurately and completely. Use your warmth and caring as your guide.

THE RULE OF THREE IN COMMUNICATION

Saying it three times to get a message across, has been around for a long time. Lee Iacocca, the man who saved the Chrysler Corporation from bankruptcy, learned it from his father (Iacocca 1984). He used it in giving talks. It was used twice in the article "Unraveling" at the beginning of this book.

The Rule of Three goes like this: First you tell them what you are going to tell them. Then you tell them. Then you tell them what you told them.

The first telling is fresh. When you do that, you grab their attention. Then, with their attention gained, you say in detail what you have to say. The third telling says you really mean it. So often in communication, we say something. Then, in the next breath, we laugh, meaning what I said was laughable, or we say in effect, "Yes, but …"; or we give a clue in the negativity we present—that we have mixed feelings about it and we shouldn't be taken seriously. That can derive from a childhood hesitancy, based on a wish not to be so offensive that we will be rejected—an intolerable option for a dependent child. But not for a grown-up who could heal and mature that.

So be clear. Do your homework. Resolve your mixed feelings. Then say what you have to say, expecting to be heard. Delete all images of rejection—the message you don't need to include— from your inventory. You expect success. You create success.

With that tool in your pocket, you can be sensitive to the person you are talking to. You are not a steamroller. If the person is giving inattention signs as you speak, having difficulty swallowing what you have to say, you can ask, midstream, "Are you having difficulty with any of this? Is the something you might share?" Your willingness to be a sensitive listener can model the sensitive listening you are requesting from them. Walk your talk.

CHILD COMMUNICATION

A special case in the field of communication is the child position. A marker of the inner child taking over control within a grown person is that person sitting around waiting for someone else to do something, say something. The grown-up finds a way to take responsible action and does that.

A child, due to lack of power, inexperience, and immaturity, is not in a position of equality with an adult. Any communication that seems equal relies on the generosity of an adult listener to lend support and be gentle. Dependency is the reality. Dependency must be maintained as safely as possible until the child is fully grown and able to take care of himself.

So the talk of a child has a strategic quality: he cannot risk interfering with the support he needs to carry him through the dependent years.

A child may be concerned about the ultimate consequences of bad behavior. But she cannot have her worst fears confirmed. The child uses a language termed "childrenese" by Haim Ginott in his book *Between Parent and Child* (Ginott 1965). The child may say to the parent: "I saw on television where a child was so bad his parents threw him out in the snow to die!" The child didn't really see it on TV. But he couldn't risk the direct question "If I was really bad, would you kill me?"

The understanding parent, the good parent, reads through the words to the true concern of the child and says, "That may happen on television. But in real life parents love their children. They would never do that no matter how badly the child behaved." The child can now relax, secure in the knowledge he needed but could not ask for directly. He knows he doesn't yet have the maturity to behave well at all times. He knows he may sometimes playfully push people's buttons, exploring what it feels like to have power he can only glimpse at for the time being.

Lying has the same strategic slant in "childrenese," quite different from a grown-up telling a lie. If a child, from careful observation, gathers the impression she could be killed if she told the truth, she is under powerful training to begin a career of lying. If she also knows it is dangerous to be found out for telling a lie, she is between a rock and a hard place: a no-win situation. The unfortunate rules are being set by a bully, the grown-up, with a strong commitment to punishment as a solution to problems, living out the errors of a previous generation, from the child position into which *she* was trained.

The shaming technique called tough love is most likely to work when there is a robust river of love supporting the action, not just a big dose of "tough" attempting to drive down a shallow, rocky creek bed.

Children have a brilliance: clear-seeing eyes that observe vital information about how we operate. The grown-up can breathe deeply. He can allow the truth of a clear set of eyes from a new, younger generation to soak in. That can bring a glorious healing to bear. Brutalizing, to shut that truth up, is bypassed.

As you respond to the child in self or others, you must consider strategic frameworks (thinking), behavior (acting and the body that carries out those actions), and intention (the feelings involved). Recognize the defenselessness and fear aspect of someone who is clearly presenting herself from the child position. Your task is to respect her dignity (not talk down to her), while reaching out with warm, connected support. Sometimes, you can set clearer limits this way.

SCHIZOPHRENOGENIC COMMUNICATION

The young man walks downstairs from his bedroom. He was given a red sweater and a green sweater for Christmas by his mother. He knows that if he puts on the red sweater, Mother will say, "Oh, you didn't like the green sweater." If he comes down in the green sweater, his mother will say, "Oh, you didn't like the red sweater." If he comes down with both sweaters on, Mother can say, "You need two sweaters? Don't we keep the house warm enough?" If he comes down with no sweater on, he was "unappreciative."

He knows his mother well. He has for a long time been in a lose-if-you-do-and-lose-if-you-don't situation. She has done that for years. It is also known as the "double bind" (a phrase coined by Bateson et al, in 1956.)[4] Transactional analysts recognize it as the game called Corner.[5] His strategy has been a tragic one. He must destroy communication with Mother. If he believes he is Napoleon, that the moon is made of blue cheese, and that he is receiving wireless signals from Mars in the feelings of his teeth, his mother can no longer control him. His behavior generates for him schizophrenia, He has created his schizophrenia. She was schizophrenogenic mother, a phrase coined by Frieda Fromm-Reichmann in 1948.[6]

Mother was not schizophrenic. It was something she did to her son. The usual history for Mother is that she was grossly discounted by her parents, who received the same treatment from their own parents, who also did not learn how to make genuine emotional contact. He takes on the condition called "schizophrenia." Hearing voices in his head can replace Mother. He can (hopefully) control what he has created. His own speech is of course disorganized. Both of these are termed "positive" symptoms of schizophrenia. Negative symptoms include restricted range of emotional expression. He never learned emotional expression from Mother. He is also poor at speaking and in developing goals for himself, not?[7]

Then it was discovered that the communication at first called "schizophrenogenic" was in fact very common in ordinary speech. Have you ever had someone put you in a double-bind,

---

4   Bateson, et al., 1956.

5   Berne, 1964, 92.

6   "Schizophrenogenic mother" is a phrase coined by Freda Fromm-Reichmann in "Notes on the Development and Treatment of Schizophrenics by Psychoanalytic Psychotherapy," *Psychiatry*. 11: 263–274.

7   See *DSM IV-Test* revision, page 299, the *Diagnostic and Statistical Manual* for psychiatrists.

a lose-whether-you-do-or-don't situation? How did you react? You may not have chosen to be schizophrenic. Only certain individuals can do that. They are actually potentially talented. One young schizophrenic patient on the ward was also a creative poet. He was scared to lose his poetry skill if he gave up his schizophrenia. If I had known then what I know now, I could have reassured him. He did not need to worry about losing his skill at poetry. All he needed to do was give up a creative strategy he had mistakenly chosen: to become schizophrenic.

How Can I Say to You "You Are Worthwhile"

How can I say to you, "You are worthwhile"
when you say to yourself that you're not?
How can I say what will bring on a smile
when you're tying yourself in a knot?
How can I reveal what I know and I feel
when you tell me you have nothing in-ing?
How can we go on to show and to grow
when you never allow a beginning?
How can I say to you I really care
and there's more of you there
than you need
to compare
when you
jump on it,
dump on it,
rump on it,
slump on it
bump on it,
stump on it
and then you say
"Nothing's there."

Love, look at the two of us ... strangers in many ways ...

—Karlin, Wilson, and James (lyric from the
Carpenter's hit song "For All We Know"

Threats

If we feel threatened, we can put up walls within ourselves. The walls become habits, which interfere. You can let the wall go. It is okay to decide when to confront a threat, then go ahead and do just that. Turn stumbling blocks into stepping-stones. It is okay to decide when to walk away from a threat. It wasn't worth the effort of a response.

As you share your concerns with me, if I see your concerns as a threat to me, I may choose to defend. I put up walls against your (supposed) threat. These become walls against your concerns. I cannot hear your concerns because of my walls. My walls block my empathy, my compassion, my possibility of reaching you, making contact with your concerns.

If what I just described for me is what you do, if this is how you deal with the concerns of someone close, you can adjust this. It is simple. It is relaxed.

You let go of the idea of threat. With that released, you breathe easily. There is no need to defend. You are not threatened. Without the walls, your hearing improves. You can see better a concerned person needing openness from you. You can give a human response. If they have built a pool of anger against the dam of your self-protection, you may need to duck the first flood of that anger. You are not to blame. No need to wallow in guilt. Behind the wall you had built and the resentment that wall invited are two people with the skills and the patience to persevere and reconnect in useful, meaningful ways.

RAMPANT LOVE

"I love you" is a healer.
Using those words, you call on power
I don't like all your actions
but I love you by the hour.
You are greater than each thing you do
I see that oh so clearly
I want you healed of all you do
so I will love you yearly.
The power of my connecting
is what I'd have you feel
please observe when you've gone wrong
and use my warmth to heal.
And as you heal you'll love me more
though that's not why I do it
I'm comfortable with loving
it's my power, I renew it.
Good company's the way to go
combined love growing stronger
the benefits reach out to all
as we all last the longer.

WHAT IS THE FEELING?

What is the emotion when you want to say to someone, "It's okay. Things will work out. Don't be worried"?

The emotion is warmth. The emotion you are feeling, the energy that is driving your choice of words is your heartfelt warmth toward your friend. It may be in the form of simple warmth. It may be friendship. It may be as strong as love. But it is the warmth in friendship and the warmth in love that is doing the job.

Words can be the train carriages that carry that rich warmth. They can also be cold: the train that left the station before letting the warmth on board.

LOVE: WATER TO THE DRY CREEK BED

When water floods down a dry creek bed or onto parched land, it penetrates everything, germinates spores and seeds, and in time produces a lush growth. Everything springs to life.

When love is allowed to flood into a human situation, it can touch everything, penetrate everything, begin a process of healing that will in time enrich the whole scene with a life and vitality that was missing before.

There are exceptions. When water encounters rocks and clams, it cannot penetrate. It is kept outside.

If a person behaves like a rock: impenetrable, or clams up and refuses to be open to the good that is flooding around, they can effectively keep it out.

If we see a two-year-old rigid with terror, we know what to do. We reach out. We hold her and hug her and calm her and reassure her with soothing until the fear melts away, however long it takes.

If the same rigidity is present in a grown human being, we may think twice before risking a black eye, even though we may see clearly the route to healing. People situations require time to heal, time during which patience and understanding are shown, time during which dignity is respected and tolerance is practiced.

Patience, understanding, dignity and tolerance—these are all properties of love.

Love is marvelous!

PATIENCE WINS

My friend told me he's feeling fright
he feels that fear both day and night
yet somehow he believes that's right.
He's crazy!
I told him Love's the way to go
try it, he will find that's so
surprised I was when he said no.
He's not ready.
Growing slowly takes its time
it will not happen on a dime
waiting yields results sublime.
But what do I do, meanwhile?
Time for me to practice patience
same applies to worldly nations
better far than conflagrations.
But cold turkey's not on the menu.

WATERING CAN

I am a loving watering can
smoothing the way whenever I can
healing warmth for each woman and man
my solid base, validating plan.

VIOLENCE WINS

The conflagrations mentioned in the previous poem, "Patience Wins," are examples of the way violence in any form at any level fails to bring home the hoped-for result.

The language of violence
exceedingly rude
results of the violence
just as well stewed.
For violence solves nothing
the energy's weak
you'll never find
the goal that you seek.
So give up on violence
lead off with goodwill
results will come flowing
your hopes you'll fulfill.
Group violence wants notice
"Please see what I'm doing
I'm needing to draw
much attention to me.
I'll do that by killing
then I'll show my power
I beat him. I did it
it's my finest hour!"
When both sides will do it
what use is the carnage?
Dead bodies amassing
can prove nothing new.

PHYSICAL NUTRITION MISTAKEN FOR EMOTIONAL NUTRITION

To eat is human, to digest, divine.

—Mark Twain

It is common to confuse physical nutrition (food) with emotional nutrition (love). If guests are taken straight to the kitchen to make sure their stomachs are filled first, that can spring from doubts or inexperience about the connecting of people through the sharing of emotions. The time to make emotional connections can be diluted. If that connection fails, the body may become tense. Commonly, this tension is felt in the stomach. This allows confusion to develop between emotional deprivation and food deprivation.

Guests were invited for dinner. The hostess opens the front door and announces, "I'm sorry we don't have any food. Will it be alright if I spend the evening telling you how much I appreciate you?" No, it won't. They came for food. They want food. No substitutes, please.

The same applies to emotional nutrition. We need emotional contact with other people and the feeding of the human spirit, which validates a connecting that happens only in that way. The refrigerator is not a source of this contact.

If you are not accustomed to this, you need practice. Practice sharing what you feel with people interested in such sharing and your skill can only improve. A lonely person who tries to get that companionship from the refrigerator can become an overweight lonely person. Problem unsolved.

Eat to live; don't live to eat.

MARITAL LOVE BASE

A husband and wife are arguing over how to handle the children. He was raised rough and tough, so he wants to bring them up that way. She was raised close and tender, so that's what she wants to do. They are operating from different experiences.

The first thing they must determine is this: do they love one another? With that base, all things are possible. Without that, they can argue forever and never reach agreement. They are continents apart, not yet grounded in a common base. If they have that shared love, they have the firm handshake that will hold them together; the safety-net trampoline on which they can bounce with joy and leap at life's issues.

For he is not a carbon copy of either of his parents, nor is she the same as her parents. They are not living in the age of the previous generation. Things are different. Furthermore, each child has his own personality, her own strengths and weaknesses, with which he or she is learning to cope with the world.

If all will work together, supported by love, they will work out responses and solutions relevant to the present and to those involved. Rubber-stamping from the previous generation and turning a blind eye to the effects of this imposition are no substitute for a solid base of love.

FEED YOUR PRIMARY RELATIONSHIP

Your primary relationship is alive: a living plant, in danger of drying up if it is not watered regularly. Feed your primary relationship; feed your marriage with the richness and variety of human emotion. Love your partner. The fairytale "Sleeping Beauty" is a metaphor in narrow terms for the far greater transforming, life-energy-changing power of love. Love, shared, awakens Beauty to live life to the full.

A common cause of anger is insufficiency of such feeding, insufficient loving. In these cases, the sharing and open receiving of such anger becomes the starting point for the healing of the relationship. It is not your *fault*. Get off your own case. There is a feeling human being here, awaiting emotional contact, empathy, and understanding. If you will put aside blame and guilt for a moment, you avoid these interrupters. You make it possible for two human beings to be in touch through the receiving of strong emotions and empathizing back.

Ongoing feeding of the relationship is important. One way to do this is to leave little love-notes in unexpected places for your partner to find. Another is gifts. Another is to do something that represents the love you feel for your partner. It can be very helpful if you can say the words *"Because I love you"* to go along with it. Some people are unfortunately struck dumb in this department. Saying the words out loud can double or even triple the power, the effectiveness of the action. That is, if you can bring yourself to label accurately what is already in your heart and speak forth the words that apply to it.

Say, "I often think of how nice you can be" (if you do indeed think that way). This polishes your own act (choosing to see positives, leaving the dross behind) at the same time as it nourishes the other.

If both people contract to do such mutual feeding, the contract gathers momentum. It is the aftereffects from such feeding that ensures the children will grow up emotionally healthy.

REACHING FOR RECIPROCITY

If I meet your needs
and continue that way
showing interest in you
and what works in your life
I need have no concern
that what goes out will come back
and if you are willing
my needs will be met
fed by purity of purpose.

RICHNESS FOR CONNECTING OR DRYNESS OF DETAILS

When a couple communicates, they must keep in mind the potential richness of the tool they are using. Communication has within it the power to bind and blend them in a way that enriches both. This allows them to leave that base, go out into the world with great capacity for reaching out with understanding, and taking relevant, effective action, time and again. Then they can return for more enriching, together.

A couple came to a marriage counselor for help with their marriage. He detected a lack of communication and recommended they talk more to one another. "What about?" said the husband. "How about what happened during the day?" said the counselor.

The man had a job on a production line. "But she doesn't understand the machinery," said the man. "She wouldn't know the names of what I would talk about."

The therapist suggested an upgrade. "You are right!" said the therapist. "Details of names and parts of machinery are not necessary. You can lift the conversation way above that level. Machines are not alive. They can't feel. You can. You carry living, feeling reactions about what has happened. Do you think your wife would like to know how you are feeling? That gives a quick estimate of your reaction to your day. Was the boss in a good mood? How was that troublesome coworker?"

Once the couple upgrades to the human element, quality responses become possible. Frustration and anger are common starters, topics begging to be shared. The healing connection asks for responses back that might include empathy and understanding. Fear as a starter invites a warm compassionate response. Sadness is softer. A warm, flooding friendliness in response to sadness shows the listener is interested, perhaps sympathetic or understanding.

Once these healing responses are breathed in and fully received, the natural response is gratitude. The person who began the sharing can respond to the warmth returned. Gratitude validates the responder's warmth and continues in the building of an open, sharing, healing relationship.

Running and masterminding an interference pattern with this natural healing is the thinking mind, often lost in a contradictory sequence of fixations that were, at different times, quick fixes for problems. The body joins in. Going along with the mind and double-teaming with it in ways that can grind all healing to a halt, are body reactions like tensions that can be either obedient to the mind or in opposition to its impositions. When you say "I'm not in the right frame of mind to do this," the *frame* for the mind, a physical thing, is provided by the physical body. The double-team has one more way to set problems up.

Taking charge, assuming responsibility, and calling all interference to a halt can be a useful way to resume healing. You can lift this to a new level by adding your human friendliness. You recognize the mind as having done throughout your life what you have directed it to do, sometimes in spite of conflicting messages you sent to it at different times. It has become a bully. You reach out to it with compassion and understanding. You gradually earn its trust because you did not attack it, helping it to reduce the intensity of its efforts:

You: Stop that.
Mind: I'm scared to stop.
You: When I receive your fear, all I can feel back is compassion.
Mind: As I take that in, I feel relief in my heart. I'm so grateful to you.

You take a similar, befriending approach to a body you may have previously shown transient, fragmentary interest in. You set a path of forgiving its excesses, reaching out with goodwill and understanding. It shows you it's hurt. You extend compassion. As it feels more and more recognized, it coheres into a valiant, supportive friend for life.

But wait! Notice what you have done with your mind and with your body. It is similar to what you intended with your partner! With mind and body on your side, move yourself ever closer to a continual blossoming of this powerful, healing, interactional state; to all situations, all people; at all times. You will clean up each of these acts better as you clean up your own act.

COUPLING BY COMMUNICATING

There is no couple worth the word
not into communication
They begin by shaking hands
then building their relation.
The words they say, the smiles they give
present their new creation
each reaching out, a mighty clout
becomes their inspiration.

MAUDE AND HERB

Maude and Herb were getting old; Maude said to Herb, "Don't you think it's time we got married?"

Herb replied, "You're right, but who'd have us now?"

Herb suffers from a communication problem called mind-intrusion. It is the chatter in his head that stops him from hearing what Maude is saying.

FEELINGS AS COLORS FOR CONNECTING

Feelings are often depicted as colors. A colorful person is one who arouses a lot of feelings in us. They have an effect on us.

Blue shares with yellow. Yellow takes blue in and is changed. Yellow sends back a response. It is green. In that green, blue sees itself blue, but colored by yellow. Blue and yellow are forever closer because of the sharing. If blue shares with red, it gets a different response: purple. Again blue is present in the response. Blue finds out about blue's nature through the common element in the response from each color it chooses to share with.

Feelings are like the colors. In the sharing, we have an effect on other people. They, in turn, effect us by their sharing.

Faulty learning from dysfunctional pasts can tell us not to be affected and thus hurt again. Feelings become equated to the narrow band of hurtful feelings, to be blocked. We are stripped of exploring the touching, warm, healing power that connects and unites us.

With courage, we can revise the learning and practice more effective contacting from a more mature competence level than we could manage years ago.

Feelings connect us. How you feel toward someone is your living response to someone else who is equally alive. Sharing that response can be done directly (by naming the feeling) or indirectly (by showing your enthusiasm, anger, fear, or other feeling) in the music of your voice or your physical posture. Sharing reaches across, connects, and invites an equivalent, alive feeling response from the other. In this way, both can intermesh. Peculiarly, they do not lose their uniqueness, their identity, in the meshing.

There is an ideal to be reached. It is white. Be white. Steadily grow more and more white. White has the power to react cleanly. White takes in yellow and returns yellow accurately to the giver. It is complete, natural feedback. White then turns to blue and gives blue back accurately to itself. It is not that it doesn't remember what it did for yellow. It has complete awareness, full memory. It is free of the thinking mind that would apply a holding action, the control and territoriality implied. White has that thinking mind in trust, to be used as needed, not to dominate.

ENRICHED BY EMPATHY

Empathy is the basis of communication. Empathy as you speak lifts what you have to say to the level of your humanity. You are not an irrelevant being from Planet X spewing out facts. Your humanity touches the humanity of the one you communicate with. You bridge the gap, a bridge that is suddenly able to take much greater loads. With a basis of empathy for the other person's condition, you become listenable, worthy, valuable. What you have to say gathers strength, the power to have an effect. If you prioritize empathy.

Empathic statements are simple. But they need to come from the heart. If you merely read from a list with no heart of yours in it, you become laughable and irrelevant.

Look into your heart to find which of the following statements you can truly make at this time. Your partner is the obvious receiver of choice as you enrich your primary relationship with the power of your empathy.

"I know what you're saying; I can feel how you feel about it. I am with you."

"Tell me more. I want to understand. I understood it when you were talking about _____ and _____. But could you tell me a bit more about _____? I didn't quite get that."

"Tell me more about how you feel about it."

"You are okay. You're going to make it. You have a good head. I am impressed with your ability. When I think back to the things you have done, I know you have it in you to succeed."

EMPATHY, THE CONNECTOR: "I DON'T KNOW WHAT TO SAY"

Empathy is a wonderful healer, a connector between people. Empathy, truly sent and truly received, can cure a loneliness that had become an ordeal, hard to bear.

Empathy is also delicate, at risk to be disrupted. The simplest form this can take is mind-interference. A flood of words, mainly aimed to reassure the listener that the speaker is not weak and incompetent in this situation, can pour out in the form of all sorts of helpful advice. The thinking process, unable to grasp the richness of the living life force, desiccates it down to mind size: words. Unfortunately, the shift to the more trivial level is often what the troubled person does *not* want. In some painful situations, the blabbermouth is the least welcome person.

So it can be a relief for someone stressed with emotional pain to hear the words, "I don't know what to say." Behind these simple words can lie a wealth of healing humanity. The stressed person can read into the tongue-tied empty space any or all of the following, and welcome it in:

I really feel for you.

I can see what you are going through.

I am with you on that.

I don't need to run from you.

I am not troubled by a personal agenda that I must do for you something observably "good," in order for me to feel okay.

I'll use my heart to connect with you, not my ego to separate me from you.

It is enough that I be with you, show to you that you are okay in my eyes, worth being with, a human being to whom I can still connect.

I can stay with you, stay the course, be here for you in case you need something.

Do you need anything?

Can I help?

I see that you are the focus, not me, and I am able and willing to stand by you, help you to stay connected.

EMPATHY'S THE WAY TO GO

Empathy's the way to go
connecting us. We start to flow
your empathy encourages me
now I know that you can see
now I know you understand
I can feel your open hand.

IT'S ALL YOUR FAULT

"It's all your fault. You're the one to blame
I now know that I will never be the same
I have no power. You're in charge of me
I am where you put me. That's the way its going to be."
As I proceed to speak this way, I give to you control
I give away my power, put myself down in the hole
all that *fault*-ing all that *know*-ing makes me fully out of breath
those mighty, fearful images scare my body half to death.
With body ever tighter and my mind in charge
I can watch the crazy, useless mess enlarge, enlarge, enlarge
double-teaming mind and body sees the whole mess much increased
guaranteeing that the disarray will never be deceased.
The situation begs for help. There's no need for no-power
I can reel in my control, thus blossoming the flower
that describes much more the me I am, not blocked and full of tension
so I can let my glory be, not leave me in suspension.

NOT CONTROLLING OTHERS

Some people dissipate enormous amounts of their time and energy exerting control over other people who are perfectly capable of doing well by themselves, given the freedom to do so. It is okay to stop doing that; retrieve your energy and become more integrated within yourself, as you retract from the territory of others. When you control others, or collude with them in the belief that you are *in control*, you are suddenly responsible for everything they do. After all, they only did it because of you. There is a huge albatross hanging around your neck, weighing you down.

It is okay. Instead, be supportive of others. Watch them as they, in their own way, at their own speed, and when they feel ready, take on the issues in their own lives. You can empathize with their fears, their sadness, their frustrations, while recognizing that all of this is not yours, that they have their own path to walk and their own time frame to do it in.

Their failures may motivate them. They may not. But they are not your failures. You can have compassion. Their successes? You can rejoice with them as they bring them in. Yet you can be clear that you have your own successes, and because of that, you do not need theirs. You can feel clearer, cleaner for having drawn your own boundary, leaving them to draw theirs.

The huge error is to be unresolved in your own emotions. You exert large amounts of energy sitting on that Pandora's box, and then trying this same *control method* on other people. Be more generous to yourself. Your feelings are okay, worthy of befriending and understanding. If your lawn needs cutting, you don't cut your neighbor's lawn! Save yourself some energy. Focus on number one.

People in positions of power and control over others can have a problem. If that is your lot in life, does your occupation interfere with your ability to sense the basic ingredients in life that make things work? Can you detect courage, goodwill, the compassion in key people that will smooth things out and bring home results? Resorting to power and control can be lonely. Holding just to that can foster mistrust. It is the fear ingredient in mistrust that is the killer. Is that basic rubble under your operation perpetuating an earthquake of your own making? What could you do to heal the fear element in any way? Can you reach out to make contact with others? Have you inadvertently been practicing not doing that?

A Loser in My Picture

If your life picture needs a loser
as you seek to fill it out
then in time you'll be that loser
as the whole thing turns about.
The loser that you play to
is the loser you'll become
as your attitude refuses
to stay underneath your thumb.
For the weakness you invite in
is a weakness you retain
what you send in expectation
turns to come around again.
So eradicate your weakness
seek to know and understand
where it came from, why you need it
what's the force that ties your hand.
With that understanding gathered
you release it to the wind
freeing up self-ties so binding
you, the lot of them rescind.

Jealousy

We say, "I feel jealous." Its pervasive nature affects us totally, body, emotional heart, and mind. It may be hard to recognize that the *feeling* arose more as an agenda, a piece of thinking from the mind.

The thinking involves an unfavorable comparison with another person: "I can't do what he does … I can't have what she has … I can't be who he is." The lateral pressure of this can interfere with or even cut off completely our natural tendency to grow, evolve, and expand in our own unique way.

Emotion is quickly added to the thought or thoughts. We may feel angry. We can add holding roots to that to form hatred or resentment. We may feel fear—fear that we will fail, never measure up, be rejected, or be forever inadequate. Fear, the crude oil of our humanity that takes us nowhere, can become rooted in body reactions like terror or solidified under a protective coating of anger, in hopes of driving away the supposed cause of the jealousy. If we want to be close to the person we are jealous of, our anger/fear can become a formidable stumbling block to achieving that closeness. We are already defeating ourselves, blocking closeness and walling in our fear of incompetence.

Deep (or not so deep) behind fear and anger, is sadness. Sadness that things became this way. Sadness that fear or anger were invoked. Sadness that even our natural ebullience and vitality were slowed down, even for an instant.

There is a way out of jealousy. Stop the comparisons. Stop the unfavorable actions. Stop the useless dissipation of energy.

Turn back. Turn back to the job of your life, the unique expansion as you evolve to become who you are designed to be. Then, you can cleanly and clearly take the next step along that path. You never were identical to someone else. There is work to be done, experience to be gained. The other guy has his own job to do. Yours is to be who you were designed—appropriately, beautifully—to be. Find ways to be grateful for that. Let your gratitude flow as the start of the river you will canoe happily for the rest of your life.

A definition of happiness: wanting what you have.

> *Be Yourself. Everyone else is already taken.*
>
> —Oscar Wilde

HEARTFELT CONTACT

When people share with you what they feel in the heart, they compliment you. They say to you, "I trust you with this personal information." If you take that confidence and blab it all over town, someone may use that information to punish the person. That person will not again trust you with what she feels.,

Tables and chairs, cars, computers, rocks, and grit—all of these are *things*, incapable of sharing a feeling or making emotional contact. When you trash the trust of someone, you reduce yourself to the *thing* level. You trash yourself. You cut the sapling to the ground. From then on, you crawl about, seeking value from life. By continuing not to value human emotional contact, you reduce yourself to groveling in gravel, sniffing the ground to find value in life. Such senseless activity can be instantly reversed any time you turn your heart back to on.

POURING OUT LOVE WHERE IT IS NOT APPRECIATED

Sometimes your teenage or fully grown son or daughter stays in the state of *needing to differentiate* (needing to become an independent adult), rather than simply owning his or her uniqueness. He or she makes the error that the best way to do that is to repel you by hurting you. Paradoxically, he or she doesn't make a clean break, but stay trapped in, close to you (to hurt you), in the name of moving away from you to make a life of his or her own.

You have always been a loving parent. You know love is good and that your young person needs love. You have a habit, developed over years of supporting the growing of that child, of providing that love yourself. You recognize that your offspring will need to get that love from friends, a mate, and that you won't be around, can't be around, forever, to provide it. Yet you have fears of letting go, just as your offspring has fears he or she won't be able to make it, to survive and get their needs met, out in the world. So both of you can be motivated by fear. This can guarantee ongoing pain and failure, in a repetitive cycle that goes nowhere. Being the more experienced one of the two of you, it can become your job to break the cycle.

Your first step to focus on is the *payoff*, the little thrill of I-win-you-lose that your son or daughter gets by going through the cycle one more time. This is his or her reward. This reward keeps the cycle attractive to him or her. Lacking experience at feeling powerful in his or her own life, they return to the consolation prize of having power to hurt you.

It is the fuss, the extra energy, that you invest that guarantees the cycle will continue. Cut that. No big "Why do you always do this to me?" No angry outbursts. No "poor me" playing.

Be calm. Be quiet. Figure things out. Make fresh choices.

In a like manner, be selective, with anyone, with the giving of your valuable advice. Do not assume automatically that someone in pain or in unfortunate circumstances is in need of what is in your brain rather than what is in his or her own brain.

Start with concern. If your warm interest reaches out, you may be able to detect warmth, gratitude, appreciation coming back. This two-way arm holding between you both can be the red carpet for the passage of many wonderful gifts between you both.

If, instead, you get the cold shoulder, such as swearing, or an icy look, do respect the message. It's "don't come close to me." This is not a situation for force-feeding someone, unless you are still needing to find out about how you bring punishing retaliations on yourself.

QUOTATION FROM SCRIPTURE

Do not give dogs what is sacred; do not throw your pearls to pigs. If you do, they may trample them under their feet, and then turn and tear you to pieces.

CHRISTIANITY: Matthew 7:6 NIV

TEENAGE SAFETY

Safety in numbers is so much the teen
eye contact with fellows no room in between.
The world of adults is their real rival
the name of the game is consistent survival
denied experienced understanding
the choice is to be underhanding.
That should make things safe, secure
'til we can feel more mature.

TEENAGERING

When a teenager's so trying
you can't be blamed for buying
that they're a pain
you can remain
in your state of justifying.
What you do not see's their straining
is what they are maintaining
to be alive
just to survive
so they'll end up remaining.
The teen has been a member
as long as (s)he'll remember
of family
so now (s)he'll see
what (s)he needs to dismember.
If ma(pa) lets separation
become the new relation
then those new ends
develop friends
transcending indignation.

CLOSENESS AND SEPARATION

It makes sense to love others, to be close to other people (those who want it), to relate, and to care—as well as to be separate when you need to. Be close. Give love to those who are capable of receiving it and who want it. Don't allow rejections to teach you that somehow your love is not valuable.

Moving away to be alone gives you time for processing, putting it back together before you make contact once more.

BE A FRIEND

Your friend is troubled. Your friend is worried and concerned. These things do not threaten you. This is your friend. It's your friend's problem, not yours. You can open your heart. You breathe in the weight your friend is carrying. You take her load. You take it all in. You watch what you are feeling in your heart.

In generosity, you give back your response. It may be compassion. It may be empathy or sympathy. It may be understanding. You want the best for your friend. You openly give your best.

Hopefully, your friend is open to what you give. The relaxing of your friend's face, the beginning of a smile are evidence of your friend's openness. But there is no guarantee of this.

Your friend's body may be physically tight. With such a lot of I-am-tight messages pounding on his brain, it may be impossible to receive your goodwill. Or perhaps your friend has a chatterbox mind that will not shut up. It is hard to hear your communication above her own internal noise. Either way, body or mind, your goodwill won't get through. In fact, these dual defense systems can alternate to block out the supposedly terrible situation of making true emotional contact.

Then you must be patient. Your friends are on their own time frame. It is not in your ability to determine if and when they will make the move toward the fullness of healthy contact.

EFFORT SAVED

Not bothering to ask, not bothering to enquire what is really behind what someone is wanting can set up a string of retaliatory problems. You need to correct your error. You can seek emotional contact by reaching out. If you don't, then *why-should-I-bother?* is the weed you are sowing. If two railway carriages don't lock into one another, they are both going nowhere together. Frustration and a wholesale belief in failing are what are being created.

> If you ask them what they want
> you can save yourself much effort
> for they undermine your effort
> by their lack of follow-through.
> How could they follow through
> with your showing such disinterest?
> Why bother is the message
> that they received from you.
> You weren't on the same wavelength!
> Back off. Use communication.
> The connection that you make
> lubricates what you both do.

PLEASERS

There are many people in this world who seem to have as their main function in life the job of making life feel better for other people. They delight in making life easier for others. The best ones have a deep understanding of love, a deep knowledge that love is the way to go. Their love greases the way and nourishes people. Others flock around to drink at their fountain.

There can be a downside to this. Some pleasers took on the job as children, in a dysfunctional environment with little love. They took care of other siblings and even the parents, who may not have been good at taking care of one another, let alone the family. These pleasers can believe, from their experience, that the flow of love goes out from them, away from them, never toward them. The urgency of meeting the family's needs for many years can become frozen in a fixed attitude of *not-for-me*. They are giving, but emotionally deprived themselves.

The physical model for this, the metaphor for it, is the human heart. Not the invisible, emotional heart but the physical pump. This gallant little instrument can do enough work in a lifetime to lift an ocean liner three feet out of the water. It pumps gallons of life-preserving blood to the entire body every day. The trickle it siphons off for itself is carried into the heart walls by the coronary arteries. It is not a lot. But take away that flow and the entire system fails, the heart suffers a coronary occlusion.

Some pleasers experience the metaphor in not only their physical heart, but also their emotional heart. They occlude their own flow, as is their policy. If you are such a person, notice the discrepancy. You love to give. You won't do much giving from six feet under. Begin to include the ounce of prevention (better than the pound of cure). Do something, one thing, each day that is just for yourself. If an over-critical part of you wants to call that selfish, give it a sleeping pill or a night out on the town. Then come back to *serving yourself.* This changes the nature of your pleaser role.

Switching to the opposite role, if you are warming yourself from the radiance of a pleaser, raise your eyes. See the face. Is this wonderful person at risk of being taken advantage of? You don't have to stay in the sucky-baby position: getting yours and then doing a cut-and-run. It might strike a useful balance for *you* to find a way to be loving to such a good person. Don't force-feed them. They may, out of their own habit, object. But can you at least be considerate?

If you need a helping hand, look at the end of your own arm.

—Audrey Hepburn

HEALING PLEASER PATHOLOGY

Being a pleaser
can be a way
to stop being a connector.
With the mind in charge
a dead agenda:
to be pleasing
replaces
the sharing of living feelings.
At the insistence
of a dominating mind
pushing the agenda
is substituted for
reaching out with a feeling
to connect to someone.
Also at the mind's insistence
live feelings are stuffed
into the body
which becomes so full, eventually
that suffering ensues.
The mind, the mess-maker
wins.
You lose.
Retrieve your life.
Steadily, insistently
tell your mind what you expect.
In the meantime
increase the warmth in your words
as you decrease the pleasing.
Warm and alive
replaces
cold and forced.

PLEASING IS UNCOMFORTABLE WITH SOMEONE WHO IS REAL

Pleasing is uncomfortable with someone who is real.
They won't accept the role, too tight, for they're the ones who feel.
All people can be real, but some aren't doing it quite yet
what you put out comes 'round, it converts to what you get.
The narrowness of playing roles may satisfy some others
for *they* are into playing a role, and all of these are brothers.
Don't bring a role, it can be hurtful to someone who is real
you'll run aground, you'll mess up, as you're challenged by their zeal.

PERFECT

It is okay to do a good job without having to be perfect. On one occasion 95 percent may be necessary, while on another 78 percent may be quite adequate. And if something low on the priority list gets 23 percent, let it be. You can't do everything at once. It will have its day.

Perfection-thinking can blind you. When only perfection can be seen, the small improvements that can build steadily to a fine result pass tragically unnoticed.

Question: What do you do with a standard that is too high?

Suppose you have polished what you have been doing to a nice shine. Then you put on an extra coat of polish "for good measure." And now you are considering polishing the polished polish. You're going to far.

What do you do with a punishingly high standard that drains you of your efforts to a point of exhaustion and uses up too much time?

Answer: Lower the standard. Be able to say "Enough is enough."

Use what talents you possess
The woods would be very silent if no birds sang there
except those that sang the best.

—Anon.

PERFECTION IS

Perfection-thinking's down the tubes
perfection-thinking's cold ice cubes
perfection-thinking only freezes
holding tightly, simply squeezes.
Perfection-thinking leads to blindness
unawareness makes unkindness
standards that were made too high
free them, let them learn to fly.
Too much polish weighs things down.
In too-high standards you can drown.
Rise above your putrid task.
What is left then, you can ask.
Being perfect is an art
being in charge sets you apart
run the show, it can't run you
all you'll do is self-renew.

NOT PERFECT

Judge: You are charged with not having been perfect in everything you did. How do you plead?

Accused: Guilty, your honor.

Judge: Guilty as charged! And for this heinous offense, you are sentenced to go into this world and be yourself.

Accused: Oh, no! No, your honor. Anything but that. Couldn't you put me on death row or something?

Judge: What gives you the right? How can you take the life God gave you and trash it so readily? What is so wrong with what you have?

Accused: Well, no one told me it was good. I've been laughed at, ignored, used, and abused. I have been trying to be perfect to bridge the gap, to become worthy of recognition by doing a perfect job. But no one seems to care, or even to notice. What's the use?

Judge: Did it ever seem to you that these uncaring people had problems? Do you think any one of them truly saw you?

Accused: They didn't know me.

Judge: Why not?

Accused: They didn't ask. They didn't care, even when I shared what I really felt.

Judge: Why didn't they?

Accused: I think they were too tied up in themselves. They couldn't see past that.

Judge: So you've been using a series of blind people to find out how best to see yourself?

Accused: I have, haven't I …

Judge: Perhaps I should charge you with *mal-cooperation*.

Accused: No. No. I'll choose better people.

Judge: Go. And do not darken my door again.

DRAWING OUT

"You bring out the best in me," you say to one person.

"You bring out the worst in me," you say to another.

"When I'm challenged, I rise to the occasion." Each situation then builds your confidence.

We all experience other people, other situations, in unique ways. Some can seem like magnets to us. They invite us strongly to react in certain ways. They pull on us, draw us out.

In a similar way, we are magnets. We have a *presence* that pulls on people, pulls on situations. Cartoonist Al Capp acknowledged this in his "Li'l Abner" cartoon. His character Joe Btfsplk would walk across in the background with his own private cloud raining just on him! Everyone else was out in sunshine. We can be amazed to come across folks who always seems to have bad luck. And then we hear of one more bad thing that happens to them. On the other hand, we can admire, even envy those for whom things always seem to go right. They may plan well, stay organized. But the average quota of bad things seems to bypass them. That's not just planning.

The TV documentary on the 9/11 attacks on the World Trade Center, introduced by actor Robert De Niro, focused on the New York City Fire Department. They understand two classes of firefighters: white clouds and dark clouds. White clouds are those firemen who are consistently ill or on days off when the dangerous fires break out. The new recruit, the original focus of the documentary, was having a day off on September eleventh. He nevertheless showed up to make himself useful. This type of draw-out shows a balance, a coordination between person and event. He is in-sync with what is going on (synchronicity is a sophisticated ongoing form of the one-step draw-out.)

Use your drawing card. Consciously watch what you do to pull things to you ("I knew that would happen"). Raise your consciousness. Take conscious control of your life. In particular, watch your *expectations*. These mischief-makers can blight our lives until we bring them under conscious control.

Expect well! Expect a good result. Correct errors of expecting things to go wrong, into expecting, imaging, picturing things going right. You may wish to allow for other possibilities; cover all the bases. (You don't want to be caught out). But set your sights clearly. What you see, what you look for, is what you'll get. It is happening already. Mixed motives blur that. You are merely raising the percentages. You can only improve.

HEAD PUPPETS

Each person in our memory holds the sum total of our experiences with that person. No one else had that identical set of experiences with the same person. A man has children who know him as a father, a wife who knows him as her husband, parents who knew him as their little boy, an employer who knows him as an employee, and friends with varying common interests who each draw him out in different ways. Each of us get a slice of the pie. No one gets the whole man. He does not even get that himself. (It is hard to see yourself clearly, wholly, easier to take feedback from someone about the slice they have of you. Ensure this is someone you trust if you want accurate feedback.)

So we carry in our heads a personal puppet of each person we know. Our puppet is unique, not the same as anyone else's puppet of that person. So two people can disagree about a third. One finds him terrible. Another calls him his best friend.

Recognize the head-puppet nature of your *angle* on each person you meet. Reach out beyond your angle, your pie slice of each person. Understand you are not getting the full picture. Expect more and you may get it!

Every person is complex. You are complex. It is one of the wonders of life to explore that complexity. Be a Swiss army knife, with ever one more instrument of your own to display, given the opportunity. Become excited about that. You have more on the ball than you may give yourself credit for.

Each personal head puppet that we keep is independent of the person the head puppet represents. The person herself may undergo a lot of changes. Yet our head puppet of her can stay the same. Or the person may refuse to change and never change. Yet we can upgrade and evolve his head puppet—because it is *our* head puppet—much the same as we would evolve any other part of ourselves, such as an unwanted habit. We can also upgrade people who have died, in our heads. They are *our* head puppets. If we had an unpleasant experience with this person or that, we can upgrade that experience too. If we loved them and miss them, we can upgrade them into a constant presence: "I know now that my father will always be with me."

You are only limited by what you will allow.

Over months, as your readiness expands, you may achieve this healing and upgrading through the meditations. There are many ways you can learn to exchange a negative version of a person or experience for an evolved understanding, a positive version that increases your ability to love rather than hindering it.

ENGAGEMENT: IF IN DOUBT, COMMUNICATE

If you are in doubt as to whether to talk to someone, talk to them. Talking has the possibility of making contact and sharing information, with the potential positive effects contact and information can have. Two people persisting in talking with one another, even when they don't intend it, sooner or later show a spark of humanity. They engage. The two fire sticks rubbing together lead on to a fanning of the life force. Something *real* happens. From that point on, all sorts of wonderful possibilities become available, despite any attempts by the intentions of the thinking process to contain, control, and exclude them.

Communicating *now* also forestalls future regret: "If only I had spoken up. Why didn't I say anything? Why do I repeatedly fail to take the courage to say what is on my mind?"

People cannot know what they have not been told. How often have you thought to yourself, "What a stupid thing to do!" when seeing someone else in action. Then you think a little deeper. You realize that the person doing the "stupid" thing lacked a key piece of information. Had they known that, there is no way they would have made the error.

(If you enjoy seeing people make mistakes, you may need some therapy for your problem: having to have *losers in your environment*. What goes around will come around).

So you communicated. See what happens. Did things work out? Did all hell break loose? Look back. The title reads "If in Doubt, Communicate." Did you know all along what was going to happen? Do you sometimes dull your senses, block your awareness, and so allow disaster? What steps can you take toward solving that?

For couples struggling with communication, a big stumbling block is often anger.

TELL ME

It would help if you would tell me
if you're wanting me to know
with your help I could see clearly
the way I need to go.
But if you do not tell me
you make sure I do not know
guarantee I will make messes
obstructing my own flow.
If indeed you tell me
what I do is up to me
you cannot force my hand
for that would not leave me free.
If I then take what you tell me
distort it in my way
and turn on you in anger
make my style live one more day
I should know your hesitation
to speak to me at all
comes from knowing what's my problem
what I need to overhaul.

OVERCOMING A PREVIOUS RELATIONSHIP

In the old mystery movie *Laura,* the hero's wife, Laura, had died, and he has remarried. But a picture of Laura stands on the vanity, as well as standing in the way of his developing a full relationship with his new wife.

If you are in a similar situation, and if you want to achieve a full relationship with your new partner, you need to do some work. The work is the job of mourning the loss of your former partner. It can be hard work, because a part of you keeps saying that the primary relationship, the *important* relationship, is with the old partner. It is as if you are having a *ménage à trois.* Every time you go to bed with your new partner, your old partner sits in between you, *as you see it.* With the holding on tight to a past that is no longer responsive, this bears the hallmarks of the controlling, imprisoning, thinking mind.

You must do your work. Otherwise, you remain forever in the past, in a situation that can no longer respond, though it may have once. You remain unaware, rendered incapable by your own dereliction, of receiving delicious emotional warmth in the present, from a partner well able to respond from a full awareness that you do not share.

PRINCIPLES

Introduction
Setting Yourself Up
Float Along Those Chores
Pulling Yourself Up by Your Own Bootstraps
Balance
Balancing Communication
Sleep Inducers
Breathe In, Breathe Out
Succeed
Quick Successes for Failure
Smell the Roses
What You See Is What You Get
Responsibility
Mind-Blind Confined
Do You Mind?
Building Storm-Water Channels: Making Practical Use of Good Intentions
Getting It Right Completely
The Way That You Do It
The Puppy Principle
Forty Percent
Okay World
Concerned
Relay Race, Modeling Clay, and Handicap Horse Race
Quotations from Scriptures
Gold in Potatoes
Sustainable Behavior
Life Lengtheners
Parenting Self
Paradigms and Boxes
Fishing Metaphor
Apples from Hardware Stores?
The Attention Demander

Warren Douglas Phegan

Giving Your Power Away
Do You Mind
Venting or Head-Tripping
I Learned Patience

INTRODUCTION

Principles. This is the last section of this book. In some books it is the first section. In the best of these, it becomes a tour guide, a plan of how to negotiate the territory when you travel to another land, or a way of assembling the ingredients as you become a better cook.

But this book is about people, about people having experiences. Putting the principles section first would run the risk of prioritizing facts. The dry fact is upgraded when you look within it for the human experience. The dry dust, watered, yields living flowers and trees.

So we put principles last. Yet each of the articles here has distinctly human aspects. Further, the sequencing of the articles makes logical sense. A line is developed a certain way, then left while another line is begun. It should be no surprise then that, at the end of a book titled *Love Is Power*, love becomes the point made.

Principles lie behind the construction of this whole book. In this separated existence we call life, there is the advantage of being able to formulate principles to help us use the gift of the space–time continuum. You can start with a good breakfast, physically as food and emotionally as well. Maintenance keeps things rolling. It does require action. You must actually do something. Above all, seek balance in what you do. "Unbalanced" is a common word for insanity. And if you would balance, be balanced with your primary relationship.

The physical body is the gift we use to do these things. It goes naturally at a slow speed, despite apparent evidence to the contrary, as in running. Yet even after that, a rest, perhaps sleep, will help you recuperate. Through it all, you must breathe. The body's vital need is life-giving oxygen. The overall aim is to succeed. Failure can be turned around. Select roses over weeds.

Perception is everything. As comedian Flip Wilson used to say, "What you see is what you get!" Full awareness rises beyond narrow seeing. Maturing involves being responsible; the mind can hold onto belief systems that cancel out awareness. You are responsible for not letting it.

The value of practice to get it right is illustrated in "Building Storm-Water Channels: Making Practical Use of Good Intentions," as it is in the poem "Getting It Right Completely." All roads lead to love.

It is often far easier than you think. Save your energy. In the long haul, your capacity to stay with the task will get the job done. Again, this may be easier than you first thought. Slow and steady wins the race. As you do all this, recognize the error built into seeing the world as anything less than an okay place.

Be concerned. Risk being that open. You will gain enormously by practicing doing that.

"Relay Race, Modeling Clay, and Handicap Horse Race" comprises three principles into one article. Each is a valuable way to look at life and to overcome discouragement. Problems can be hand-me-downs from previous generations. Things are not always as they seemed at first appearances.

Assumed by a number of the above principles is that what you are doing is sustainable. Being aware of what you feel is a good perception for lengthening your life. Throughout, you take care of yourself.

Sometimes what is needed is to think outside the box. In the area of using just enough energy, the "Fishing Metaphor" says it all.

Looking once again at what you have always done can remove old discouraging ways of seeing life.

Someone demanding our attention can become infuriating—if we choose that reaction. You can be proactive and set it up on your terms. Children are very aware of not having power. They become familiar with giving it away. Grown-ups can retain childhood patterns. You can rise above that; again, be proactive and set it up on your terms. Mischief mind, intent on retaining the status quo, can be the source of retaining patterns. We'll also examine mind-dominance from other points of view. Patience is the recommended strategy for letting the array that is life slowly assemble itself.

Principles abound in *Love Is Power*. Scarcely a page can be turned that does not have a principle underlying it. These are here to help readers grab them easily.

SETTING YOURSELF UP

A good breakfast is the recommended way to start your day—lots of energy and vitamins for the work and activity ahead. But you are human. You have feelings. It is the nutritious, caring emotions you need to start your day: supportive love, understanding, empathy, and other warm emotions. These are far more useful than the emotional junk food we so often chew on: fear, anger, and hatred. Find ways to give and to get for yourself emotional warmth. It is an exchange process.

FLOAT ALONG THOSE CHORES

We all have to do chores. There are always maintenance things to be done. They carry on the successful operation of a business. They ensure the family keeps functioning.

"I hate to do chores!" is the common complaint from a child. How often do you hear the child inside yourself say exactly those words? Hatred is a poor path to walk. You slip and slide over gravel and rocks no matter how tight you keep every muscle. It is exhausting walking backward when you want to go forward.

Try floating along. Canoe the river of your goodwill and love. Feel the bounce and rhythm of the song "Whistle While You Work" from *Snow White and the Seven Dwarfs*. Feel the flavor of "Don't Worry, Be Happy," from musician Bobby McFerrin. Don't be the stern teacher standing over the terrified pupil issuing a command. Let that go. That way doesn't work. Feel your love. Let it flow. Then ride that river.

Let this be the basis of your day, the way you live. Not that every moment has to follow a prescription. Don't be the stern teacher. If you are fully alive, you will feel many things, face a variety of situations as the day evolves. But always be able to return, to canoe the river of your warm emotions. Have a cupful of that healing water available for yourself, for others, as needed.

PULLING YOURSELF UP
BY YOUR OWN BOOTSTRAPS

In order to do it
you have to start doing it.
There'll be no history
if it doesn't start.
It isn't hard
to do something one time
you simply see it
then think it and do it
then it's behind you
you've made it a fact.
Doing it once
jumps you over the speed bump
now you are rolling
so do it again.
Now you've done it twice
that wasn't so difficult
you gather momentum
to smooth the third time.
Remember what happened
make notes, celebrate it.
You're now in action
from here it's downhill.

BALANCE

Balance is beautiful. Your face illustrates this. The face that has one side balanced off by the other is what we perceive as beautiful. The face with one side much different from the other invokes fear, only because it is unbalanced.

Always balance. See the elements of what is going on. Ignore none of them, lest the one you ignore becomes the one that trips you. Move forward, but always in a balanced way. The weight lifter does best when the weights at one end of the bar match those at the other end. The power is at the middle. The lift that is balanced is the lift that succeeds. With practice, you perfect.

We classically underachieve. We are capable of much more, if we would just take the grind out of what we are doing. Changing our attitude to others can have a huge effect on what we become able to do.

So things are tight for a while. An ongoing Dagwood sandwich of things packed into your life can put powerful pressure on you to stay focused, but you can do it. You don't have to burn out. Your potential is enormous, just waiting to be tapped.

The person caught up in burnout can bring to himself immediate relief. Don't imagine for a moment that what you have been doing is the only way to go.

That's the problem with habits. They become addictive. It is as if the habit was saying, "I'm the only game in town." It isn't. Don't put up with such nonsense; see "Changing an Old Habit Using Healing Emotions."

Soak in the possibilities of changing habits; use healing emotions as if you were taking a delicious bath. Bring joy back into your life.

Situations can be demanding. If you have to go excessively in one direction for a while, you can always return to balance it later.

Liberal use of the warm friendly emotions in any problem situation by all concerned moves the situation toward balance. Love and goodwill have this power. Moving over to a loving way of operating keeps you right-side up, focused, aware. The presence of such warm emotion from each individual offering it has this righting, balancing property.

The warm emotion tends to act on the rock-in-the-river aspect of a fixed attitude, moving it toward the status of floating debris and no longer such a problem. This it does by acting on the fear that so often drives the attitude, refining and upgrading this crude-oil fuel to more competent levels. Your household pet can be a living breathing demonstration of this power.[3,4] The actual situation will then work out as it needs to.

There is an overlap between the human qualities of being centered, being balanced, and being grounded that is way beyond the simplicity of *things* photographable, *things* grabbed by gravity.

The back-up-against-the-wall feeling into which we can feel forced is a weak place to be. We can feel hopeless and without choice, neither of which are true. The back-up-against-the-wall was just an old habit we were repeating. It often involves fear or anger feelings, unless you can apply acceptance.

Prefer to take charge of yourself and your reactions. Move your back away from the wall. Find the weight lifter's middle point. Be able to face left or right and experience both possibilities. Breathe easily. Relax. Have power.

As you seek balance in your life, as you repeatedly look for that middle point, you will find dross dropping away. Excesses are not needed. You develop the light touch that does things with ease and does them well.

BALANCING COMMUNICATION

You tell me how it is for you
you can't say how it is for me
when you ask, then I can tell
then we're balanced very well.

SLEEP INDUCERS

This book is a smorgasbord of chewable pieces for life. Each piece of *Love Is Power* taken in as new practice produces a feeling of relaxation and peace in the body. The body is slow by nature. It needs rest to catch up to the state set up by the new practice. As you take time during the day to practice those pieces of *Love Is Power* that work for you, take a little extra time afterward to rest. You may need that. Genuine psychological work done carefully is demanding of time, effort, and attention. This can be exhausting. You deserve rest after such expenditure. If you are awake in the night, *Love Is Power* can get you back to sleep.

If the body is having an uptight reaction to the novelty of *Love Is Power*, the threat of change, you may need to extend compassion and understanding directly to the body. Such empathy can help the body to relax. Then you may sleep.

BREATHE IN, BREATHE OUT

Breathing is vital to life. The oxygen we take in burns sugars in the body, creating warmth and energy. The next time you hear someone say, "I feel terrible," see if they have stopped breathing. Holding the breath can give us that momentary suffocation, our contribution to the "terrible." We're saying, in effect, that if terrible has to happen, we will gain some sense of control by contributing to it. If you can't beat them, join them. Right?

Wrong! We need to understand situations so as to gain control of our responses and contribute usefully. Understanding can become impossible if we are not only feeling terrible, but compounding the problem by suffocating ourselves.

Breathe. Breathe slowly. Breathe gently. Not so hard and fast that you turn your chest into a pressure can, forcing back the low-pressure blood trying to return to the chest to pick up oxygen for another tour of the body. At times of stress, make sure enough oxygen is supplied to your body to make it an ally in the situation, rather than a dead weight. Correct bad breathing habits by good practice.

Then use breathing to be a metaphor for handling life. When you breathe in, you take in oxygen and other unwanted ingredients. When you breathe out, you breathe out both what you didn't want to tolerate, plus carbon dioxide, a waste product from your body.

Turn your head to the left. Breathe in. Breathe in your past, your history, all the things you have been up until now. Feel your body taking from it all that is useful.

Turn your head to the right. Breathe out all the waste, all that you never needed. Feel it leaving you cleansed, refreshed, free to do what you need to do.

Do this exercise many times a day, every day. You deserve nothing less.

SUCCEED

It is okay to succeed. It's okay to set goals and, better still, to reach them. It's exciting to discover your expanding potential. It is great to put together, piece by piece, a growing, moving picture of the story of your success.

Eighty percent of success is showing up.

—Woody Allen

QUICK SUCCESSES FOR FAILURES

So you think of yourself as a failure. You've been doing that for years. You believe it. Others believe it—particularly those you have convinced. We can build a convincing picture if we plan it well, turn all our thoughts in the same direction, and add in the pieces of behavior that fit the picture.

These things create a mess. Are you happy with the mess? Would you like to continue it? For how long? Are you punishing yourself for something? How much more punishment do you figure you need? Are you having fun yet?

Would you be willing to do something that might turn this broken-down road show around? Would you be willing to accept something less than instant, total success? When would you start? How about right now?

What you need is some quick successes. They don't have to be huge. They do have to be observable as successes, something you would accept as a success. You need to stock your memory with these. It is already overstocked with the opposite. You need no more of those.

Is it alright for you to succeed at reading one page? Could you allow that in? You succeeded at getting up this morning. There are some people who cannot do that.

Begin small. Do any little thing. Then say, "I did it! I succeeded! This is me in action!" Say it out loud. That is your mouth speaking to your ears. They need new input.

Buy a blank book you can keep in your pocket. Title it *Successes* and write down any and all your daily successes in it. Small successes help at first: *I succeeded at making a shopping list. I succeeded at telling someone something. I succeeded at completing this task, that task.* Build the list.

Then, when you are feeling down, open your book. Drink in the encouragement you have written. Recycle your successes.

SMELL THE ROSES

Smell the roses. Don't chase weeds.
The positive is what succeeds.

WHAT YOU SEE IS WHAT YOU GET

With thanks to comedian Flip Wilson

What you see
is what you get
what you picture
you attract.
You pick out
from what's around you
things to which
you give importance.
All the others
you let go.
They are not there.
They don't exist.
Then you look
at your collection
rocks and cushions
mixed together.
Rocks can block
and irritate you
challenge you
to rise above them.
Cushions, lying there
support you
stroke your life
for better coping
nourish, recognize
enrich you
they are people
understanding.
Rocks are people
irritating
those who will not
get it right
challenging
your way of being
calling you
to rise above them
with support
from welcome cushions
nourishing
your way of being.
Challengers

225

can truly help you
giving light
to your reactions
leave behind
the crud within you
as you rise
to stronger levels
nourished by
supporting cushions
feeling freedom's
loving presence.

RESPONSIBILITY

"I didn't do it."

"I didn't mean to do it."

"The devil made me do it."

Responsibility involves a balanced use of memory, full awareness, and self-control—managing the thinking mind and the agitation it can invoke inside of us.

As we progress along life's path, we can collect a series of holding and blocking strategies. These were each designed as a quick fix for a problem that may well have been unsolvable at the time. But the strategies, well represented in the physical body in which we feel a steady build-up of lack of freedom, add up to a prison. The prison is metaphorical even though it involves the body. There is no real prison. But it does drain a lot of life energies to maintain the tension implied in the metaphor. This living reality can leave us feeling tired, exhausted, with an accompanying sense of weakness, powerless to deal with life.

The thinking mind is a participant. With its ability to set up an incessant, draining monologue, it can mastermind holding and blocking out. When this has built to obsessive or psychotic levels, there has been such a progressive giving up of life energy, that it can seem to be irretrievable. A life of weakness and incompetence can appear to be the only option.

A life of healing can resemble walking on a beach in search of seashells. We clean and identify, one by one, the holding and blocking strategies. We consciously release them, recognizing that the patterns of behavior may have become arthritic. They may not instantly release the moment we recognize them. It may take a number of attempts, extending over time.

Meanwhile, an underlying river of supportive warm emotions in ourselves and in those we choose as travelling compassions can ease our passageway. If we allow within ourselves compassion and forgiveness for the holding we have been doing, if we can receive warmth and understanding from well-meaning others instead of repeating old block-it-all-out choices, we set up for ourselves a light at the end of the tunnel. This light becomes the goal we aim for, in our move toward freedom, joy, and enlightenment. We take responsibility for past choices, for presently refreshing choices. We make no attempt to offload responsibility for actions we have taken or attitudes to which we have held. We are not, by our own habit, in need of offloading responsibility for our actions onto someone else.

Holding and blocking strategies can restrict us to childlike levels of incompetence. It is hard to be mature and responsible for our thoughts and our statements, as well as what we do, when we feel restricted and childlike. Releasing the restrictions, cleaning the seashells, allows us to expand, to *grow up* in the way we deal with life. We become capable, mature individuals, trustworthy for our abilities to discern and be responsible.

MIND-BLIND CONFINED

Mind
you have me mesmerized
because of you
I can't see past
what you'd have me believe.
Your actions
make me blind
to what is going on.
Because of how
you rush and pressure me
I cannot smell the roses.
You deprive me
isolate me
confine me
with your fear
to the prison
in which you hope
I'll be safe.

DO YOU MIND?

The joke went as follows: The ship's physician had forty different medications for the forty commonest ailments. If the patient had disease #2, he would give him medication #2. If the patient had disease #8, he would give medication #8. If the patient had disease #10, but the doctor was out of medication #10, he would give him #2 and #8.

That joke is easy to understand. There is no logical connection between human ailments and a numbering system. Yet we laugh. As in the article "You Can't Get There From Here," we are again looking at the difference between *experiencing life* and the culled, fragmented expression of that in words: the *functioning of the mind*. You would not appreciate it if someone suggested cutting off your head and limbs and then sewing them back together. The process that is the way of logic does disservice to the life it is trying to represent. The abstract (unreal) does not replace the *real*.

If a couple in a troubled marriage separate from one another, they give themselves the chance to find out what is real. *Do they love one another or do they not?* If they don't, there is nothing there, nothing that is a real basis for a human relationship.

They may choose to have a marriage of convenience, a business arrangement. But without that solid heartfelt connection, they remain always at risk to drift apart.

In a like manner, many a failing marriage needs the feeding of the sharing of emotions, in a heartfelt process of connecting to one another. This is not having sex. The body doing it is not where the living power lies. That occurs from *heart* to *heart*.

227

BUILDING STORM-WATER CHANNELS: MAKING PRACTICAL USE OF GOOD INTENTIONS

Act healthy first and pick up the garbage later

—Eric Berne

You long to be able to do a particular thing smoothly and well, and to feel good about it as you do it. But you are not there yet. You don't have a feel for it. That will take time. For now, all you can do is go through the motions.

It is like building a storm-water channel. You lay down the pieces of pipe partly submerged in the ground, with spaces between them so water can run in to join the flow down the pipe. But there is no water. There is no flow.

Then one day, it storms. Now there is reason for the pipe. The water floods down the well-prepared passageway.

Practice is like that. Fake it until you make it. Well before you have a feel for it, you are getting it right, doing it over and over again the correct way. Then one day the penny drops! Now, the feeling floods through it. It has taken on the vitality, the reality you had been hoping for.

Part of the mind does not understand the difference between *doing* something and *thinking* you are doing it. So you can be bedridden. Still you can build storm-water channels. You merely picture yourself going through the paces. If indeed you are bedridden, you can do much more than lie there. You can move yourself toward healing. If your friend is in a coma, know that people in a coma can hear. Read to your comatose friend this page. Read "The Illness Paradox." Look for tiny movements that signal understanding. The movements may guide you to further articles if you grow to understand movement language.

GETTING IT RIGHT, COMPLETELY

I wanted to get it right
so I practiced getting it right
and though I practiced
and I practiced
still it didn't feel I was
getting it right.
Then one day it happened
I practiced getting it right
and when I least expected it
the feeling flooded in.
Now it felt like it was right!
I had gotten my act together.

THE WAY THAT YOU DO IT

It's not what you do
it's the way that you do it.
It's not what you think
it's the way that you swing it.
It's not what you feel
it's the way that you show it.
All roads lead to love.

THE PUPPY PRINCIPLE

If you chase a puppy, it runs away. The more you chase it, the further it runs. It thinks it's a game. You never catch it. If you stop chasing the puppy, it comes right up to you and licks you on the leg. You have the puppy.

There are many situations in life like that. There are times when no effort is required. Effort is counterproductive. Any effort you put in turns around to bite you. You must let it be. You must let it go. If your helping hand becomes your strangling hand, you must stop the helping to stop the strangulation.

This seems to fly in the face of the Golden Rule: Do unto others as you would have them do unto you. Do nothing … and get benefits?!

Life is larger. Some things are bigger than the narrowness of our thinking, the restrictions of our best intentions, the length of our reach. The lasso with which we would catch them falls short, doesn't catch anything, merely strangles the situation. Our efforts are not needed. Things will work out. If we had loving intentions behind doing unto others, we must let it be, in love. Our empathy is the length of our useful reach. Reaching further is merely mess making. Reach out with goodwill. Extra may mean intrusion.

Parents face this with teenagers. They want to be a good parent, when the biological urge of the teenager is to break away and start a new life, a new and different family. The parental job is done. Where there was a parent to a child, there now needs to be a friend to friend. Both may find the new role difficult at first. With practice all around, it can work.

If you tell a friend what to do, you may lose your friend. The telling is not friendly. It is *true* friendliness that is the healer. Can you be a friend without telling? It is the urge to control, to be able to say to yourself, *Look how wonderfully I did* that you are renouncing. Your friends need to work out their own problems. Your brain can never replace theirs. Empathy is a vastly better alternative.

You need to be their friend. You cannot do their wanting. They must do that. Some people are too preoccupied with themselves to be friendly and responsive. Do not frustrate yourself with your own friendship energy. Keep it available. Spend it wisely—where it is accepted.

FORTY PERCENT

The pamphlet in the bicycle shop asks the question, "How can a long-distance cyclist keep going and cover all those miles/kilometers?" The answer—the cyclist pedals at 40 percent of his or her capacity.

At 40 percent you can carry on forever. You are never pushed. You can speed up to 50 percent, slow down to 30 percent, return to 40 percent. There is no strain. The person who goes at 85 percent, speeds up to 95 percent or 100 percent, eventually collapses. It is 0 percent for a while. That is also harder on the body. Forty percent just cruises on by. There is a life message in this.

It is the story of the "Hare and the Tortoise" all over again. The tortoise wins. The moral is slow and steady wins the race. Look around you at the people who have achieved something in their lives. How many are the flashy, dashy spectaculars? Did they stall quickly? How many are those who kept their eye on the goal and worked steadily toward it?

Forty percent is sustainable. Time passes. The long haul reels in the results. Your body approves of that. It will work along with you. If your sudden extreme forces are part of a pattern of self-abuse to your body, they will stop you in your tracks. With severe illness, you will achieve the 0 percent you have been working toward.

Speed and rushing are unfortunately still fashionable as the new millennium revs on. Put your efforts into the 40 percent rule as your contribution to a better "New Age."

Okay World

The world really is an okay place. You don't have to see some bad things and believe that the world itself is bad. It is okay to find out where you belong in the world. Be the amoeba reaching out sensitively to make contact, as you become the jigsaw piece that has found its niche in the living, moving puzzle of life.

Concerned

It's important to be concerned with the world, with all existence—but not worried. Let worry go. Concern is your reaching out from the heart, not corralled by a mental process, an attitude that is supposed to make you safe, but instead imprisons you. Allow concern to float out from you in a free fashion. You will find that relaxing. It is freeing for you to do that.

Relay Race, Modeling Clay, and Handicap Horse Race

The human race is a relay race. Each generation runs a certain distance; then passes the baton on to the next generation. They take the baton from that point and run a further distance.

Another way of saying the same thing is this: There is a room with a table in it on which is placed pieces of modeling clay. People come in through doors, go to the table, work on the clay (shaping it for a while), and then leave. The next generation comes in and shapes the clay further. Some people go sit in the corner and do nothing for the clay. Others may try to smash it. But over time, the actions of several generations work the clay into a nice shape. The clay represents a problem that the family has taken on.

Individuals react to the problems life has presented to them in different ways. Sometimes the reaction borders on resentment: "Why me? The guy next door doesn't have half the problems I have. Why do I have to deal with all this stuff?"

An interesting answer to the apparent unfairness, lies in the concept of the Handicap Horse Race. The stronger, faster horses are given lead weights in the saddle—and perhaps a heavier jockey. The idea is to have all the horses cross the finish line nose-to-nose. If you find life has presented you with extra things to deal with, maybe you are one of the better horses!

Sometimes a patient will say to his or her psychiatrist, "Why me? The person next door doesn't have half the problems I have. Why is all this happening to me? Am I being victimized by God?"

The psychiatrist can reply, "No. You are not being victimized. Don't look at it that way. Prefer to see it as a challenge. Take courage and rise to the occasion. Maybe you are one of the better horses!"

QUOTATIONS FROM SCRIPTURES

For I the Lord thy God am a jealous God, visiting the iniquity of the fathers upon the children unto the third and fourth generation of them that hate me.

JUDAISM: Exodus 20:5 KJV

He punishes the children and their children for the sin of the fathers to the third and fourth generation.

JUDAISM: Exodus 34:7 NIV

The Lord is long suffering, and of great mercy, forgiving iniquity and transgression, and by no means clearing the guilty, visiting the iniquity of the fathers upon the children unto the third and fourth generation.

JUDAISM: Numbers 14:18 KJV

GOLD IN POTATOES

An old man, as he was dying, told his sons there was a pot of gold buried in the field he owned. It was theirs for the taking.

The sons dug up the field from one end to the other. No pot of gold did they find. All they had was a dug-up field. Then it occurred to one of them that they could plant potatoes. They had a bumper crop! *That* was their pot of gold. The riches they had sought were there for the taking. It wasn't in the form first thought of.

Life is like that. There are many riches to be had from life. Sometimes it comes in a form different from the way we first conceived it. Money, for all its advantages, can be shooting for the lowest of the low. We can develop a habitually narrowing tightness to the way we approach situations. If we are not plagued with *holding* actions, we are more free to feel the full joy of what we achieve. We lift it out of the mud of the physical, out of the realm of money, things, possessions and into a realm that is living.

That is where the glow is to be found. That is what enriches and strengthens you for the rest of your life. That is what can connect you in deeper ways to others who are capable of giving you genuine living responses.

SUSTAINABLE BEHAVIOR

It is important for each of us in every moment to be involved to some degree in behavior that is sustainable. We have such power to do things large and small that are *not* sustainable. When our actions destroy our own self, *we* become the unsustainable. Destruction as a way of life, a lifestyle, goes against the positive, striving nature of our vitality. We drop a rock in the water and watch ripples of destruction extend and extend until their backlash returns to us from the far side of the lake.

We readily destroy language by lying. That removes language as a reliable course. Which statement of the habitual liar is the lie? It can be exhausting figuring it out. Trying to get value out of the tattered clothes of a language so destroyed is not worth the effort. Lying as a habit is not sustainable.

If you launch a career of lying, your mind must exhaustingly do double-duty. To whom did you tell which lie? If you are now talking about it, what statement must you make that will not give up the lie to the previous statement? Quickly. Quickly. Think. Think. Pressure, pressure leads on to exhaustion or to anger, from trying to repel the questions.

We destroy forests, our atmosphere, the beauty of our planet with actions that are not sustainable. In our excited rush to stand on one another's faces, we destroy the one thing that is being asked of us in the global village: the skill to manage and sustain long-term human relationships in an environment that will sustain us.

LIFE-LENGTHENERS

Feelings
are expressions
of aliveness.
If someone
covers up
what they feel
you cannot know them.
To you
they are dead.
If they continue
to cover
what they feel
from everyone
they progressively
deaden themselves.
You cannot live
for very long
doing that.
A prescription
for longevity
is to familiarize yourself
with what you feel
and spend time
with friends
who are interested
in what you feel.
Get those feelings out
so they won't fester and pollute.
It helps
if you have a similar interest
in what they feel.
The road to heaven
is a two-way street.

PARENTING SELF

Say to yourself, "I love you very much. I am your new, warm, nurturing parent-in-residence! I am with you. I will always be here for you. Take love from me whenever you need it." Be protective of yourself, with love. Let love be the universal sponge to blot up hurts, leaven life's insults, the spring suspension that bounces you along.

"But isn't that selfish?" someone asks. That someone may be your own mischievous mind. It wants to retain control of the status quo. Parenting yourself in a mature way is not part of that. The answer is "Yes. It is selfish." You require sufficient attention to your nutritional needs and your recuperative needs. No one else will do these for you. You must do them for yourself. You also have emotional needs. You must be sufficiently self-interested *(selfish)* to meet those needs yourself. So parent yourself. Then, with self being served, you will be free to float along a life of generosity, good for you, good for all.

Staying the course, say these words, "I will never leave you. I'll always be here to say good things to you and help you feel better. I love you too much to leave you. We are in this together."

Paradigms and Boxes

One of the most difficult tasks to negotiate is the paradigm shift: thinking outside the box. If you feel dizzy thinking through the following, regard it as your mind setting up a barrier by taking the vibrations up to mind-speed (and out of healing/changing range). If you get a headache, consider whether your mind is recruiting the body for backup.

Terms used in this book for aspects of mind functioning include:

cull/culling—the process of selecting out certain parts, discarding others

desiccating—the process of turning a rich living experience into a dry fact or a worded description

extract—taking from the original. If what is left behind is water and its lushness, the result is a concentrated, unreal version.

reduce/reduction—taking a part that is less than the original

The mind, in an apparent attempt to simulate life at a level it can manage, strings word descriptions and facts into logical sequences, reaching a conclusion, at which point it stops. The stop signifies the end of mind processing, the edge, the wall beyond which it cannot go, the need of the mind to contain, confine, and control.

The difficulty for any human being in living seamlessly from one experience through to the next is the potential for insult and denigration. It is *undignifying* to be so reduced.

The mind's process has a useful function in a world of separated parts, clearly seen as distinct from one another. In applying a balance, you can be the conductor, seeking to coordinate a mind that often wants to dominate with a body that gets you around on this planet. A studied use of feelings and emotions, themselves unbound, can help bring this all together beautifully.

If you ever feel that things have become too dry, extracted, and reduced, you can enrich the situation easily. You dip into your stock emotions and add warmth to the mix. In tight, intolerant situations, you can do this silently within yourself. Love always helps, always brings relief. The simplest way to practice warm emotion is to evoke gratitude whenever you can. An attitude of gratitude can become a habit that requires no thinking to add the advantages, the enrichment, the re-enlivening whenever you choose.

If reading this article has made you dizzy or given you a headache, practice gratitude now. Think of someone, a person, a pet that you love and put your focus there—love that person, love that pet. Watch the headache release, the dizziness drop away, dissolve, and re-enliven by the emotional warmth.

Fishing Metaphor

Our world is full of metaphors. Little things can be metaphors for big things going on around us. Large things can be mirrored in the minutiae of life.

Grasping the metaphor, you can focus on healing that small thing; then watch the spinoffs into other areas! Your life is metaphoric!

Question: How do you land a ten-pound fish with a five-pound rod without breaking the line?

Answer: You *play* the fish. When the fish is rushing, swimming hard and fast, you give it all the line it wants. Never do you let the tension in the line go above five pounds. When the fish is tired and stops pulling, you gently reel it in. You don't let the line go slack, lest it snag around a rock. You maintain the tension.

Another burst of speed from the fish, and again you let it go. Tired again, you reel it in. When it is finally close enough, you lift it out of the water with a net.

This is a metaphor for human relationships. It says, "Stay in touch. Keep the faith. Retain your caring and interest, your connection. Don't let it snap from too much pressure or get snagged from too little attention."

In fact, the fish metaphor falls short. While there is life, there is hope. People are alive. Aliveness qualities remain in even the most troubled, hung-up people, just waiting to be revivified. There is no broken line. You can't make the choices others need to make. But you can be ever clearer on the quality of the invitations you send out. Maintain *attention* in the line between you and others, the right level of intensity, particularly in your primary relationship.

Use the metaphor for your goals. There was that idea you had, that thing you would like to do—it still comes to mind occasionally. You have been letting the line go slack. Think about it more often. Reel some tension into the line. Give it enough emotional warmth to make it real. Don't sweat the details. You risk snagging the line on those rocks. *Know* that all the brilliance needed to do the problem-solving healing is built into the emotional warmth you are using.

To use another metaphor, merely water the garden, watch, and wait. Relax.

APPLES FROM HARDWARE STORES?

You go into a hardware store and ask for a dozen apples. They tell you they don't have any. Do you have a temper tantrum on the floor? No. You go where they do sell apples and get your apples.

Life is like that. We all have needs. Sometimes the place we customarily go to get our needs met does not have what we want. Yet we can develop the habit of going back and back, never getting what we need.

If you want recognition, a listening ear, understanding, and acceptance, you can have those things. They are available. In generosity, you can give unto others what you yourself want to receive. Notice who are the ones capable of responding in kind.

It makes no sense to continue to ask of someone what they have repeatedly shown they cannot give. They only feel frustrated and put down by you. You in turn lose, because you don't get what you want.

Develop skill at life. All people have something to offer, even if it is only a moment to talk about the weather. By pausing with you, they tell you that you are worth talking to. Feel thankful toward them for the time they spent with you, their gift. Go on to others whose gifts are different. Collect for yourself the exact interpersonal diet you need. Surround yourself with people of like mind.

It will help if you ask cleanly and openly. Resentment at the ready, in case you need it, won't attract emotionally nutritious responses. You will get better with practice.

THE ATTENTION DEMANDER

Some people demand our attention. They weasel and needle their way into our presence in ways that can be infuriating, *if we choose that response*. They feel like the demanding, attention-seeking child that won't take no for an answer. We can say, in anger, "Okay. So you have my attention. What do you want?" The anger you invest in this has a repulsive quality that lacks the nutritional value, emotional feeling they need.

It is possible to reverse this whole process. You can reduce the time you spend, make it much more pleasant, and do it on your terms.

How? You become proactive. You recognize the needy state. You pause. You *feel that state*. You approach the person. You say hello. You can ask how the person is today. You can allow warmth in your voice. If it is someone you run into often, *you* can be the one to initiate emotional contact. Lean slightly toward them. This clicks something in you that makes it much easier. You may share a few words after that. It will likely not take as long as the last (negative) exchange. It will serve a need inside "needy" and put you in the driver's seat at the same time.

GIVING YOUR POWER AWAY

A child does not have much power. A child is small, lacking the strength of an adult. A child is immature, not yet fully developed mentally or emotionally. A child is inexperienced. She has not yet been there or done that. A child, so constantly aware of her lack of true power due to her smallness, immaturity, and inexperience, can grab for power at any opportunity. In the case of the schoolyard bully lording it over another child, this can come from her experience of bullying from parents who seem to the child not to understand her.

One of the delights for grown-ups is to see how the child is all eyes and ears, looking with wonder and delight at things the grown-up has long since forgotten about or relegated to the category of boring. This gives the child power to remind the adult of the way things can be seen and reacted to. Adults can release their habitual deadness habits and come alive again. The child has that power.

In a well-functioning family, this wonder and delight is encouraged and developed. The parent is ahead of the child, removing danger and threat, presenting the child with tasks he can master, allowing the child to learn *success*. The child paddles its little canoe on the supportive river of love, the environment provided by the parents.

The learning of *success* is carried through to adulthood. Such an adult has eyes and ears to perceive things fully, with freshness. The habit of *success* carries through to become *potency and effectiveness*, as you gather maturity and experience.

Parents cannot spend all of their time doting over a child. There are other children, other affairs that must be attended to, to maintain family and personal stability. Another factor is that not all people, not all children are identical. Everything else being equal, one child may be born with twice the need for attention as the other children. This child is destined not to have his needs met.

All too often (perhaps it is the norm), the family was not so supportive. Dysfunctionality encouraged the child to learn a false lesson: the world is unappreciative and inhibiting. The natural tendency of the life force to flow forward, involve, and succeed is blocked. The child learns to retain that energy in the body.

With this dysfunctional habit well practiced, the now-grown child can go on to further under-achievement: seeking to control other people. Such a position statement reads:

"I am a child, small, inexperienced, and incompetent. I am angry about that.

"(I am also deeply afraid that the prison, childhood, in which I feel trapped, will be there forever. I repeatedly tell myself I can never escape. Desperate attempts to escape prove useless.)

"So instead of finding out who I really am and exploring how to make that work, I will side with the inhibition. Fear will underlie my actions. Anger will give that 'bite.' To make myself feel less uncomfortable than I already am, I will distract myself from my problem by seeing if I can control others. To the extent that I succeed, I will gain a moment's respite from my prison. I will have created company for myself in my prison, by giving myself the illusion that power over others is somehow power over myself."

The clear alternative is to give up a life committed to fear and anger and the maintenance of dysfunctionality.

Turn 180 degrees. See the dysfunctionality taken on as a gift, an opportunity to face down a problem and gain mastery over it. Such power will forever outshine any trivial, temporary, tattered control over other people. It is real. It is rewarding. It is permanent.

VENTING OR HEAD-TRIPPING

Feelings can be held. Feelings can be stored in the body. Unexpressed emotion can be experienced as a feeling of heaviness on the chest. The chest, that would function as a bellows to vibrate the vocal cords when you speak, is being *held back* from doing that. The expression *getting it off your chest* refers to the sense of relief that follows successful venting. Feelings can build to such a pressure that you can feel you would burst. There is an urgency to get them out. The most versatile and useful way to do that is to "vent," to let the feelings out by using words that will carry, like the carriages of a train, the cargo of unexpressed emotion.

The mind, which cannot grasp and contain that flooding life force, is best diverted from mischief. You give it the job of manufacturing train carriages—selecting the words that will most ably express the emotion in manageable form.

Problems develop when this process is subverted. The mind can head trip. It kicks the feelings out of the carriages and uses the train for barnstorming: to promote its own political agenda. It changes the subject. It asks questions and seeks answers. These are processes foreign to plants and animals in general, but highly developed in the human being. Once you buy into these mental processes, you effectively block processing feelings (unless you deliberately turn back to the feelings).

From there, the mind can go to imagery: pictures worth a thousand words. Bouncing around thousand-word aliquots can be great fun for a mind bent on power and control. You can feel like "fighting off the bats" as you try to cope with this overworking mind.

More power is felt when the images are scary. The mind, not able to grasp, contain, or manipulate compassion, love, and understanding, makes an ally of their crude form, fear. Instead of refining crude-oil fear up to higher grades, thinking can more readily *downgrade* warm emotions to cold fear! Then it can play king of the garbage heap, sitting atop the mess.

Challenge that. Reverse the mess making. Take charge. Generate courage. Create warm emotions. Use a sponge of love to mop up the fear and upgrade it to more useful forms.

I LEARNED PATIENCE

I learned patience
by loosening the stranglehold
time had had on me
the right I had given *time*
the concept
to squeeze the life out of me.
For life
is now
is real
is alive
there is no past
but movies we can recycle
in our heads
to distract from now.
There is no future
except for what we construct
our patchwork editing
of those same movies.
Life is now.
If I stay in the glory of that
watching the freshness
of each evolving moment
like the opening
of a flower
I have no need
to push
for something *better*
as I might imagine it.
For *better* evolves
in the natural scheme of things
through *worse*
which we may retain
in stranglehold
until
we release
the effort.
So *patience*
as a concept
gains meaning
in the natural flow of things
and impatience
becomes the false construct
that is not needed.

Now, you may try my patience
by what you do
as you dig a little deeper
into my tight spots
and evolve our relationship
to a deeper, softer, broader level.
But you are here for me to enjoy
and you know it.
May our play together
be the reward
that carries the deeper meaning.

GOD SPEAKS

All things are of God, there is nothing that is not God. God is everywhere. Understanding that, is everything. It means you cannot get away from God. God is all-seeing. God is omnipresent.

God is simple. It is easy, straightforward, it requires no strain to understand God, see through God, get inside God, and be a participant in God's power.

God is ineffably complex. It is impossible, beyond the grasp of a simple human being to comprehend all of God, reach around all of God.

Better to rest in the security that God is present and gently, reliably supportive of each of us. We need have no fear. Fear represents turning our back on God. We usually do that to keep hold of a fear habit that has become too familiar—never mind that it never worked in the first place.

All things are of God. Destruction *is*; it exists. Therefore destruction is of God. This may run in the face of long-held beliefs we have about a special place, separated out, for evil. In the life we live out on this planet, we have an excellent opportunity to experience separateness in space and separateness in time. That is a unique property of life on earth as we know it. But do not confuse properties of life-as-we-know-it with the nature of hell, heaven, or God. These are omnipresent.

Even destructiveness is present in heaven. We come here, the better to sort it out. Does it work? Does it help? Am I better off to destroy? In time, we can see the immature child rising up through the middle of destruction, crazed, trying vainly, weakly to take charge, while knowing she is beaten before she starts.

Death itself is an image, an event relative only to the physical existence we live out on this planet. It has little to do with the ultimate reality, the *oneness*.

The body dies. In this life the body reflects fear as tension and pain. Pain gives our concerns an undue urgency—*Deal with it! Deal with it!*—inviting far more energy than is needed. But your basic nature is the stuff of which God is made. It is that which is doing the learning. You are making God more godly, an important task.

Regret can burn up a lot of energy and render it useless. Anger is another feeling that can generate destruction. Terrified is a kind of dead-end state with mind and body double-teaming you out of relevance.

Imagery has great power—a thousand-word power—in the broad scheme of things. High speed can outfox the slower healing/feeling speed.

All of these details circle back to who we are. We are of God. Any discussion of God only makes sense in the context of ourselves. It is not selfish to do that. It is merely recognizing our true nature. We start life as a child with immature perspectives. It is our job in this lifetime to upgrade that. We use life-stuff/God-stuff as grist in our process of refining. What an honorable job that is!

We can have and build relationships with other human beings in a specific God-to-God manner, building at a speed exponentially faster than our private efforts.

Failures are merely misnomers: one-step-backs on a sequence of two-steps-forward-one-step-backs that guarantee success at the end. We must succeed. In no matter how many lifetimes. All roads lead to God, lead to ourselves. We progressively validate ourselves, building and building on a basic quality core of self-validation.

All things are of God. Humor exists. Therefore, humor is of God. Thank the heavens for that. What a droll existence this would be if everything was devoid of humor. Humor relaxes what would be a heavy existence on this planet. It lightens things up.

Music is of God. The immediate image brings choruses of angels singing of God, praise music, which resembles feelings in that both are invisible and pervasive. You can hear invisible music around a corner.

Light is of God. We think of radiance: the glory of God.

ABOUT THE AUTHOR

Warren Douglas Phegan is a recently retired family psychiatrist of over thirty years experience, currently residing in London, Ontario, Canada.

An Australian physician, he entered molecular research in the United States; then trained in psychiatry and family therapy in Canada. He is also a pianist, composer, photographer, cartoonist, and poet.

REFERENCES

1. Basen, Ira, prod. *Spin Cycles* (A radio series broadcast by the Canadian Broadcasting Corporation about those in power manipulating facts.) January and February 2007. Available as a six-CD set. http://www.cbc.ca/shop/ or contact barbara_brown@cbc.ca.

2. Bateson, G. et al., "Toward a Theory of Schizophrenia," *Behavioral Sciences* 1 (1956):251–264.

3. Beck, Judith S. *Cognitive Therapy: Basics and Beyond.* New York: The Guilford Press, 1995.

4. Berne, Eric. *What Do You Say After You Say Hello?* New York: Grove Press 1972

5. Berne, Eric. *Games People Play.* New York: Ballantine Books, 1964.

6. Boyce, Mel. "Twelve Permissions," *Transactional Anal.* J. 8(1), January 1978, 30–32.

7. Cole, K.C. *The Universe and the Teacup: the Mathematics of Truth and Beauty.* New York: Harvest Books (Harcourt), 1999.

8. Fromm-Reichmann, Freda. "Notes on the Development and Treatment of Schizophrenics by Psychoanalytic Psychotherapy," *Psychiatry* 11:263–274.

9. Ginott, Haim G. *Between Parent and Child.* New York: Avon Books, The Hearst Corporation, 1965.

10. Hatterer, J. *The Pleasure Addicts.* A. S. Barnes and Co., Inc. 1980.

11. Iacocca, Lee, with William Novak. *Iacocca: An Autobiography.* New York: Bantam Books, 1984.

12. Kahler, Taibi, with Hedges Capers. "The Mini Script," *Transactional Anal.* J. 4(1) January 1974, 25–42

13. Kant, Immanuel. *Fundamental Principles of the Metaphysic of Morals.* Thomas K. Abbot, trans. Indianapolis, IN: Bobbs-Merrill Company, Inc., 1949.

14. Karpman, Stephen. *Drama Triangle,* "Fairy Tales and Script Drama Analysis", Transactional Analysis Bulletin April 1968, Vol. 7. No. 26.

15. Lewis, C. S. *The Four Loves,* Houghton Mifflin Hardcourt, November 1991.

16. Lewis, C. S. "The Weight of Glory," *Screwtape Proposes a Toast,* New York/MacMillian, 1949.

17. Lowen, Alexander. *The Language of the Body.* New York: Collier Books 1976. (Originally published as *Physical Dynamics of Character Structure.* New York: Grune and Stratton, 1958.)

18. Mabey, Juliet, ed. *God's BIG Instruction Book: Timeless Wisdom on How to Follow the Spiritual Path.* One World Publications 1996.

19. McKenna, Paul. *The Golden Rule: Quotations from Scriptures* (a poster). Toronto, ON, Canada: Scarboro Missions, http://www.scarboromissions.ca/Interfaith_dialogue/poster_order.php. Reprinted with permission from Scarboro Missions. Available through Broughton's tel. (416) 690–4777.

20. Peterson, Eugene H. *The Message: The Bible in Contemporary Language.* Colorado Springs, CO: NavPress Publishing Group, 2002.

21. Phegan, Barry PhD. *Developing Your Company Culture: The Joy of Leadership: A Handbook for Leaders and Managers.* Berkeley, CA: Context Press, 1994.

22. Sanders, Tim. *Love Is the Killer App.* New York: Three Rivers Press, 2002.

23. Sandweiss, Samuel H., *Sai Baba The Holy Man and the Psychiatrist.* San Diego, CA: Birth Day Publishing Company, 1975. 203.

24. Satir, Virginia. *Self Esteem.* Berkeley, CA: Celestial Arts, 1975.

25. Schreibman, Phillip. *My Cat Saved My Life.* Wisconsin Rapids, WI: Dog's Bark Publishing. 1998

26. Smith, Penelope. *Animal Talk.* Hillsboro, OR: Beyond Words Publishing, Inc. 2008

INDEX

W